Derek Prince
A Biography

Derek Prince
A Biography

Stephen Mansfield

Charisma
HOUSE
A STRANG COMPANY

Most STRANG COMMUNICATIONS/CHARISMA HOUSE/SILOAM products are available at special quantity discounts for bulk purchase for sales promotions, premiums, fund-raising, and educational needs. For details, write Strang Communications/ Charisma House/Siloam, 600 Rinehart Road, Lake Mary, Florida 32746, or telephone (407) 333-0600.

DEREK PRINCE—A BIOGRAPHY by Stephen Mansfield
Published by Charisma House
A Strang Company
600 Rinehart Road
Lake Mary, Florida 32746
www.charismahouse.com

All Scripture quotations are from the King James Version of the Bible.

Cover design by Joe De Leon

Library of Congress Cataloging-in-Publication Data:
Mansfield, Stephen.
 Derek Prince : a biography / Stephen Mansfield.
    p. cm.
 ISBN 1-59185-794-5 (hardback)
 1. Prince, Derek. 2. Biblical scholars--Biography. 3. Christian educators--Biography.
I. Title.
BS501.P75M36 2005
277.3'082'092--dc22
                              2005015064

First Edition

05 06 07 08 09 — 987654321
Printed in the United States of America

To the daughters—

Tikva, Peninah, Ruhammah, Johanne, Magdalene,
Kirsten, Anna, Elisabeth, and Joska—

Who have loved much and endured much

His life was gentle, and the elements
So mix'd in him that Nature might stand up
And say to all the world "This was a man!"

—JULIUS CAESAR
ACT V, SCENE 5

❇ Contents

Foreword

IT IS MY great honor to be chosen to write the foreword to this volume celebrating the life of Derek Prince, who was a world-class scholar and one of the greatest spiritual generals who ever walked on the battle-fields of spiritual warfare.

I met Derek Prince in the early seventies when a demonized man walked up the aisle of my church with a pistol and tried to murder me before my congregation. The assassin fired every shot in his gun from a distance of eight feet and missed only because the hand of God supernaturally spared my life.

The next morning I began calling America's leading pastors for anyone who had personal knowledge of demons and deliverance. I was told, "There is an Englishman in Ft. Lauderdale, Florida, who has personal knowledge and Bible balance."

I contacted Derek, and there was an instantaneous divine affection for this "prince" of a man. He came to minister at my church many times, and in every service there was a supernatural breakthrough that took our church to higher ground.

My wife, Diana, and I miss Derek Prince! In our darkest hours, we would receive his letters of strength and encouragement. He had an inner fortitude that was without limit. Derek was my spiritual mentor and teacher in the field of spiritual warfare.

Derek Prince was an epistle of living love! He loved the Lord with a passion few men ever know. He loved his family. He loved Israel and defended Israel's right to the land God gave to Abraham by an eternal blood covenant in the Book of Genesis.

He was, in every fiber of his being, a servant of God. The Bible says, "He that is the greatest among you is the servant to all." Derek's ministry circled the globe. His brilliant teaching and anointed ministry made him an apostle to the nations of the world. He was a man whose name was a synonym for integrity.

This mighty spiritual general is buried in a small cemetery in Jerusalem, wrapped only in burial cloths, just as the Lord Jesus was. He is now awaiting the resurrection of the righteous to see the risen Lord he loved and served with unlimited passion.

I, and millions like me, loved Derek Prince. I have in my library every tape he ever produced and every book he ever wrote. And still he speaks from the grave to the nations of the world through the voices of his spiritual children who rise up to call him blessed.

—JOHN HAGEE, PASTOR
CORNERSTONE CHURCH
SAN ANTONIO, TEXAS

Introduction

Remembering a Life

I DID NOT NEED help to believe that Derek Prince was a great man, but I was about to get it anyway. Never mind that I had nearly grown up to the sound of this man's voice. By the miracle of the audiocassette, Derek Prince had for years taught the Scriptures in my childhood home, often while laundry was folded or the evening meal was prepared. He was part of the family, though if he got long-winded and the family routine was threatened with delay, my mother simply increased the speed on our 1970s tape recorder so that the revered Mr. Prince sounded like a British Mickey Mouse or a BBC newscast with technical difficulties. But he was always there, his voice providing much of the soundtrack of my early life.

What a privilege it was, then, to have lunch with Derek on that sparkling November day in Jerusalem. We met at the Ramat Rachel, the kibbutz hotel on the "Heights of Rachel" still pockmarked by bullets fired during one of Israel's wars. The rich tapestry of history reached to us. Through one window we could see the much-contested West Bank. Through another lay Bethlehem. And a mere hundred yards in a third direction were the scattered ruins of a citadel built thousands of years before by the kings of Judea, a bath built by the Tenth Roman Legion, and a Byzantine church: all the stony legacy of the centuries left to this strategic location on the south of Jerusalem and at the crossroads of history.

The voice of the past was never lost to Derek, and as we ate he reflected on the meaning of what surrounded us. He spoke of history with a casual mastery borne of years in reflection and study, and while he did, I took in his features. Though he was eighty-seven, he still had those intriguing eyes that were both intelligent and soulful at the same time. Still there was the full, jutting forehead, as though his brain was pushing itself forward. His face was yet long and narrow. His mouth was still lined by full, expressive lips, and his nose a testament, surely, to the presence of Rome on British shores. When he concentrated, his face congealed like an impassioned symphony. When he laughed, every feature conspired with glee. And I could picture how anger might animate those same features to make him fearful indeed. I hoped I would not see it.

Yet, I had feared displeasing him since I first agreed to author his biography. When his grandson Derek Wesley Selby approached me with the idea of writing the Derek Prince story, I was interested but cautious. It was an honor to be asked, and I knew enough of Derek's history to know how it might appeal to a new generation. But I wasn't sure just what kind of book Derek Prince Ministries expected. Did they want a hagiography, what I insultingly called at the time a "preacher puff piece"? If so, they needed to find another author. Nothing would be more mind-numbingly boring than just another boastful book on just another famous preacher.

But I discovered to my delight that they wanted a genuine biography, a work of poetic scholarship that would capture the truth of Derek's life and let God breathe through both the triumphant and the tragic. I was glad to hear it. I had long believed that history is best written as we find it in the Bible. Human beings are spared nothing in Scripture. We find them starkly exposed as vile and low and craven and yet approaching the angels in their better selves and delighting the heart of the Creator with their friendship. Scripture captures it all. I had come to believe that the way to write a life is to tell the truth with compassion and let the beauty arise from both the darkness and the light. The good folks of Derek Prince Ministries agreed, but I wasn't sure that Derek would feel the same way. This was, after all, his story, and he might not want it fully told.

In fact, I feared that he might not think me the man to whom he should unfold his heart. After all, I was half his age, an American, and far from the Cambridge scholar he might have preferred as his biographer. But I need not have worried. Derek had read my other books, understood what I was about, and, more in honor to his God than in deference to me, he opened up from our first meeting. In fact, his transparency took my breath away. He seemed to delight in surprising me and chuckled that he was ashamed at how much he enjoyed talking about himself.

Our friendship was sealed by our love of humor. His sense of play was undimmed by the years, and we were not far into our relationship before the jostling began. Derek and I once spoke over dinner of what would happen to the biography if he died before it was finished. The mood grew heavy. To lighten the moment, I told him he could not die because I needed someone to explain the game of cricket to me. He didn't miss a beat. Never taking his eyes from the food on his plate, he said with disdain, "Cricket is too sacred to explain to an American." He was only half kidding.

I would remember those first steps into humor when we shared our final laugh together. He was in the Shaare Zedek Medical Center in Jerusalem just days before his death. Nurses were constantly fiddling with him while we were trying to talk, and finally I said, "You're not here because you're sick. You just like all these beautiful women fawning over you." He lifted his nose slightly, looked at me with the most condescending Cambridge-bred expression, and said, "Well, of course." Only after the words left his lips did his eyes betray his teasing solemnity.

By that lunch at the Ramat Rachel, Derek and I were well on our way to the kind of friendship a biographer hopes for: respectful, playful, and brutally honest. But the other dynamic a biographer hopes for was just about to make itself known. There must be the inspired moments, those unexpected revelations that cannot be scripted and that make the writer feel as though God is smiling on his undertaking. As Derek and I ate our lunch and spoke of generations past, God remembered us.

I had noticed at the far end of the vast restaurant at Ramat Rachel a large group who looked to be Eastern European. From time to time, they would look up from their food and conversation to stare our way. Some were nodding their heads, and others were soon talking as though trying to convince the group of an important matter. Then there was a change. I noticed that more than a few began to weep. Some knelt by their lunch table as though it were an altar and began to pray. Others held each other, as those consoling friends whose hearts are overcome. This continued for some time. Derek continued talking, unaware of the growing stir across the room. I was distracted and tried to listen to him while becoming increasingly aware that we were the focus of a commotion.

Soon a young man approached from the group and asked if he could join us. His English was excellent, and he began to explain what was happening across the room. They were a group from Hungary, he told us, and they were in the Holy Land to bless Israel and learn the geography of their faith. They had decided at the last minute to have lunch at the Ramat Rachel, but when they arrived, they quickly realized that God had ordered their steps. We did not understand at first, but the young man soon explained that in the months leading up to their trip, many of the group had begun to pray that they would see Derek Prince, who they knew made his home in Jerusalem. For some, it was the main reason they had come, and when they looked across the dining room and saw the very man they had prayed to see, they were overcome. And the tears came.

Derek and I were still confused. The young man, whose name we learned was Andras Patkai, patiently explained. In 1978, a Christian couple in Budaors, Hungary, named Sandor and Judith Nemeth, wished to improve their English. Already Judith was fluent in Russian, French, and German. Her English needed work. The couple soon found a tape entitled *Deliverance for Children and Their Parents*. It was by Derek Prince, and the truths they heard changed their lives. They played the tape for their home group of some seven college students, with Judith interpreting. The effect was astonishing, and soon after they wrote to the address on the tape to see if this man Derek Prince could pay them a visit, if he would come teach the gospel in the communist realms of Hungary. Two of Derek Prince's friends, Jim Croft and Terry Bysinger, responded to the invitation. This paved the way for a visit from Derek several years later. By then the small group of seven college students had grown to an underground church of three hundred, meeting on the outskirts of Budaors.

At this point in the story, Derek, who had been silent while Andras spoke, grew animated. He remembered it now. He and Ruth, his second wife, went into Hungary on tourist visas. They were taken to a small house crammed with people. The shades were pulled on every window for fear of the secret police. There was a strong sense of God's presence, he recalled, and he had seldom felt such power as he taught for days on end. He knew a bit of what had happened after. The church had grown, the pastors had come under persecution, and the communist government had tried to close the little church. Typical of Derek, he remembered that Judith was an accomplished pianist, and her husband, Sandor, was always brave in the face of threats on his life.

Derek paused for a moment, and Andras picked up the story. The church had survived, he relayed. In fact, it was now nearly forty thousand people. It printed a national newspaper, was a center for the arts, and was arguably one of the most powerful cultural institutions in Hungary. What was more, the church had been built on the ministry of Derek Prince. His tapes and books provided the foundation from which their whole movement sprang. The people of this church saw Derek as their father. Little Hungarian babies were named Derek in his honor, and, in fact, several young men and women at the Ramat Rachel were named for Derek or his wife Ruth.

It was a holy moment. Derek was overcome. While he wept uncontrollably the group of Hungarians surrounded us, and the weeping and the hugging continued. Some knelt at Derek's feet. Others gingerly touched his arm. Derek turned to me and said through his tears, "It is good you are here. God has ordained our time together." Cameras flashed, and many in the group pressed young Andras to give Derek messages in English. "I left my life of drugs when I heard your tape," said one. "My communist father converted and turned our family to Christ when you spoke," reported another with sobs. "What you have started has changed the history of our nation," a student insisted quietly.

It all seemed to have lasted but a few minutes, and then a tour guide was calling the Hungarians to their bus. Time had been suspended by beauty and remembrance. When the group was gone, I looked at Derek. He was sitting alone with his thoughts, dabbing the tears from his eyes and telling me over and again what sweet people these were and how thankful he was that God had given him this moment.

They do not give awards for ministry. There are no Emmys or Pulitzers for preaching the gospel. Yet Derek had just received an early trophy, a triumphal bouquet, from his Lord. And he knew it. Before we left the table, he turned to me and said, "Who am I to be honored in such a way?"

It struck me that day how scenes of similar tribute could easily be repeated the world over, with a rich tapestry of tribes honoring Derek for what he had planted on their soil. A conference designed to thank God for Derek Prince would have to include delegates from nearly every nation on the earth, for he touched most all of them. And besides the nations, there would have to be representatives from the many unique gatherings he had attended. There would be delegates from the band of British soldiers who drank from Derek's life during the horrors of war in northern Africa. There would also be ambassadors from all the thousands who heard him preach the gospel at London's Speakers' Corner. Certainly the hippies of America and the expatriate Jamaicans of postwar England and the converted blokes from Down Under would all be there—and thousands more. There would even have to be some in attendance to stand for the millions around the world who had heard a tape, read a book, or seen Derek in person at any of ten thousand meetings around the world. He had touched so many lives and fathered so much of what a new generation enjoyed, whether they knew it or not.

Yet, this was the challenge I felt as Derek drove away that day. How was I to capture all that this man's life had meant, all the history his years encompassed? I let his seasons flow through my mind. He was born under the British Raj in India, educated in the radical post–World War I years of 1930s' England, and shipped off to war as Japanese Zeros pounded Pearl Harbor. He was there at the birth of Israel, there when America unraveled in the 1960s, and there when the greatest spiritual renewal since the resurrection of Jesus filled the nations. The span of his life was daunting. He came into the world when George V ruled England with Asquith as his prime minister and when Woodrow Wilson was the American president. His first wife was born before the White House had electricity. Yet, in the last year of his life, Derek and I discussed how the Internet would change ministry and how the man who then lived in the White House was not yet alive when Derek was already in his fourth decade of life.

It was also in the last year of his life that Derek spoke the words that became my personal commission. We were sitting together in the brilliant sun of a September day in Jerusalem. It was obvious that Derek did not have long in this world. He was in pain, hard to understand, and deeply frustrated that he could not make his meaning clear. In fact, without the help of Pat Turner, his faithful assistant, I rarely understood anything he said. But I heard one sentence with a clarity that would never leave me. After some of our usual banter, there was a long silence when Derek spoke in a sudden burst of clarity. Taking my forearm in his hands, he leaned toward me and said, "I must apologize to you." I was confused and asked why he felt he had anything to make right with me. He then said, in carefully measured words, "I must apologize for asking you to write a book about a man who no longer exists."

My eyes filled with tears. This was Derek. A humble man who could admit he was not as he had been and a proud man who was frustrated with what he had become. It was an admission that I could not escape, and I took it as a challenge. In my heart I said, "No. He will not cease to exist. This man is too dear, too much a verse of God's crafting, to allow his life to descend in obscurity." And though I had already been researching his life for a year, I lit my torch anew and determined to impress the wonder of Derek Prince's life on a generation who could not know how desperately they needed what his story had to offer.

He is gone now, and he is missed. His unique brand of biblical wisdom and insight is desperately needed in our time. Yet perhaps because of this retelling of his story and the devoted labors of those who now extend his legacy, it may be that the life of Derek Prince has yet to have its greatest impact in this world. This is as he would have wanted it to be, for he always knew that his life was not intended as a monument for future generations to admire but as a well from which future generations could drink.

Come, then—drink deep. The water is sweet, and our age is exceedingly dry.

1

1915:
India and the Sacrifice of Empire

DEREK HAD JUST settled into his chair and was cradling his cup of hot tea with both hands. He was quiet, pensive. I think he was changing gears.

Weeks before when his staff had told him about his time with me and how the biography was going to delve into the depths of his life, Derek had seemed pleased. "It will be good," he said with obvious relief, "not to tell the same old stories."

So it was time to begin. We were alone, a majestic stretch of the Judean wilderness visible through the window of our room on the Heights of Rachel. Derek shifted about a bit, sipped his tea, and then fixed his penetrating eyes expectantly upon me.

I knew he was ready. Finally, at the end of his life, he was willing, even eager, to tell it all. I had only to launch him.

"Tell me," I said, "of India."

Derek smiled slightly. He knew my spare words formed a challenge: "If you are ready to talk," I was saying, "then run and I will follow. You are long past needing someone to pull it out of you."

He sighed wistfully and turned his eyes to the region where Jesus withstood Satan for forty days. There was a pause. "From the beginning," he nearly whispered, "I believe that India laid claim to my soul…

Derek Prince was born in Bangalore, India, on August 14, 1915. He thus drew his first breaths just as much of the Old World was dying and much of the new was making itself known.

In 1915, the Old World was dying in the breasts of thousands of Europe's young who took with them to the grave the noble ideals of centuries. Just the year before, on June 28, Archduke Francis Ferdinand of Austria-Hungary and his wife had been assassinated on the streets of Sarajevo, Bosnia, by an anarchist named Gavrilo Princip. From this seemingly small beginning, a wicked brew of entangling alliances and ancient animosities exploded into what came to be known as the Great War, the first one to "make the world safe for democracy."

With crisis upon them, the European powers summoned their young to martial glory by appealing to patriotism and manhood. Traditional concepts of honor still lived in those days. The boys and men of the nations swelled to the call and streamed into the muddy trenches. But no one was prepared for the butchery. Technology had outstripped military tactics by 1915, and whereas just decades before war had been fought with rifles, cavalry charges, and cannon, this new war would be fought with submarines, tanks, machine guns, planes, and, most horribly, nerve gas. Human beings began dying at the hands of their brothers in greater numbers than ever before in history.

Though 1915 was far from the bloodiest year of the war, it nevertheless typified much that was to come. The battles of that year tell the tale. At the Second Battle of Artois, for example, an astonishing 400,000 men were lost. At the Second Battle of Ypres, the Germans used chlorine gas as a weapon for the first time in history and so thrust warfare to new levels of human devastation. It was also in 1915 that the blunders of the Gallipoli Campaign left more than 100,000 dead Allies on Turkish soil and almost ended the political career of England's First Lord of the Admiralty, Winston Churchill.

England was tempted to be cruel to her statesmen because she was already reeling from her losses. Though the war had lasted barely a year, her killed and wounded together totaled more than 550,000. By war's end English dead alone would total 680,000. It was madness. Surely nothing could justify such slaughter. But the nations found no way out of the darkness, and the sacrifice of a generation continued.

The Old World, both its men and its meaning, was dying. And Derek Prince was born just in time to hear its funeral dirge.

Yet a new order was rising to fill the vacuum left by the old. On May 7, 1915, a German submarine sank the *Lusitania* off the coast of Ireland. Some 1,198 lives were lost, 139 of whom were Americans. The United States was incensed, and tensions with Germany rose dramatically over the ensuing months until, two years later, the Americans joined the war and sent some 4 million men into battle. More than 53,000 never returned home, a number almost insignificant beside Europe's millions, but still a deep wound to the American soul. More lasting, perhaps, was America's appearance on the world scene. Forced by the war to break from her long-standing isolationism, America would so dominate the era just then dawning that many would conclude at its end that it had been "the American century."

Another nation was just then emerging as well, from the sands of Ottoman Palestine, from the pages of the ancient writings: Israel. It had all begun with Theodor Herzl, the Jewish journalist who was so outraged by the shameful anti-Semitism of the Dreyfus Affair in France that he raised his voice to issue the call for a Jewish state. Dreyfus had been a French army officer who was tried and found guilty of treason on false charges fabricated by his fellow officers because he was a Jew. He was later acquitted, but not before France's outpouring of anti-Semitism convinced men like Herzl that the Jews could never be safe in Europe: they would need a country of their own. Hearing Herzl's trumpet call, the Jews of Europe began pouring into Palestine. This became the First Aliyah, or return to the land. When Herzl died in 1904, though, the movement he founded nearly died with him.

Great Britain gave it life again. Both to win Jewish support for the war and out of genuine sympathy for Zionism, England made a promise in the years just after Derek Prince was born that became the founding oath of Israel. In a 117-word note to Lord Rothschild, head of the Jewish banking family, Foreign Secretary Arthur Balfour assured, "His Majesty's Government view with favour the establishment in Palestine of a national home for the Jewish people." Immigration was slow at first, but the message was not lost on a persecuted people. By 1936, when Nazism was just stepping onto the world stage, more than sixty thousand Jews had made their way to the land that, twelve years later, would become the nation of Israel. And Derek Prince would be there at its birth.

Yet, in 1915, Derek Prince was but a newborn babe. He knew nothing of wars or nations on the rise. He could not have known that in the year of his birth a man named Charles Lawrence developed the first successful air-cooled airplane engine, making long-distance flight possible. Nor could he have known that in that same year a man in New York named Alexander Graham Bell called his friend named Watson in San Francisco, thus achieving the first transcontinental phone call. Young Derek could also not have known that a man named Einstein had just announced his general theory of relativity or that a man named Ford had just produced his millionth automobile. Yet each of these breakthroughs, achieved in the year of his birth, would have a profound effect upon his life. This was 1915, the year that marked the death of the old, the birth of the new, and the beginning for young Derek Prince.

Yet Derek's beginning was as much about *where* he was born as it was about *when*. That he was born in India, that he spent the first five years of his life there, and that the men he revered in childhood devoted themselves to serving their monarch in that land are, certainly, among the most important realities of his life.

Today, Bangalore is at the heart of India's Silicon Valley. Internet commerce abounds, and there are sections of the city as modern as any in the world. Yet in 1915, Bangalore was one of the cities from which the British ruled "the Jewel in the Crown." In those days, the Union Jack flew high above manicured lawns as khaki-clad soldiers drilled, turbaned servants served whiskies on cool verandas, and officers' wives sporting parasols read Kipling and Dickens to their young.

The English had begun in India a century and a half before under a general named Robert Clive. In the name of "trade, not territory," Clive had subdued a warring tribe outside a Bengali village called Plessy and thus opened the gates of northern India in 1757. All good intentions aside, the century that followed was marked more by conquest than commerce. In fairness, most English thought of themselves as the liberators of an enslaved people. Historian John Stuart Mill, writing in 1823, captured the dominant English view of Indian natives at the time:

> By a system of priestcraft, built upon the most enormous and tormenting superstition that ever harnessed and degraded any portion of mankind, their [the Indians'] minds were enchained more intolerably than their bodies; in short; despotism and priestcraft taken together, the Hindus, in mind and body, were the most enslaved portion of the human race.[1]

To their credit, the English did indeed, in Kipling's phrase of later years, "take up the White Man's burden." They instituted the Pax Britannica, which allowed legal, administrative, and educational institutions to thrive. They graced India with order, cleanliness, sport, the accumulated wisdom of the Western canon, the English language, and, perhaps above all, Christianity and a Christian idea of progress.

Still, India wanted to be ruled by Indians, and in 1857 a savage mutiny proved the point. British troops prevailed, though, and beginning in that year India became the possession of Queen Victoria. Her viceroy and his few thousand aides would determine the destiny of nearly one-fifth of all humanity. Indeed, by the year of Derek Prince's birth, more than 300 million Indians were subject to some 100,000 Englishmen and their Indian officials.

Interestingly, it was the slaughter in the trenches of Europe that ultimately led, in part, to the English departure from India nearly two centuries after Clive. The war left nearly a million British males either dead or incapable of service abroad. As a result, Indians were increasingly welcomed into the civil service, the officer corps, and the courts of law.

Indeed, one Indian lawyer, who plied his trade first in Bombay, then in South Africa, and then again in his homeland, was named Mohandas Karamchand Gandhi. He would combine the law he learned in the Temple of London with the language of his nation's captors and merge both with a uniquely Hindu passive resistance to convince the English that they ought to leave India to the Indians. In 1947, he would victoriously hail the English decision to grant India her independence as the "noblest act of the British nation." In 1915, though, India was solidly English, and few expected it would ever be otherwise.

✖

The men of Derek Prince's immediate family were the kind of warriors who made the British Empire great. They were all army officers, all men of deep Victorian values, and all devoted to the belief that England was a force for righteousness in the world. When tourists view monuments in London fashioned to commemorate the character that built the Empire, that prevailed on far-flung battlefields, it is men like those of Derek's family whom they are meant to remember.

Chief among them was Derek's grandfather, the quintessential British imperial officer. His name was Robert Edward Vaughan, and he was born in Felhampton on August 12, 1866, to Thomas, a farmer, and his devoted wife, Eliza. When Robert came of age, he left home to join the army, possibly to escape a farmer's life, and by the time of Derek's birth was living in Rawalpindi as a lieutenant colonel in charge of supply and transport for the Indian army. He possessed an astonishing ability to organize, to plan in the abstract but execute in the particular. The army found him invaluable and promoted him to major general in recognition of his skill. One of the few surviving pictures of "the General" is a study in character. Sporting a bushy mustache and a bulldog's jutting chest is a man of stern bearing and movie-star good looks, regally adorned in a red uniform draped with tiger skin.

On October 18, 1890, Robert, then a handsome twenty-four-year-old lieutenant in the Bengal Staff Corps, married Amy Mountjoy Woodward. Amy would become a major figure in the Derek Prince story, for she was a deeply pious woman. At a time when most Englishmen were officially Anglican but personally uncommitted, Amy was a praying, Bible-reading Christian who genuinely believed what she affirmed every Sunday in the liturgy. She also believed in the exceptionality of her grandson. Much of what he learned of faith and piety in his early years was gleaned at her knee.

The true military hero of the Vaughan family was Robert and Amy's son, Edward. The year Derek was born, his uncle Edward was a lieutenant in the storied Bengal 2nd Lancers (Gardner's Horse). He had entered the service on January 22, 1913, and eagerly joined the legendary horsemen who fought

14

ferociously and had a reputation for melting women's hearts with their gallant manner and striking blue uniforms.

It was during World War II that Edward most distinguished himself. While a lieutenant colonel fighting in the western desert of Africa, he was captured by Italian troops and taken to Italy as a prisoner of war. He then lived in a squalid prison camp for three and a half years. Finally, in an act of exceptional bravery, he escaped and made his way southward down the spine of Italy until he met up with invading British troops. Celebrated, decorated, and given a field promotion to the rank of general, Edward was made the "commander of Delhi Command" in India until independence ended that position in 1947.

Edward's career ended painfully, though. His file in the India and Orient Room of the British Library contains a troubling series of letters in which he fought valiantly to have his retirement pay set according to his highest rank. The army argued in return that Edward's field promotion did not count for purposes of retirement, and thus he would have to settle for the pay accorded a colonel. Edward seems to have ended the exchange bitterly, retired, and then died not long after of complications arising from his long imprisonment. He was a true hero of the realm, and it is of more than passing interest that the blood that flowed in him also flowed in the veins of Derek Prince.

General Robert Vaughan's daughter and General Edward Vaughan's sister was Gwendolyn Chrysogon Vaughan, Derek's mother. Like her son, Gwendolyn was also born in India, in Goomarg. Photographs of her reveal a trim, athletic figure with raven hair and eyes that blend British determination with a hint of the Indian dreamer. She was the highly cultured, overachieving daughter of a British general abroad. She read voraciously and was so skilled on the piano that she was often called upon to give impromptu concerts after the sumptuous dinners served in the general's home. She also loved tennis, hiking, and hunting, a contagious passion in British India. Clearly, she lit the early fires of learning and culture in Derek's soul. Yet throughout his life, Derek would see her as a tragic figure, a woman of great gift and beauty squelched by the stifling expectations of Victorian culture. Both her gifts and her pain would deeply shape Derek's early view of life.

On February 10, 1914, Gwendolyn married a dashing young captain by the name of Paul Ernest Prince. The single wedding picture that survives is a breathtaking tribute to the glory of British India. The men—Colonel Robert, Lieutenant Edward, and Captain Paul—are in their dress uniforms, helmets under arm, medals gleaming, and tiger skins grandly draped over broad shoulders. The women are adorned in Edwardian finery, delicate creatures radiating a strength and nobility borne of army life in India. Though they could not have known it, they stood that day at the end of an age, symbols of a glory soon to pass from history. Little more than four months after the wedding of Paul and Gwendolyn, Archduke Ferdinand would die of an assassin's bullet. Weeks later the guns of August would change their lives forever.

Derek's father was an extraordinary man whom Derek would refer to with honor and longing all his life. Paul Prince was born in Derbyshire on April 27, 1882. His father, Edwin, was a cotton manufacturer who, along with his wife, Agnes Ann, provided a good life for young Paul. Yet, like his future father-in-law, Paul left the agrarian life behind and won an appointment to the Royal Military Academy at Sandhurst. Graduating in 1900, his commission was one of the last documents Queen Victoria ever signed in her own hand.

Lieutenant Prince was assigned to the Royal Engineers, and after training in general engineering and submarine mining at Portsmouth, he steamed to India on the SS *Sicilia* to serve in the Queen's Own Sappers and Miners. He would give himself to India for twenty years before returning to England to instruct young engineers for another decade. Retiring in 1935, he would live another thirty years, and it was only during these latter years that he became truly accessible to his son.

These then were the characters who filled the stage of Derek's early life. It is fitting to speak of them in just such terms for, as valiant and as gifted as they were, to Derek they were not unlike players on a stage with whom he had no personal connection. It is important to remember that in the Victorian and Edwardian eras, people rarely spoke of religion, seldom spoke of personal matters, and thought displays of emotion a sign of weakness or instability. This was particularly true among military men. Though Derek revered his family members and always remembered them with pride, he barely knew them and was at a loss, even at the end of his life, to speak of them in any relational terms. They were symbols, examples, and influences, but they were never intimates. This makes Derek's early years largely about the impartation of a heritage that both empowered and imprisoned him. It is the defining dichotomy of his life, one that makes the successes of his later life even more remarkable.

When Derek Prince was born, then, on that August day in 1915, his proud parents undoubtedly intended to fashion their son into a champion of the empire. At his baptism on October 12, the Rev. Hatchell of St. John's Church in Bangalore would have held the baby aloft and offered him to God as Peter Derek Vaughan Prince, "Christ's new faithful soldier and servant." These were the venerated words of the Anglican liturgy of baptism, but they were also the dearest hopes of the Vaughans and the Princes who stood misty-eyed in attendance that day.

❈

Not long after Peter Derek Vaughan Prince was born, his mother declared that she did not like the name Peter and that the boy would henceforth be known as Derek. How he came to be given a name his mother didn't like is not known, but the incident does say something of the strength of Gwendolyn's personality. Derek's lifelong attraction to strong-willed women was probably an extension of his own mother's forcefulness.

Derek's early life was as much Indian as it was British. In the manner of the times, he was reared more by his Indian nanny, called an *ayah*, than he was by his own mother. In the tradition of centuries, British children of that age lived largely under the tutelage of servants and had time with their parents only at predetermined times of the day. Derek spent the first five years of his life, then, as the temporarily adopted child of an Indian woman and, often, as part of her family. He started life speaking Hindustani as well as English and knowing Indian lore as well as the poems of Rudyard Kipling and the legends of Nelson and Clive. In the same way that British nannies in London took the children of aristocrats on strolls through Hyde Park and down the tree lined Pall Mall, Derek's *ayah* took him to the markets of Bangalore and to busy corners where the other *ayahs* of British families collected to share the gossip of the day.

Derek's early childhood was similar to the romance of a Kipling novel. He lived in an exotic, violent, clashing world where East did indeed meet West. Americans would know the culture of Derek's early life as "frontier." Native uprisings were common, thieves were hung, and wild animals sometimes carried babies off in the night. Derek witnessed it all. Shortly after birth, Derek would have been laid upon tiger skins. There were many in his family homes, most of them shot by his father. Two were his mother's prizes. Danger was everywhere. During the years Derek lived in Bangalore, two officers were killed in an elephant stampede. He knew men who had been mauled by the big cats or crippled by snakebites. These images captivated him and inspired him to write the first "book" of his life, entitled *My First Game Animal*. He was barely six when he wrote it.

The dinnertime conversation he overheard would have been filled with speculation about Indian uprisings and assassinations. The year before Derek was born, Gandhi had returned to India from South Africa, and there was rebellion in the air. The British despised this man that Churchill called a "half-naked fakir," but their spite was mixed with fear. The natives were listening to Gandhi. Times were tense, and little Derek must have sensed it. Moreover, the talk of war in Europe and of German intrigue in the East must have filled his young imagination with flaming images.

The most important images from his first five years of life, though, were inspired by Derek's father. Captain Prince was an unusual, often contradictory man. He was, on the one hand, a successful and respected British commander. Yet he had a nonconformist's soul. He chafed in the regimentation of military life and was never happier than when far from headquarters with his fellow officers and an Indian crew building a bridge or laying a road. He loved the freedom, the beauty of an open sky, and the solace of a quiet wilderness. Derek's earliest memories of his father were of the captain's unrestrained joy upon being assigned to build in some remote backwater of India. Oddly, this meant that Derek knew his father was happiest when away from home, a message his young soul could not have failed to absorb.

Yet Paul Prince was also a man of unusual compassion and conscience. Unlike many of his fellow British officers, he learned to love India, to befriend Indians, and to despise the Western arrogance that he believed was poisoning the empire. Other officers thought him strange. He gave exceptional responsibility to deserving Indians on his crew. This shocked his British peers. He was also generous and personable with the "natives." He often spoke up in their defense before his superiors and seemed to prefer Indian company to British in some cases. He was accused of "going native" or "going soft," but he didn't mind. Paul Prince served his king in uniform, but it was his conscience that ruled his life—a lesson not lost on his son.

Captain Paul was also unusual as a father. It would be natural to expect that a graduate of Sandhurst and a career military man would be a strict disciplinarian. Sometimes this was indeed the case. Derek once collapsed into hilarious laughter when a cousin was visiting and seemed unable to recover himself. This infuriated his father and earned Derek the worst spanking of his memory. It may have been that Captain Paul was simply embarrassed by his son's behavior in front of peers. This was certainly the case with Derek's other major offense: his failure to stand when "God Save the Queen" was played. Every loyal subject of the queen was expected to rise to attention at the first notes of this anthem. Derek never did. Captain Paul thought his son was being disrespectful, and Derek was repeatedly punished until his parents discovered that he was horribly tone-deaf, a defect easily detected by those who heard him sing throughout his life.

In another break from both the Edwardian and military cultures in which he lived, Derek was always encouraged to address his father by his first name. Derek's boyhood friends would have been addressing their fathers as "Papa" or, more formally, as "the Major" or "the Colonel." Derek used the name "Paul" and never that he could remember addressed the man as "Father" or "Dad."

Perhaps more significantly, Captain Paul never once told his son that he loved him. It is one of the most defining deficits of Derek's life, though not unusual in that age. Derek never remembered climbing into his father's lap, never remembered a fatherly hug, and never remembered an intimate word between them. Such acts of tenderness may have occurred, but if they did, they were so infrequent that the adult Derek could not recall them. It is a heartbreaking reality, and all the more so when we reflect that the man who would be internationally known for his family life, who would have a global reputation as a spiritual father, and who would teach love to millions—this man had never known the love of his earthly father.

What Derek did know from an early age was the expectation, the standard, the rule. This was the primary message of his early life: there is a way chosen for you, so walk in it. But it was not a way chosen by God, personality, or gift. It was a way defined by culture, class, and dictate of tradition. The Indians called this *pakkah*: what is expected of a man, the way he ought to be. If Derek heard this word once in childhood he heard it a million times. If he was loud at play, his mother scolded that his behavior wasn't *pakkah*. If he mussed his clothes, his father warned that others would know he wasn't *pakkah*. It was the defining rule of life. A man has a role to play as determined by the past and his peers, and he dishonors both if he refuses to fill the form.

Obviously, such expectations can be stifling, soul-numbing, and vain. Yet there was in this inheritance a good and noble understanding of what a man ought to be, and this too seeped deeply into young Derek's soul. It is captured best, perhaps, in Rudyard Kipling's oft-quoted poem "If—." Kipling, the poet laureate of the British Empire, had written the poem to commend to a new generation the heroism that made England great. Published in 1910 as part of *Rewards and Fairies*, the words came to define the manly ideal of the age.

The impact of this poem on young Derek is hard to exaggerate. At his parents' urging, he memorized it word for word by the time he was five. He was often called upon to recite each verse as votive confirmation of the man England destined him to be. A fatherly rebuke might begin with the words, "As Kipling said..." only to be followed by several lines of the poem in answer to some transgression on Derek's part. Even in old age, Derek would lean back with his eyes closed and recite the poem flawlessly, tears streaming down his cheeks.

Indeed, so critical are Kipling's words to an understanding of Derek's life that they bear reprinting. Hearing the words again, particularly through the ears of a five-year-old desperate to please his father and a waiting world, will take us far in understanding the cultural soil from which Derek grew.

> If you can keep your head when all about you
> Are losing theirs and blaming it on you,
> If you can trust yourself when all men doubt you
> But make allowance for their doubting too,
>
> If you can wait and not be tired by waiting,
> Or being lied about, don't deal in lies,
> Or being hated, don't give way to hating,
> And yet don't look too good, nor talk too wise:
>
> If you can dream—and not make dreams your master,
> If you can think—and not make thoughts your aim;
> If you can meet with Triumph and Disaster
> And treat those two impostors just the same;
>
> If you can bear to hear the truth you've spoken
> Twisted by knaves to make a trap for fools,
> Or watch the things you gave your life to, broken,
> And stoop and build 'em up with worn-out tools:

If you can make one heap of all your winnings
And risk it all on one turn of pitch-and-toss,
And lose, and start again at your beginnings
And never breathe a word about your loss;

If you can force your heart and nerve and sinew
To serve your turn long after they are gone,
And so hold on when there is nothing in you
Except the Will which says to them: "Hold on!"

If you can talk with crowds and keep your virtue,
Or walk with kings—nor lose the common touch,
If neither foes nor loving friends can hurt you;
If all men count with you, but none too much,

If you can fill the unforgiving minute
With sixty seconds' worth of distance run,
Yours is the Earth and everything that's in it,
And—which is more—you'll be a Man, my son![2]

As moving and instructive as Kipling's words are, we must remember that they are about the externals: behavior, character, duty, and skill. But they are not about the soul, about that hungry inner man of whom prophets and poets speak, and it is precisely in this tension between the inner and outer life of man that we find the defining tension of Derek Prince.

England taught Derek to perform. It taught him honor as the way of a man fulfilling his role. India, though, taught Derek mystery. In the Hindu gods, in the Indian superstitions, in the barely conceivable ideas of reincarnation, karma, and Brahma—the invisible pressed itself into Derek's worldview. England was mind and body. India was spirit. England was reality mastered. India was reality as prison. England lived in the visible. India looked past the visible to what it thought was the real. England taught man to achieve. India taught man to cease.

Derek would spend the first decades of his life torn by the pull of the two. He was a son of the upper class who would early learn his duty and strive to fulfill it. In school, on the playing field, and in society as a whole, he would give his all to become the man of England's dream. Yet he would always feel a mystical draw, the lure of a world outside his own. Dangerously, though, what he felt was not the lure of Christian mysteries but the seductive appeal of pagan spirituality. It would haunt him until a greater power intervened.

He first felt the intrusion of "the dark side," as he said later in life, during an innocent fatherly prank. Men of Paul Prince's generation believed that teasing their sons made them better men. Once during a family picnic, Captain Paul removed a piece of melon from Derek's plate and hid it while the boy's head was turned. When Derek noticed his fruit was gone, he erupted. Screaming at the servants in Hindustani, he insisted they return the fruit he mistakenly thought they had stolen. The family simply laughed at the five-year-old's tantrum.

Derek remembered in later years how it was in that moment of anger that he felt something enter him. It was a strength, a power beyond his own that filled his words and caught him up in great torrents of rage. Even after the heat of his passion passed, he knew something was different and that it wasn't good. For years, he would feel it return, welling up inside of him when emotion summoned. This was more than the spirituality India offered. It was, as he would later learn, spirits of evil occupying the territory offered them. Only after Derek had learned of their existence and how to defeat them was he able to offer similar victory to his generation.

Yet it was because of this occupation, this embedding of force into his soul, that Derek would always say that India had laid claim to him. He clearly believed that in India something had reached for him, sought to own him. Though he would return to England at the age of five to take up the duties of his station, he knew he carried within himself something that he acquired in India and that sought to exert control over his life. It would make him miserable, drive him to immorality, distance him from meaning, and leave him exhausted. All the while, he would live the pristine existence of the English upper class in the Edwardian era. He could not deny the struggle though. England and India were wrestling in his soul.

2

The Gray Streak:
Lonely Is the Child

THERE WERE TIMES in listening to Derek when I wondered if he was ever touched by his own story. He had told it so many times before and had lived such a long time, I sometimes couldn't tell if he remembered from the heart.

Then a moment would come when I knew he did. Often, though, I had to stop him and remind him to feel.

I had studied Winston Churchill, and I remembered the agonizing loneliness young Winston felt in his early years. He was packed off to what the British call public school—Americans would term this private school—and often didn't see his parents for months at a time. His letters home pleading for a visit are heartrending. Cruelly, his father sometimes gave a speech two blocks from his son's school but wouldn't drop by for a visit. The stamp of loneliness never faded from Winston's soul, forming itself into depression and rage in his later life.

As Derek spoke of his own experience in public school, I listened, but I was disturbed. He was describing an experience just like Churchill's, but he betrayed no feeling. The emptiness in his voice troubled me.

Stopping him, I asked, "Wasn't it lonely? Wasn't it painful to be so alone?"

Derek looked a bit shocked, because it wasn't my habit to interrupt. He was kind, though. He stopped, reflected, and then uttered the words that were so painfully beautiful they almost capture the human condition.

Slowly he said, "Life was a gray streak," and then, looking away as though to distance himself from the memory, he said pleadingly, "but I had nothing to compare it to." It was then that I knew Derek had forgotten nothing and still felt it all.

It is odd how our earliest memory in life comes back to us again and again. Something about that first lasting image seems to capture everything about our beginning. Once it becomes fixed in our mind, it forms into a symbol we draw from for the rest of our days.

One of Derek Prince's earliest memories was of climbing the railing of a huge ship to look over the side into the waves. He remembered that his mother called out for him to climb down, that it wasn't safe, and Derek remembered the feeling all little boys have when a big adventure is thwarted.

The year was 1920, and Derek, then only five, was on a steamer leaving India for England. What had probably fascinated young Derek was a ritual all Englishmen observed as they left the subcontinent. Typically, each passenger took off his solar topee, the canvas "pith helmet" popular among the British in the tropics, tied a rope to it, and let it drag in the water as the ship steamed home. It was a way of saying good-bye, of tipping one's hat to the home now left behind.

Derek probably remembered this voyage all his life both because every boy remembers his first time at sea and because his life was about to change forever. His parents had decided that he should be educated in England and not in the colonial schools of India. So, in 1920, Derek and his mother made the long voyage back to England so that Derek could live with his grandparents and go to a proper English school.

Though no one could have known it at the time, Derek's life would never again be the same. In India, he had known a stable home, doting servants, and the security of a tight community. Now, at the tender age of five, he was beginning a lifestyle that would define him for decades: separation from parents, months away at boarding school, and the family constantly relocating, making community and lasting relationships virtually impossible.

When Derek and his mother finished their long voyage to England, they were met by Derek's grandparents, who had moved home from India and retired some years before. Robert and Amy Vaughan lived then in Sussex in a small village called Cookfield, and for a few months Derek and Gwendolyn stayed with them. After arrangements were made, though, Gwendolyn returned to India, leaving Derek with his grandparents.

His mother's departure marks the beginning of an agonizing time for young Derek and the introduction of a force that would haunt him the rest of his days: loneliness. One of the themes that surfaced often in Derek's adult conversations about his life was his struggle with this foe. It seemed to want to own him and press itself into his soul until his heart would break and his vision would dim. In his early days, he was its victim. In midlife, he conquered it, but he always knew it was stalking him. Then, in his latter years, he heard its voice again and fought it valiantly. Yet all his life he felt as though loneliness was an enemy on assignment against him and that he had to master it to be of any consequence.

His second early childhood memory reveals how he first met this foe. His mother had returned to India some months before. Derek was playing in his grandparent's home. Suddenly, he heard footsteps. His first thought was, *Mother! She's home.* Then he realized it was only the footsteps of the maid on the floor above. The tears came, as did the crushing realization that he was all alone, that his mother and father were on the other side of the world. He never forgot that moment and, later in his life, came to believe that a destructive form of grief set its hooks into his soul at that moment.

Robert and Amy sensed their grandson's plight and tried to make him happy. There were walks in the park, pony rides, and games with the neighborhood children. The retired general seldom let young Derek miss an army parade, and there was no lack of toys and gifts. The truth is that Robert was intensely proud of young Derek and showed him off wherever he could, always betraying a glowing fondness for the boy.

Still, Derek could not have helped thinking of India and his distant parents. The Vaughan's home in Cookfield was filled with treasures acquired from a distinguished military career. There were Indian army uniforms hanging in the closet, tiger skins on the floor, and furnishings all through-out the house that called the mind to the East. In the manner of people who have lived abroad, Robert and Amy often spoke in partial phrases of the Hindustani they had learned, never letting Derek forget the land of his birth. Though his grandparents did not intend it, their chatter in the language of India only kindled the longing in his heart.

It was during these years, though, that Derek first witnessed the kind of piety that would later define his life. One evening he walked into his grandmother's bedroom and found her on her knees, opened Bible before her, praying aloud. The boy thought it strange and asked her about it. She told him that every evening at seven o'clock she read the Bible and then knelt in prayer. It had been her habit for years. Though Derek could not explain it, he immediately had a sense that his grandmother spent much of her time praying for him. Years later, he was sure it was her prayers that drove a wedge between his soul and the surrounding culture and drew him ever further in his spiritual journey. Even on his deathbed, he would tear-fully remember her intercessions.

When Derek was seven, he began attending a school in the Sussex town of Worthing. It was a small, privately owned school run by several ladies who prepared the children of the upper class for England's elite preparatory schools. Derek would have been drilled in all the basic academic subjects, but his teachers would also have emphasized manners, character, and religion. Given what he would become, one of the great benefits of Derek's school years was the required study of the Bible, Christian history, and Anglican polity. Though he had no active faith of his own in the early years, Derek's mind and heart were nevertheless being filled with the words and the truths of the Bible: from the Anglican liturgy, from the scriptures he was required to memorize, from his study of the Greek New Testament, and from the many religion classes he was required to take. Time and again his life would be changed as these early plantings sprang to life.

In 1924, Derek's parents returned to England. It had been four years since he had last seen them, and when he glimpsed the figure of his mother dis-embarking from the huge ship along the Portsmouth dock, he ran to her and collapsed tearfully in her arms. He was only nine, but nearly half his life had been spent away from his parents. This was not an uncommon separation in those days. Parents serving abroad understood that they were sacrificing their children to the empire. The children, though, paid a huge price emotionally, a price often unrecognized until those children reached adulthood.

After a short time in Worthing, the Prince family moved to Kent and settled in a tiny village called Bobbing, near where Major Prince served with the Royal Engineers. Oddly, the family lived in an oast house, a building designed for drying hops during the brewing process. Why a major in the army chose to settle his family in such a simple dwelling is not known, but the setting filled young Derek with a sense of adventure. The house had no electricity, and Derek helped his father keep the oil lamps trimmed with military precision. Behind the house there was a walled peach garden with fruit so luscious the memory of it brought a dreamy smile to Derek's face for years after. There were sometimes fires, too, and one of Derek's lifelong memories of Bobbing was the fiery vision of a nearby oast house burning to the ground in the night.

This boyish bliss was short-lived, for in a manner consistent with the pattern of his life, Derek was soon sent away to school. His parents had chosen a prestigious institution called Hawtrey's, some two hours away at Margate, a quiet coastal town on the southeast coast. Derek would spend most of the next four years of his life there.

Hawtrey's was founded by the Rev. John Hawtrey, an assistant master at Eton, one of England's premier schools devoted to preparing young men for Oxford and Cambridge. Seeing a need for better schools designed to prepare candidates for Eton, Rev. Hawtrey first set up St. Michael's School at Alden House in Slough in 1869. The school continued there for thirteen years, producing some of England's finest scholars and leaders. In 1881, Rev. Hawtrey visited his sister at Margate and was so impressed with the healthy climate of the little coastal town that he moved his school there. It quickly gained a reputation for being, along with The Dragon School, one of the two primary preparatory schools for Eton and was renamed in honor of its founder when he died in 1916.

Derek remembered the trauma of his first day at the school for the rest of his life. His parents took him to Margate in the family's snub-nosed Morris automobile, and Derek's lasting impression was of being deeply embarrassed by how his father's car compared to the Daimlers driven by the parents of the other boys. It is odd that the normally nonconformist and unflappable Derek would be embarrassed by such a thing as a car, but perhaps it says something about the culture of the school and the sense of competition that infected him as soon as he arrived.

The Major and Gwendolyn registered Derek, toured the three brick buildings of the school, and then turned to say good-bye. Derek always remembered that his mother kissed him and his father simply shook his hand and walked away. The boy was left alone—again. Immediately, though, the new students were herded into a room to have the "procedures" explained to them. It was a pitiful scene. Several dozen nine-year-olds, many already in tears, stood at attention while the school's policies were explained. One boy could stand it no longer and finally cried out, "I want my mommy." Other boys began to cry aloud in sympathy. Derek did not cry, but it was just at that moment that he felt it again: that paralyzing, gnawing loneliness, the feeling that would become his enduring memory of Hawtrey's.

Fortunately, he was given little time to wallow in emotion. The headmaster of Hawtrey's during Derek's time there was a man named Frank Cautley, a handsome, dashing scholar/athlete who was married to the founder's granddaughter. Cautley knew that the only antidote to homesickness was industry, and he quickly herded the new class into their routine. There were studies to begin, sports to master, and the ever-pressing need to keep things clean, pressed, orderly, and neat. All the while, Cautley taught the boys that they were the elite, that they must learn to perform the duties of the ruling class in service to God and country. This was their mission, their calling—and Hawtrey's intended to teach them how to fulfill it.

Despite his loneliness, it was at Hawtrey's that Derek began to stretch his wings and explore his powerful natural gifts. Cautley's bold example captured Derek's young imagination, and he quickly rose to the challenge the school issued to him. The boy immediately found that he had a clear, systematic mind, perfectly suited for languages and study of the classical literature that comprised the core of the curriculum. With Cautley's urging, he gave himself to athletics and found that he had untapped abilities that won him the admiration of the other boys. He played rugby, tennis, football, and cricket, and he excelled at all of them. Almost effortlessly, he became the lead student in the school. He was tall, handsome, gifted, and popular.

Yet, he was also becoming an odd combination of proud, distant, and disgruntled. Apart from Cautley, he had little respect for his teachers and actually felt superior to them. Some of this, surely, was adolescent arrogance, and some was a genuinely higher intelligence, but it left him cynical and bored. The admiration of his friends was sweet to his soul, but he was still a loner, ever aloof. He had no warm relationships, was self-sufficient in the extreme, and often seemed drawn into himself.

On a visit home, his mother noticed her son's loner tendencies and asked him to explain. "You're not like other boys," she said, "You have no friends, no hobbies."

Derek thought for a minute and replied, "But I do have a hobby."

Surprised, she asked, "Well, what is it?"

"I won't tell you," he teased and then said, "But I'll tell you the initials: HN." His mother was perplexed, and only after a good deal of time passed did he explain that the letters stood for "human nature."

The exchange is revealing. His mother is deeply concerned about her son's increasingly odd nature. Derek toys with her, gives only a partial answer, and then explains that his hobby is human nature. Gwendolyn could not have been comforted by her son's strange answer and increasingly strange ways. Derek was, after all, only twelve at the time.

By the time he turned thirteen, Derek had absorbed everything Hawtrey's had to give, and Headmaster Cautley decided his gifted young scholar should attempt the entrance exams for Eton. Derek took the train to the legendary English school and found that his examination consisted of an essay on the proposition "if it is good, fight for it." It was a typical theme of the age, a time when men were still reeling from the losses of the war and wondering if any cause could be worth such horrible bloodshed. The masters at Eton clearly wanted to get a sense of Derek's soul as well as his mind. His essay must have been stellar. Returning home the same day, he stepped off the train at Margate only to be met by Cautley, who was waving a telegram from Eton declaring that Derek had already been accepted. The decision to admit Derek to Eton was made in half a day.

In July of 1929, Derek Prince entered Eton College and so joined the ranks of England's emerging elite. He would walk in the footsteps of nineteen prime ministers, two signers of the American Declaration of Independence, and some of the greatest thinkers, artists, and explorers the world has ever known: Aldous Huxley, George Orwell, Percy Shelley, Randolph Churchill, Ian Fleming, Henry Fielding, John Whitehead, Thomas Merton, and John Maynard Keynes. It was assumed at Eton that its students were destined for greatness.

Derek's scholarship earned him a place as the tenth best student in the 1929 entering class, or what Eton called an "election." He was fortunate. When Henry VI founded the school in 1440, he had made provision for seventy deserving young scholars to receive a free education. In the slang of Eton, these seventy came to be known as "Tugs," short for the Latin word *toga*, a reference to the black gowns these seventy students wore. Yet, through the centuries, the school grew beyond these initial seventy until by Derek's day there were more than a thousand. These other students were called Oppidans, or "town dwellers," because they lived in the surrounding town rather than in school quarters like the Tugs. The Oppidans also paid their own tuition, something Derek's father could never have afforded on his modest army salary. Clearly, Derek's intellectual gifts were paving his way to power.

Derek initially found Eton a disorienting place. He was required to wear a top hat, tailcoat, stiff white-collared shirt, and white bow tie. Because he was among the new students, the "election of 1929," he was forbidden to put his hands in his pockets. It was a light form of hazing, as was the requirement that he could only walk on one side of the street. There was also the tradition of *fagging*, in which an older student made a new student his servant. Usually this arrangement was gentle on the new boy, but sometimes it became a nightmare. Beatings were not uncommon at Eton, committed both by older boys against their "fags" or by school officials to correct abuses.

Derek escaped the worst of this and settled into the routine largely through the comfort of new friends. The boys he regularly dined with were called his "mess" in Eton-speak, and these became his dearest comrades. There was John Waterlow, whose father was the British minister in Athens at the time. He was the top student of Derek's election. There was a Greek student named Vlasto and a boy called Holmes, among others. Even at the end of his life, Derek softened into sentimentality as he spoke of them.

His life was defined by the small number of men who ruled his days at Eton. There was first the kindly Dr. Alington, headmaster, whom Derek loved. A man who reveled in the company of youth and often treated disciplinary problems with humor, Alington inspired Derek with his love of history and his poetic sense. The two occasionally walked together across the school grounds, a huge treat for any Tug. Yet, Alington could be firm, even harsh, in the long tradition of the school. Once Derek's election was found to be too "uppish" and were all caned. Another time they received the same punishment for speaking ill of a teacher.

Some of the teachers, or masters, deserved to be spoken ill of. Derek lived for a while in a house run by a man known for his repressed homosexual behavior, often trying to kiss the boys when saying goodnight. Derek and his housemates simply avoided him when possible, but his behavior did not endear him to his charges. Still, students at Eton had learned to expect odd behavior from some of their masters and took it all in stride.

Another of Derek's masters was more difficult to endure. In fact, Derek hated the man, and he was not alone in despising him. Writing years later, one of Derek's classmates, Freddie Ayer, captured the venomous attitude of most of the boys who had encountered this master in mathematics and housemaster. He had a long history with Eton, Ayer wrote, which:

> ...at least led him to take an interest in boys, which might have borne better fruit had he not been a sadist and a repressed homosexual. He used to prowl about the passages at night and I could not go to the lavatory after lights out without his coming to my room and asking me where I had been. Being an innocent boy, I did not realize until long afterwards that he was suspecting me of homosexuality. He was not allowed to beat the boys himself, but he contrived to have them beaten by his sixth-formers (older students) and later when he had an Oppidan house he blackmailed at least one boy, to my knowledge, into letting him beat him. He was much concerned about our masturbation and used on his nightly rounds to question us about our apparent loss of vitality...I hated him at school and for some time after, until I saw him drunk at a Christ Church dinner and thought him more pathetic than odious.[3]

Ayer was apparently not exaggerating the master's extremes. Once when a boy was late returning to his house because he had been dining at Windsor Palace, the master insisted the lad get a note of explanation from his host. The boy did so, returning with a note handwritten by King George VI. The master read the note and, seeing that it included no date, threw it in the trash can before issuing punishment. When he died in 1967, the wife of a housemaster told a friend, "I've been going to funerals all this week and [his] was *much* the nicest because no one could possibly mind."

Though Derek was tormented by the likes of these housemasters, he nevertheless thrived in the rich intellectual life of Eton. He threw himself into the classical literature that his masters demanded, reading Horace, Virgil, Euripides, Pelham's *Outlines of Roman History*, Bury's *Greece,* and Plutarch's *Lives* with relish. He had already achieved some competence in Greek and Latin at Hawtrey's, but within two years of entering Eton he could read competently in both languages. His assignments included translating English poems in Latin and Greek and writing poems of his own in classical style. He was once asked to rewrite the hymn "On Christ the Solid Rock I Stand" in Latin verse. The grace of the hymn never left him.

The written word captivated him. He wrote for the school newspaper, joined the Essay Society, and became wild about Shakespeare, winning the school's Shakespeare Medal in 1933. He also won the Assistant Masters' Latin Prose Prize and was "sent up for good"—commended to the headmaster—four times for his proficiency in Latin verse. Probably in a misguided literary experiment, he wrote a Greek iambic that was so odd that one of his masters entered it into his personal journal. Literally translated, it meant "Dropping dung is unexpected to me." Strangely, the master added the words, "Sad, but true."

As he had at Hawtrey's, Derek thrived in athletics. He played cricket, tennis, rugby, and an odd Eton sport called "The Wall Game," which one old Etonian called "large boys fighting in the mud." Derek himself said later in life that "it was a silly game that nobody ever won because the rules were so complex." Yet, as with other sports at Eton, the objective may not have been athletic excellence so much as character development and the venting of adolescent energy. Typical of boys his age, Derek played games with a wild adolescent passion. His housemaster once wrote after a rugby match, "Prince at times looked extremely well, but was always erratic."

Some of the most intriguing references to Derek's time at Eton are found in the journal of the College Debating Society, which he apparently joined in 1933. The record of his words portrays a budding wit, a sharp mind, and a rather unformed worldview. It also reveals the joviality of college life. One entry, written by a fellow debater, contends, "Mr. Prince, who diffidently proceeded to murmur a few indifferent truisms on the already well-worn subject of the debate, continued." In another entry, Derek condescendingly challenged a speaker who made the statement, "The Classics are not what they were." "Really?" Derek replied. "Have they changed?" When Derek once spoke for too long, a fellow debater recorded, "Mr. Prince decided that it was time to do some more dancing."

The playfulness of the debates aside, though, there were shining moments when it appears that Derek was wrestling with his faith. One of the society's debates had to do with whether the British government should purchase the Codex Sinaiticus from the Soviet Union. Discovered in the rubbish bin of a Mount Sinai monastery in 1844, the Codex is a very ancient manuscript that includes large portions of the Old and New Testament in Greek as well as the apocryphal Gospel of Thomas and The Shepherd of Hermas. It eventually came into Russian and then Soviet hands, which is why in 1933 England was considering buying it for a price of £100,000.

In the debate, Derek stood against the purchase. "First," he insisted, "the government is not entitled to spend other people's money on mere objects d'art such as a Codex. Second, the money spent on its purchase would probably be used to finance a Soviet anti-God campaign." At first, his words appear to be those of an economic conservative and a man of faith. Yet, the more he talked, the less clear his views became, though he did betray some of his thoughts about God.

> The Soviet anti-God campaign was not really a campaign against God, but against priests. There was little of God left in the world and what there was, was far too deeply and cunningly concealed to be affected by a Soviet campaign. In any case, what did it matter to the Church of England what happened to God in Russia, provided that in England he received a fillip from the purchase of the Codex? In short, hurray for anti-God!

Later in the debate, another student raised the question of whether Russia should be required to spend the £100,000 it would get from the purchase of the Codex in the English economy. Derek took the position that it didn't matter.

> They will merely be able to devote the hundred thousand pounds, which they would normally have spent in this country, to some other purpose—such as, for instance, the anti-God campaign. Of which, by the way, I neither approve nor disapprove. I merely say that the purpose to which the money is devoted is a matter of consequence indifferent to those who supported the purchase of the Codex.

What is odd is that Derek seems to have dragged God into the debate when it wasn't necessary. The subject was buying ancient Christian documents from the Soviet Union. It wasn't whether God exists or whether He has revealed Himself adequately in the world. God must have been very much on Derek's mind. He was clearly wrestling with his own soul, having an inner dialogue about how true all the Christianity that had been forced upon him really was.

His tastes in literature at the time also reflect this inner grappling with truth and the state of the world. While casually scanning the books in a section of the Eton library one day, Derek happened upon the writings of Anton Chekhov, the famed Russian storyteller and playwright. Soon he was devouring Chekhov's short stories and reading plays like *The Wood Demon* and *The Seagull* aloud to his friends.

Chekhov's work reached to a growing darkness in Derek's soul. Increasingly, Derek had begun to see the world in tragic terms, a view not uncommon in the despairing culture of postwar England. The world was cold and threatening, and mankind was at the mercy of titanic forces of harm. For Derek it was more a mood than a philosophy and one not unique to him among adolescents, but it dominated his outlook in these years. Derek might have described his understanding of reality in very much the same terms that Chekhov used to describe the central message of his work.

> All I wanted was to say honestly to people: "Have a look at yourselves and see how bad and dreary your lives are!" The important thing is

that people should realize that, for when they do, they will most certainly create another and better life for themselves. I will not live to see it, but I know that it will be quite different, quite unlike our present life. And so long as this different life does not exist, I shall go on saying to people again and again: "Please, understand that your life is bad and dreary!"[4]

If Chekhov framed the world as Derek saw it, Plato framed the world as Derek wished it to be. He had discovered Plato at Hawtrey's in his study of ancient Greek and was immediately captivated by the alternate world the great philosopher proposed. Plato had suggested that the material world is but an imperfect copy of the ideal world. The present world, he argued, is filled with *forms*, or copies of perfect objects that exist in the ideal realm. Thus, a table in this world is but a form, an imperfect derivative of a perfect table in the land of the ideal. The same would be true of a man, a tree, or even an idea. They all exist in perfect form in the ideal world. This idea answered Derek's souring view of reality with the hope of something better. "I loved the idea that there is a perfect world somewhere," he often said when remembering these years.

What Derek yearned for was heaven, but his grip on the Christian truths that promise heaven had long been slipping. It is hard to say when it began. Perhaps he had been herded into too many disappointing chapel services, forced to witness too many lifeless rituals. Perhaps he had, like many of his generation, turned from the traditions of Christian England in the disorienting aftermath of the war. Whatever the case, he had clearly begun to reject the truths that provided at least the backdrop if not the passion of the Edwardian era.

This distancing from the faith of his fathers was evident several years into his time at Eton when it came time to be confirmed in the Anglican church. Many of the boys at the school were confirmed at the age of fifteen and everyone, including Derek's parents, expected that he would be as well. Yet when the time came, Derek wrote his father and explained that he didn't want to be confirmed, that he wasn't sure he believed what a man had to believe to receive the sacrament. The letter he wrote his father has been lost, but Derek never forgot his father's response: "All the other boys of fifteen are being confirmed, and you will be, too."

It was an unfortunate decision. Paul Prince insisted upon what must be done, upon what a boy of Derek's age ought to do. He was making sure his son was *pakkah*. Yet by insisting that Derek observe the rituals when they clearly meant nothing to him, Prince forced the boy into the world of religion as heartless duty. The fact is that Derek may have had more respect for confirmation than his father did. He knew that it was a weighty experience that ought to have deep meaning for those who observe it. Derek had searched his heart and found that confirmation meant little to him, not to mention that the whole of Christian theology was in question in his mind. Perhaps if he had been encouraged to wait or if someone had coached him to understanding, Derek might have taken a different path in his early years.

Instead, at his father's insistence, he became a candidate for confirmation. He met, not with a minister, but with a history teacher who made sure he learned all the relevant scriptures by heart and that he could answer the standard questions in the appropriate way: What is your name? Who gave you this name? The answer? "My godparents at my baptism, wherein I was made a member of Christ and an heir of the kingdom of God." And so it went. The mind was engaged but seldom the heart.

Surprisingly, confirmation brought a sense of conviction. Though he underwent the ritual of confirmation in the most dismissive fashion, he nevertheless found himself confronted with his own failings. "I thought to myself," he said decades later, "confirmation has really come at the right time. I'm not nearly as good as I ought to be. So I'll turn over a new leaf when I'm confirmed. You know, I'll go to Communion and I'll brush my teeth and anything else that I know to do."

Derek had embarked on the well-worn path toward moral perfection. Like Benjamin Franklin, John Wesley, Martin Luther, and an army of others before him, Derek had decided to respond to spiritual hunger with a program of moral improvement. The yearning of the heart would be met with changed behavior, the aching of the inner man answered by a reformed outer life.

Of course, it didn't work. In fact, "The harder I tried to be good the quicker I got bad." He was confronting his own powerlessness. As intelligent and talented as he was, he could not make himself good. In fact, he could not even make himself disciplined or nice to others. Like the apostle Paul, he found that when he would do good, evil was present. The conclusion he drew was disastrous. "I concluded that religion didn't work, at least it didn't work for me, and why should I bother with it. So really, it had the effect of turning me away from Christianity and from religion."

It is painful to watch. A teenage Derek finds this world wanting and begins to look for an alternate reality to give him meaning. The Christianity he has known leaves him cold and empty, so he leans to Chekhov for wisdom and Plato for hope. Yet when confirmation is forced on him, it works something into his soul. He tries to be good, thinking this is what it means to be Christian. He fails and concludes that Christianity may be true, but it isn't true for him. He grows darker, emptier, and less hopeful.

He also grows angry: "Then I began to lose my respect—I didn't have much—but I began to lose my respect for Christianity. I regarded it as a sort of crutch that weak-willed people needed to hobble through life with. I decided I didn't need the crutch. However, as long as I was at Eton, we had to go to chapel once every weekday and twice on Sundays. When I went up to Cambridge I decided that I'd done all the churchgoing I needed to do in my early years and I wouldn't do any more."

He was angry, yes, but the truth is he was lonely and secretly disappointed that his faith had no answers for his aching soul. That familiar fiend, that isolating loneliness, had plagued him at Eton. He called the school a "nest of snobbery," a realization that only comes to one who feels himself an outsider. In 1934, he heard Christmas carols sung by the college choir and felt so lonely he wept and ran from his companions to hide the tears. "I can't really say that I had a very happy life at Eton. I don't think happiness was really much esteemed. You did what you were supposed to do, conformed to the customs and traditions, and probably developed a certain amount of cynicism." It is just such cynicism, though, that doubts everything and leaves nothing. For one already susceptible to a disabling loneliness, cynicism means only greater isolation still.

It is not hard to imagine that India and England were in tension in his soul. He was a leading student in one of the finest schools in the land, an institution designed to press duty and imperial values into the hearts of England's young. Yet, he was longing for the invisible, the mystical, that perfect other world that Plato promised and that India had first suggested.

Typical of his age, his other world would take a second place to the press of the real one. Duty called. Expectation reigned. He must be *pakkah*. If his loneliness and spiritual longing were not quite buried, they were at least silenced and silenced by the roar of his generation's march. His philosophy at the time is perhaps best captured by his favorite poem, one he often quoted aloud and the boys of Eton chanted to each other as the mantra of their emerging worldview. It is the Longfellow poem entitled "A Psalm of Life," and with its call to action over contemplation, to doing over philosophizing, it fit the eager energy of a generation weary of outworn ideals and longing for the bold action of a new century.

Tell me not in mournful numbers,
"Life is but an empty dream!"
For the soul is dead that slumbers,
And things are not what they seem.

Life is real! Life is earnest!
And the grave is not its goal;
"Dust thou art, to dust returnest,"
Was not spoken of the soul.

Not enjoyment and not sorrow,
Is our destined end or way;
But to act, that each to-morrow
Find us further than to-day.

Art is long and Time is fleeting,
And our hearts, though stout and brave,
Still, like muffled drums, are beating
Funeral marches to the grave.

In the world's broad field of battle,
In the bivouac of Life,
Be not like dumb, driven cattle!
Be a hero in the strife!

Trust no Future, howe'er pleasant!
Let the dead Past bury its dead!
Act—act in the living Present!
Heart within and God o'erhead!

Lives of great men all remind us
We can make our lives sublime,
And, departing, leave behind us
Footprints on the sands of time;

Footprints, that perhaps another,
Sailing o'er life's solemn main,
A forlorn and shipwrecked brother,
Seeing, shall take heart again.

Let us, then, be up and doing,
With a heart for any fate;
Still achieving, still pursuing,
Learn to labour and to wait.[5]

Derek loved the poem and took its meaning as his own. Perhaps, though, he interpreted it a little differently than others of his time. When his five years at Eton were done, he refused to attend graduation and sailed off to Europe with a few friends. As he later said, "The wild was calling, so I left the constrictions of Eton to heed its voice."

3

Cambridge:
The Haunting of the Dead

"You're kidding?"

"No, I'm not."

"You just left?"

"Yes."

"You were the number four student at one of the most elite schools in the land, and you just walked away?"

"Well, I finished my studies first, but, yes, I just walked out."

"Where were you going?"

"To Europe. I wanted something true and beautiful. So, I went to the continent. It seemed wild to me from afar, and that's what I wanted—something different and untamed. So I left."

"And you didn't even attend graduation?"

"No, it didn't mean anything to me, the pomp of Eton and all that. So I left before all the fuss."

"Did you go alone?

"No. Another Etonian named Alan Clifton-Mogg was going to Vienna to learn German. It was decided that he would be tutored by a certain family, and all the arrangements were made. He said, 'Why don't you join me in Vienna?' So I said, 'OK.' My father quite approved of the idea and gave me twenty pounds a month for everything: travel, food, lodging—everything."

"Your parents didn't mind that you missed your graduation?"

"No, they were quite unconventional about those things, and you must remember that graduations didn't mean then what they do now."

"So in May of 1934 you simply left England behind and went off to Vienna. What did you end up doing?"

"We stayed in the home of a woman named Frau Jutta Popper. She was German, and her husband was Jewish, and looking back now I realize that she was already distancing herself from him. I didn't understand the German/Jewish issue at the time. Politics didn't interest me. Alan and I spent our time at museums and art galleries."

"Did you master the German language?"

"No, we reneged on that idea. I had learned some German in school, but we got around on English, mostly. We were restless, and one day my friend said, 'Let's buy some bicycles and go westward.' So, we did."

"But the Alps were to the west, weren't they?"

"Yes, and I realize now that this was a crazy thing to do. I mean, it's uphill all the way. I never have enjoyed a bicycle, and ever since then I've never wanted to ride a bicycle again."

"Where did you stay?"

"We would stay in *Freundinzimmer*, what you might call 'youth hostels.' We could get a bed for five Austrian shillings a night. We went to Salzburg and then to Innsbruck. Actually, at Innsbruck my bicycle was stolen, and I was really quite grateful for that. I decided to go south to Italy by train."

"By yourself?"

"Yes. I became adept at saving a night's lodgings by traveling on the train at night so I could sleep. It took me a month to get to Italy. I went to Venice, then Florence, and stayed with Sir George Dick Lauder, a baronet who had a villa. He let me stay with him. Then I went to Rome."

"What was going on in your mind? You seem almost like a hippie then: always on the move, sleeping on trains, living on the change in your pocket. What was driving you?"

"Oh, the feeling of freedom was exhilarating, I must tell you. Yes, I was a hippie before there were hippies. I guess I just wanted what was real, and I knew that the culture around me wasn't real. I did anything I could to push back and just be me. I painted my toenails pink and..."

"Say again? You did what?"

"I painted my toenails pink. I wore sandals, and my toenails showed, and I just wanted to be different. So, I painted them."

"You know, today people would probably think you were..."

"Yes, I know."

"Well, were you?"

"No. I was around it all the time, but I never was tempted or had any desire. You have to understand that we felt the traditions had failed us. What society gave us for answers had been tested and found false in the Great War. I wanted to shout a big 'No!' to the world around me. One way I did it was by painting my toenails."

"But you were Eton, upper class, and heading toward Cambridge. You weren't exactly a radical, toenails aside."

"I was caught between two worlds: the path my class put before me and the hunger that haunted my generation. Some of the most miserable people I knew were young men my age who felt they were being shoved onto a stage to play a role that had become a tragic farce. I felt somewhat that way, and it was painful."

"Were the toenails your only act of rebellion?"

"Oh, no. I had arranged to meet my friend John Waterlow in Athens. His father was the British minister there. I joined up with John, his sister, and another girl, and we sailed around the Mediterranean on the yacht of the admiral of the British fleet."

"That sounds pretty tame."

"Well, we not only did what young people often do when males and females are thrown together, but we rented a sailboat called *The Emmy* and proceeded to sail around the Greek isles nude. That made quite an impression on the Greek sailors and fisherman we passed."

"I bet it did."

"Then there was the time I almost got married."

"You what?"

"I almost got married. My friend Alan Clifton-Mogg had met a Russian girl from Ukraine who needed to marry someone in the West, or she would have to go back to Russia. Her name was Kitty. She was pretty in a

Slavic way. When I heard of her plight, I agreed to marry her."

"Were you in love with her?"

"I don't think so, but I wanted to help."

"What happened?"

"We found out that in France, where she lived, you could not marry unless both people had been citizens there for six months. So, no marriage. She eventually married an American and wrote me during the war."

"Did you tell your parents?"

"Yes, I did. I wrote my father and told him I planned to marry Kitty. He wrote back deeply concerned. In fact, I think what I told him aged him considerably. I must tell you, though, that our exchange of letters about Kitty was the first time I ever realized he cared about me. It is strange now, looking back, that this was so."

"What an amazing time this was in your life. You leave Eton, live a wild and nomadic life in Europe, and then return to Cambridge. How long did this time abroad last?"

"Well, about five months. I entered Cambridge in October of that year."

"So for five months you pressed the boundaries of freedom, morality, and even your sense of yourself. What did you learn?"

"I had my momentary thrills. Ultimately, it was empty. I returned to England no wiser, a bit ashamed, and ailing."

"Ailing? What do you mean?"

"I had contracted a serious case of diarrhea that I couldn't master. Perhaps worse, my skin had broken out in a miserable case of acne that got so bad I couldn't carry my backpack on my shoulders. And I was exhausted. I rode a train from Athens to Somerset, third class. That meant that I rode on wooden seats, I couldn't sleep, and I had little to eat. The trip lasted six days. I arrived late one night at Langport. Thankfully, my mother had sent a taxi for me. I was never so glad for a trip to end."

"Did your adventures do anything to you religiously?"

"No. I probably came home concluding that faith and doubt, pain and pleasure were all the same. I felt nothing, hoped nothing, and believed almost nothing."

"It sounds like you were returning to India in your heart, that you were moving eastward in your worldview."

"That's probably true. The absolutes of the West weren't proving real to me."

"And then you landed at Cambridge. That must have been a jolting experience!"

"Yes. It was quite difficult. Not academically, because I always achieved in my studies. But it was difficult because Cambridge was still affected by the war and the loss of so many. More the loss of belief, really."

"I have read that Cambridge was a troubling place in the 1930s. Is that true?"

"Yes, it was. There were no answers, but there was a heaviness. We felt trapped by history. The truth is, Cambridge was haunted by the dead..."

✕

There is a scene in the movie *Chariots of Fire* that tenderly captures the dawn of the postwar era at Cambridge. It is the college dinner, a "sumptuous affair," the narrator tells us. The deans and faculty are seated at a head table, years of wisdom and study etched upon their faces. The entering class of the college is before them, their tuxedos illuminated elegantly in the light of the candelabras on the long rows of tables. High on the walls above the seated college are pictures of the ancients who seem to peer knowingly down upon the proceedings.

In the movie, the dean stands, looks tenderly at his students, and says in practiced voice, "I take the war list and run down it." He begins then a speech intended to inspire the incoming class with visions of those former students who fell on the battlefields of the Great War. It is a beautiful scene, designed to reveal how the memory of the First World War fashioned the aspirations of a new generation. A new kind of man must emerge, we are given to understand, to lead the Old World from its timeworn ways into the promise of a new era.

It is a wonderful bit of filmmaking, and it would be tempting to believe that it is but a scriptwriter's fancy. The truth is, however, that something very much like it happened. In 1919, the year after the Great War ended, Rev. H. F. Stewart, the dean of Trinity College, Cambridge, gave a sermon at a commemoration of the war that provided the inspiration for the scene in *Chariots of Fire*. The sermon was both poetic beauty and a revelation of how the elder generation viewed the sacrifices of their sons. Speaking at St. John's, Dean Stewart said:

> I take the War List and I run my finger down it. Here is name after name which I cannot read and which my elder hearers cannot hear without emotion—names which are only names to you, the new College, but which to us, who knew the men, bring up one after another pictures of honesty and manly beauty and goodness and zeal and vigour and intellectual promise. It is the flower of a generation, the glory of Israel, the pick of England; and they died to save England and all that England stands for.[6]

This was the prevailing view of the English ruling class in the years just after the war: The Great War was a war to save our world. The death of our sons was a tragic necessity. Let us honor those who died to keep England safe.

As the years progressed, though, a different view arose among all classes. It grew from the poetry of men like Siegfried Sassoon, Wilfred Owen, Rupert Brooke, and Thomas Hardy. It took form in the tales of legless veterans, in the cynical visions of the Versailles Peace Treaty, in the dawning awareness of war's lasting devastation, and in the conclusions drawn from weighing nearly a million English dead against the meager winnings of war. England began to believe that she had indeed yielded up the "glory of Israel" but with the realization in the end that it was nothing more than a costly tribute to national pride, racial vanity, and base bloodlust. Even the patriotic poet of empire, Rudyard Kipling, grew angry by war's end. In his "A Dead Statesman," he took aim at the political rhetoric that led to needless slaughter.

> I could not dig, I dared not rob;
> Therefore I lied to please the mob.
> Now all my lies are proved untrue
> And I must face the men I slew.
> What tale shall serve me here among
> Mine angry and defrauded young?[7]

In the 1920s, a toxic brew of anger, despair, grief, and moral uncertainty poured into the souls of Europe's young. They became, in the words of Gertrude Stein, "a lost generation." As F. Scott Fitzgerald wrote in *This*

Side of Paradise, both the few who returned from war and their younger brothers with them soon found "all gods dead, all wars fought, all faiths in man shaken."[8] Their parents had lived in an age of certainty, with unshakable confidence in the remaining pillars of Victorian society. War changed everything. Now the young found themselves a generation without faith, without country, without morality, and without even a humanistic hope in the betterment of man. As if in summary of the times, one of Fitzgerald's characters said, "I know myself, but that is all."[9]

By the 1930s, Cambridge had become a repository of the spirit of the age. The only certainty was that the old certainties could not be true. In fact, the possibility of truth in any ultimate, final form had long been discarded. Students and faculty alike adopted atheism, celebrated socialism, and toyed with every pleasure as challenge to the moral vision of the Old World. Homosexuality was the rage in those years. "Bed and boy" tours of the Middle East were common for those who could afford them, and drugs were just then becoming the fashion for an escapist generation. The belief in an elite still survived from the canons of the old, but that elite was no longer expected to be exemplary in character and virtue. Instead, the elite were to be the experimental vanguard of a new consciousness, of a new understanding of man and society.

The spirituality of Cambridge in these years was perhaps best symbolized by Charles Raven. By the time Derek Prince entered the university, Raven had become vice-chancellor. Already in his career he had been an Anglican priest, a lecturer, dean at Emmanuel College, and the canon of Liverpool, among other influential roles. Even when Raven took positions away from Cambridge, he maintained contact with the school and held sway over the best minds. He was nearly a legend both because of his persuasive preaching and because he had been a decorated army chaplain with the Royal Berkshires during the war when he was famously exposed to snipers' bullets and gassing at La Basse. Every new student at Cambridge learned the tale.

Raven was typical of a new breed of churchman. He held to the authority and the forms of traditional Christian faith but drained them of all content. He was a humanist, a convinced socialist, and a rationalist wrapped in liturgical garb. He once proclaimed in a widely printed sermon that "the new physical sciences have rendered untenable the traditional ideas of authority of the supernatural, of miracles and in fact of the whole method of

God's operation." His goal, he said, was to "formulate and defend a Christ-centered view of the universe in such ways as to heal the breach between science and religion." But what did he mean by Christ? A fellow traveler of Raven's, one Bishop Barnes, expressed the view of both in a 1934 sermon preached at Cambridge. "Christ lives," the bishop proclaimed. "It is well nigh impossible to go to a meeting of the League of Nations Union and not feel His presence."

Raven became a thoroughgoing pacifist and tried to take the youth of Cambridge with him. He had the positions to do it. In 1932 he was the regius professor of divinity, and by 1949 he had become the master of Christ's College. As T. E. B. Howarth, historian of Cambridge, has recorded, "In 1934, he [Raven] gave a series of singularly unprophetic lectures entitled 'Is war obsolete?' and in March 1936, the very month in which the Nazis occupied the Rhineland, he was taken to task by *The Times* for saying in a speech in Birmingham that it was almost certainly true that nine out of ten of the most virile young men in Cambridge would go to prison rather than go into the army."[10]

What makes Raven of such note is not just that he was typical of religion at Cambridge in the 1930s, but that he was also deeply influential in the life of Derek Prince. Charles Raven's son, John, was one of Derek's best friends. Derek, often far removed from his own family, frequently vacationed with the Ravens and sat with the elder man for hours of conversation over tea and cakes. Raven the pacifist and socialist, Raven the rationalist and theological modernist, was the most decisive force in the shaping of Derek's religious views during his years at Cambridge.

But we are ahead of our story. In the *Protocollum Books Recording Admission of Scholars and Fellows—1933–1934*, now located in the Cambridge Archives, is this entry: "At a meeting of the Fellows for the Admission of Scholars holden in the Combination Room, Sunday, October 13, 1934, admitted Peter Derek Vaughan Prince, born the 14th of August at Bangalore, India, son of Paul Ernest Prince of the Hollies, West Tarring, Sussex, Colonel. (Eton, Classic)." It is the first mention of Derek in the archives of Cambridge, and it is the start of a career described at the time as both "brilliant" and "colourful."

The skeletal facts of Derek's time at Cambridge have been rehearsed often through the years. His first lodgings at the school were off King's Lane at 63

Trumpington Street. This meant that Derek's room faced outside the grounds of King's College but granted access to the interior. Because his room was at ground level and had a window that opened just above the street, Derek soon discovered that his room provided a secret entrance for students in violation of curfew or who wanted to sneak women into the building. Throughout the night, Derek would be awakened by fellow King's students crawling through the window or, in some cases, by the amorous sounds of fellow students and their dates who were unable to wait until they reached "digs" of their own. By Derek's second year, though, he had moved into Gibb Hall and was no longer the unofficial late-night gatekeeper of King's.

He chose philosophy as his course of study both because he had shown some aptitude and because it interested him. He also found that philosophy classes didn't have lectures in the early mornings, a revelation that pleased him. He had come to believe that an academic lecture before nine in the morning was an exceptional cruelty.

Academically he was brilliant. He won scholarships for Greek and Latin within months of enrolling and was considered for the vaunted Hallam Prize a year later. He was the only fourth-year candidate considered for a university scholarship. He completed what Cambridge calls a classical tripos—a three-part mastery of classical literature and languages—with First Class Honors. Not only was he a John Stewart of Rannoch Scholar in 1936, but when he completed his bachelor's degree, he did so with such distinction that he was in a class by himself, his test scores setting a new high in the field. An article in the *London Times* recording this fact called him "an exceptional among exceptionals."

Upon completing his BA, he decided to pursue a master's degree. His path was decided by an odd combination of intellectual interest and personal passivity. "I never really was ambitious. I just took the course of least resistance. It was easier for me to stay at Cambridge and continue my studies than it was to do anything else." So he stayed, earned his MA, served as a professor in classics, and wrote his dissertation on "The Evolution of Plato's Theory of Definition." He was awarded his degree in March 1941.

These are the broad facts of Derek's life at Cambridge. They are true and significant, and they form the backdrop to the Derek Prince story that has reached almost legendary status in the retelling. Yet it is possible that in focusing on the successes and the humorous episodes, those who tell

Derek's story, including Derek himself, have neglected to capture the pain and despair of those years. In doing so, they may have denied the pained and the despairing an opportunity to engage the Derek Prince story at its most meaningful level.

The truth is that Derek Prince was miserable most every day of his life at Cambridge University. The picture of his entering class in 1934 shows a dark and dour Derek, clad in mortarboard and gown, with an expression completely void of interest or hope. He was only nineteen years old, but there would be little to change that expression in the seven years of his university life.

We should try to picture the Derek of those days. He is tall and thin, a few inches above six feet in height but certainly no more than 130 pounds. He has horrible acne that accents a face often drooping and soulful. Friends speak of him in terms that are reminiscent of Lincoln: "Melancholy dripped from him as he walked." He is wiry and athletic but trods the old college town slowly and always lost in thought. His eyes are beginning to show that ancient, soulful quality that will only deepen with the passing years. He already has a light stoop in his shoulders, evidence of the scholar's life.

Perhaps above all, it was at Cambridge that Derek's old nemesis achieved the upper hand. Loneliness, of a darker, more grasping kind than he had ever known, filled his life. "I felt a supernatural loneliness at Cambridge," Derek later said. "I stayed in my thoughts, mainly, because I only wanted what was real and found little of it around me." The blackness that enfolded him sent him into a panic. He felt defenseless, without the weapons he needed to drive the depressive dragon away. In desperation he threw himself into anything that brought even temporary relief.

He started to drink. At first it was just a sherry or gin with his friends. Soon he developed a taste for whiskey, and then found that he wasn't satisfied with just a drink or two but urgently needed to reach that warm, insulating ooze on the other side of half a bottle. He did not get drunk often, but he did like drinking until he was "blurry." It was the way of his fellow students and the fashion at the time, but Derek sought something he could not tell the others: he did not want to feel the stabs of loneliness, the force that sucked the meaning from his soul. Sometimes the drinking got out of hand, and he found himself taking his exams with the alcohol still working on his mind. "I am drunk," he once said aloud to himself during a test. No one heard him, though, and no one knew him well enough to know what warred against his soul.

He also took comfort in women, an easy thing to do at Cambridge in those years. Girls from as far away as Norway and Sweden knew that the university men of England were good marital prospects and flocked to Oxford and Cambridge to find mates as a path to prosperity. Derek was tall and handsome, and his acne was healing as he aged. He had no long-term relationships, but he did date and he did begin to explore the female body. He had a number of partners through the years, which was tame by the standards of the day, but what he wanted was relationship and not just sex. He knew only that he was lonely, but he found that sex merely pressed the blackness deeper into his soul.

Though there were drugs and homosexual opportunities all around him, he was never tempted. He would seem a likely candidate for both: the loneliness, the theme of escapism in his philosophy, his nihilism. But neither laid claim to him.

He turned, instead, to music and film. He was tone-deaf, and he felt left out of the musical pleasures others enjoyed. He decided to fight back by listening to the great composers. He started with Beethoven and Bach. We can visualize him in his King's College rooms sitting under the nine-foot-long horn of his old gramophone with a whiskey in hand, spinning out the great musical works of mankind. He came to know Mozart's Italian operas by heart and even began to feel a "kinship" with the rest of Mozart's work. He worked his way up to the jazz era, and then discovered Duke Ellington. He was smitten. The Duke made him want to dance, something he never could do well. The fact that he wanted to do so—perhaps for the first time ever—is telling.

He fell in love with movies as well. He saw everything that starred Fred Astaire and Ginger Rogers. He sat enraptured through popular comedies of his day, and then paid extra to see them over and over again. *Top Hat* was his favorite movie, but any comedy of the period gave him laughing relief from the blackness at the door.

In the manner of the scholar, he read voraciously and well outside his academic field. He reveled in Keats, Shelley, and Shakespeare. He mastered all of Shakespeare's sonnets, committing many of them to memory, and he recited them aloud to friends whether they wanted him to do so or not.

Like King Solomon of old, he also gave himself to folly. He was trying to escape his inner prison. He wore a blue "Teddy Bear" coat and sang bawdy songs at inappropriate times. A friend once bet him half a crown that he wouldn't jump off of a bridge into the icy water below. Derek, the least likely among his peers to do so, jumped. Dozens of students stood astonished as Derek pulled himself from the frigid waters, bemoaned his broken watch, and walked back to his room—half a crown in hand.

He was trying too hard, though. The fact is he was the embodiment of discontent. Asked decades later what his inner dialogue was at the time, he said, "I will be independent. No one will rule me. I will not be dictated to." He was angry: that life seemed an ill fit, that the faith of his fathers had failed him, that he was among "the best and the brightest" of his age and it meant nothing.

Having tried to master loneliness with energy, he grew exhausted. The darkness enclosed him. He sank. Depression enveloped him and worked its way into the fabric of his thinking. Shut away in his room, he recited a haunting poem over and again. It was "Finis" by Walter Savage Landor. It drips the very nihilism and preoccupation with death that shrouded him at the time.

> I strove with none, for none was worth my strife.
> Nature I loved and, next to Nature, Art:
> I warm'd both hands before the fire of life;
> It sinks and I am ready to depart.[11]

More telling, perhaps, is a sonnet Derek wrote himself. He penned "In the Slough of Despond" sometime in 1937 while in a deep depression. Ever the scholar, he composed it after the Shakespearean pattern.

> This I know: Men's minds and bodies must
> Both wax and wane by seasons like the year,
> Their fertile springs be choked in summer's dust,
> Their autumns bleed on winter's icy spear
> Yes, this I know, for all around I see
> Men ceaselessly restored, made fresh and whole
> By some mysterious power. Yet for me
> There is an endless winter in my soul.

Endless or not, it matters little now.
In my soul's forest spring can but reveal
The wounds—each naked root and rotten bough—
With too clear light—the wounds it cannot heal.
So might a single poppy lean its head
Over a shell hole—a brief patch of red.

It is a revealing piece. Derek admits to a "mysterious power" that restores men, but he feels himself untouched by it. Instead, the winter in his soul covers wounds that even spring cannot heal. But to what wounds is Derek referring? He often spoke of loneliness and depression, but is there something more? Is he speaking of the distance of his parents or of his father's inability to express love? Has he been harmed by friends or a failed love? Does he feel wounded by life as a whole? We cannot know for sure, but we do know that Derek believed himself damaged in a way that could not be healed. It is a torturous state for any man.

�֍

There is an interesting medical note that emerges from the record of these years. Derek's acne apparently reappeared and grew worse than ever, horribly covering his back and shoulders. It had first arisen during his tour of the continent after Eton, yet, while it cleared for a season, it obviously grew worse during his later Cambridge years. Doctors at the city's hospital were at a loss for a solution, and the condition became chronic, plaguing Derek with horrible pain and embarrassment.

The dozens of ointments they had prescribed failing to do much good, Derek's doctors decided to treat him with X-ray therapy. This was a fairly innovative approach in the late 1930s, and it came with risks. Derek's head, neck, and shoulders were bombarded with heavy doses of radiation in an attempt to clear the acne from his skin. According to his medical records, the treatment proved successful, and though Derek suffered a number of skin ailments throughout his life, he never battled severe acne again.

Seventy years later, experts in the field have described the therapy Derek received as "barbaric" and "unwise." Derek was subjected to doses of radiation that are beyond those used today for a large tumor. Asked what the results of such exposure might be, doctors today say that the most likely result would be a cancer of the brain that might not be diagnosable for decades.

Despite the pain of his interior life, Derek's years at Cambridge brought him into contact with some of the luminaries of the age. He studied, for example, under the famed philosopher Ludwig Wittgenstein. Derek was fascinated with the man. Wittgenstein was just the kind of eccentric professor who commands the admiration of students and whose odd legacy fills lives for years. He lived strangely, in a room with a single bookshelf and deck chair in it. He slept in the deck chair and met with students while they sat on the floor. He was Jewish, homosexual, and wildly popular among his students.

He was also a genius. He came to believe that all philosophical problems are essentially the result of language ill-fitting the world of facts. Philosophy, he argued, is essentially a therapeutic activity, employed to relieve the puzzlement philosophers experience at the misuses of ordinary language. If language fit facts more suitably, philosophy would die. With this and other novel ideas, Wittgenstein not only transformed the fields of philosophy and linguistics but also presaged much of the postmodernist worldview.

Derek loved Wittgenstein both because of the man's eccentricity and because the man spent time with him. The truth is that Wittgenstein may have had a crush on Derek, though the younger man would not have recognized it and nothing ever came of it. Derek's lonely soul simply needed the attention of an older, wiser man, and this became the basis of their relationship. This did not mean, however, that Derek believed everything Wittgenstein said. Once Wittgenstein was visiting with a group of students in Derek's room. The professor offered the question of why two plus two equals four. He was making a point about language, but Derek interrupted and said, "Because God says so." It was a remarkable response given Derek's distance from religion, and it may also have shown his weariness with unending sophistry.

Wittgenstein was not the only luminary Derek knew. The poet A. E. Houseman was at Cambridge in those years, as was literary master Arthur Quiller Couch. He would also have known Abba Eban, later the venerated Israeli statesman and scholar. In a different vein, Derek dated Margot Fontaine, the famous ballerina, and in fact became infatuated with her. He sent flowers to her before all her performances for years afterward.

Among the most fascinating episodes of Derek's time at Cambridge, though, was his involvement in "the Apostles," the famed secret society. At first glance, Derek's involvement in the infamous group seems at odds with his introverted, scholarly ways. Yet the fact is that he was an active member and at a time when some of the most notorious personalities in the society's history were members as well.

The Cambridge Apostles began in the early 1800s as a Christian discussion group. The members, largely composed of clergymen, pondered questions such as, "Are the Gospels presented honestly in their interpretation by the clergy of today?" or "Is the Bible used as an instrument for keeping the poor quiet?" With the rise of political radicalism associated with the romantic movement in the 1830s, the discussions changed. "Is there any rule of moral action beyond general expediency?" was the topic of one debate. "Is the practice of fornication justifiable on principle or expediency?" was another.

In the mid-1800s, the society turned to open acceptance of perversion. Belief in the "higher sodomy" prevailed, the view that since men are superior to women, love between two men is superior to the love between a man and a woman. Oddly, this view did not necessarily mitigate against the Christian moorings of the Cambridge Apostles. As Richard Deacon has explained in his history of the society:

> Homosexuality was paradoxically related both to fervent Christian believers and to atheists. In the case of the former quite a few of the clergy and those preparing to enter the Church entertained a hypocritical and sophistical theory that in some esoteric way all was well if one's sexual adventures were confined to the same sex and not to females. Some practicing Christians among the earlier Apostles had subscribed to this theory, one which has been sustained and upheld by some Church of England Clergy (bishops among them) well into the 1980s. But, more importantly, homosexuality was also a revolt against the Church and its teachings, a protest against that most dubious and controversial of all Christian doctrines that people are born sinful.[12]

In the decades following its introduction into the society, homosexuality began to define the group and the morality of its members. The society gained a reputation for its perversion and amoral living. "The Apostles repudiated entirely customary conventions and traditional wisdom," wrote member John Maynard Keynes. "We were in the strict sense of the term immoralists."[13] Atheism and sexual innovation soon marked the society. Its membership was typified by men like Bertrand Russell, who advocated the abolition of organized religion, and historian Lytton Strachey, who once wrote, "Parents would die if they knew what we were really like."

By the 1930s, the society as a hotbed of homosexuality had dimmed, and it became more a hotbed of radical ideas. In this, it was not that far from the culture of Cambridge as a whole. Derek would have been invited because of his leading academic status and because those who invited him assumed he would be a fascinating conversationalist but also open to new ideas. Thus, Derek Prince, the future preacher, sat in meetings with John Maynard Keynes, Guy Burgess, and Anthony Blunt to discuss whether the English nation was worth preserving. Given that Blunt and Burgess would join men like Kim Philby and Donald MacClean in some of the worst spy scandals of English history, it is fascinating to wonder at Derek's association with them.

The greater likelihood is that Derek enjoyed the friendship but remained as much on the fringe as possible both socially and philosophically. Throughout his life, he would exhibit a tremendous capacity for detachment. He could be part of a group and never truly connect to its core. He could be present in body yet absent in mind and spirit. This ability may have come from years of duty from which he removed himself mentally, or it may have come from the tendency of the lonely to find their inner life more interesting than anything around them.

Regardless, Derek seems not to have made much connection. Asked in his latter years about the Cambridge Apostles, he said simply, "It never seemed to mean much to me." Possibly, he did not mean much to them either. In Richard Deacon's history, *The Cambridge Apostles: A History of Cambridge University's Elite Intellectual Secret Society*, the entire mention of Derek in the text is as follows:

> But not all Apostles served in civilian posts during the war. Peter Derek Vaughan Prince (elected in 1938), another colourful King's character and Old Etonian, went out to Palestine to serve with the Royal Army Medical Corps. A Craven Student in 1939, he later ran

a school for Christian and Jewish children in Jerusalem until the British mandate ended. He briefly returned to Cambridge as a fellow in 1948.[14]

What is ultimately of importance is that Derek was among the elite, enmeshed in a secret society that might have meant access to power had he chosen it. His membership would have guaranteed him the networking needed to achieve any ambitions he might have had in politics, academia, or in the rarified climes of aristocratic society. When he turned to faith, when he left his socially upward path for a more spiritual one, he turned his back on the kind of access to power that others of his age longed for.

It may have been, then, that Derek's very disregard for the culture around him—his disillusionment with his life—served him well in the long run. He had weighed the world as he knew it and found it wanting. It did not answer his loneliness or the longing of his soul for "something that was real." When he found what he believed to be "real," then, it took little thought for him to decide to lay aside all that he possessed as a member of the English elite and to follow where the "real" took him. This may be the central message of his early life: having been offered all that his age could give him, he was wise enough to know that only something outside the age could make the winter in his soul turn to spring.

4

The Conscience Objects:
Ireland, the Army, and the Change

EREK WAS IN tears. I was, as well. I was telling him of the day in the Cambridge archives when the staff brought me a large leather volume called the *Porter's Book*. I had thumbed through the immense tome and thought at first it was little more than a lengthy handwritten list of students, their degrees, and their span of years at Cambridge.

Then I came to the years Derek was enrolled. The lists changed. There were still names, degrees, and dates, but there were also long red streaks through many of the entries. I was confused. There would be a name, a streak, and then words in red like "Dunkirk" or "bombing of Britain." I asked the attendant, who could not have been more than twenty, what the streaks meant. With an almost holy quiet in her voice, she said, "They are the men of Cambridge who died in the war."

It was then that I came to understand what it meant for a nation to lose a generation to war. There were pages in that *Porter's Book* on which every name was stricken in red. They had all died at war. They had entered Cambridge in the 1930s, devoted themselves to the great intellectual pursuits of mankind, and then met death while still in dreamy youth. I pictured the porter, who would have known and loved those boys when they were the rowdy sons of King's College, searching the death lists and sadly, wearily striking out the names of England's youthful glory.

I told Derek of all this over tea in his home in Jerusalem, but I think I went too far. In my typically American way, I was crashing about in memories that should have been treated more tenderly. Derek was holding his head, trying to speak but too broken to be understood. Finally, his words separated by weariness and tears, he said, "They were such fine men. They were so vitally alive when I knew them. And then, as though in an instant, they were gone. We lost more than we knew in those years."

And we wept together.

It is one of the most fascinating aspects of famous lives that destinies are often decided in very short periods of time. In the single year of 1895, for example, Winston Churchill was commissioned as a lieutenant in the British army, buried his father and the nanny who shaped his life more than anyone else, and—during a visit to Cuba—came under gunfire for the first time. In a similarly short period of time, Lincoln lost the love of his life, met his future wife, and decided he might one day be president. Destinies are fashioned in brief and lived at length.

Derek Prince's life reveals a short, decisive season as well, and it is virtually impossible to understand what he *became* without first understanding who he *was* during his own crucible of destiny. It is a troubling tale, much at odds with the later public image of the man yet very much the anvil on which that greater man was fashioned.

In 1939, Derek Prince was near completing his master's degree in philosophy, teaching at King's College, and wrestling the vacuousness of his inner life. During the summer of that year, just as he was beginning to write his dissertation on Plato, Derek was invited by John Raven to join his family on a trip to Ireland. John's father, Charles Raven, was then the chancellor of Cambridge, but he was also an Anglican priest who enjoyed leading a small church in a remote area for a few weeks every year. It worked out well for everyone. The local rector could take a needed vacation, the congregation would get to hear the revered Dr. Raven, and the

Raven family could explore some new and exciting portion of the world.

Derek set off with the Ravens to Galway, which lay on the west coast of Ireland. Throughout his life, Derek would recall these weeks in Ireland with great joy, as perhaps the last hurrah of unburdened youth. Everything seemed light and frivolous. John Raven once bumped up against a framed cross-stitching of the Lord's Prayer on the wall of the vicarage where Derek and the Ravens stayed. Seeing it, Charles Raven said aloud, with deep, Trinity College gravity, "The Lord's Prayer has fallen." Everyone in the house erupted with laughter and often repeated the words in the silly manner of friends enjoying an inside joke. Sixty years later, Derek could still be reduced to tearful laughter by someone saying with mock gravity, "The Lord's Prayer has fallen."

What Derek also remembered were the hours spent diving for flowers. Charles and John Raven had a hobby of painting British wildflowers, and this was part of the reason for their yearly jaunts abroad. There were only three wildflowers that they had never painted by the summer of 1939, and all three were to be found on the west coast of Ireland. They were flowers that grew on a riverside, and to retrieve them someone had to swim into the river and pull them while under water. For some unexplained reason, John Raven could only swim on his back, which made pulling flowers while swimming nearly impossible. Derek, who loved to swim and swam well, volunteered. He spent days pulling the right specimens, waiting while they were drawn, and then pulling other specimens with the features the Ravens required.

Derek Prince was nearing his twenty-fourth birthday, but he was probably having his first summer of watery abandon, the kind most children have every year. The memories never left him. In fact, he could recite the Latin names of each flower he pulled—*Ellatine trilongus* and *Ellatine hexandra*—until the day of his death.

With summer's end, the Ravens returned to England, but Derek decided to visit some distant cousins in another part of Ireland. It is easy to imagine that he simply could not bring himself to leave. He enjoyed the peace and beauty of Ireland, and he enjoyed, too, something he had never known in large doses: family life. With the Ravens, he found belonging, laughter around a table, and hobbies shared by father and son. This was new to him, and it is not hard to imagine that he didn't want to leave this new experience too quickly. As the only son of an army officer, he had never known the informal warmth of a large family, so he decided to immerse himself in another family in yet another part of Ireland.

Derek went to visit his cousin, Sean Riley,* who worked a farm on the east side of Ireland just outside of Dundalk. Sean and his wife, Clare,* had five children and farmed in a manner that was as primitive as Irish farming could have been in those days. Something about their life captivated Derek, though. He intended to stay two weeks. He ended up staying six months.

It is hard to say what it was about their lives that won Derek's heart. Perhaps it was the love of the children who crawled up in his lap after dinner or woke him with a tickle early in the morning. He had no brothers or sisters and had spent very little time with children in his life. They alone may have won him. Or perhaps it was the alternate world that Irish farming opened to Derek. He had gone to Europe because it was natural and wild and otherworldly. Perhaps the openness and the green of Ireland were so different from those of Cambridge that Derek felt connection to land and the rhythms of the earth for the first time. Then too it may have simply been the life of a family: the kitchen before mealtime, the hearth fire late at night, and the smell of Sean's pipe mixed with black earth and sweat. For a young man in his twenties who had known only cities, schools, and loneliness, a boisterous Irish farm may have provided just the place for the soul's winter to find its spring.

Whatever the lure, Derek made himself at home. He grew a beard, began smoking a pipe, and started wearing the boots and sweaters of an Irish farmer. He learned to snig turnips and wring laundry with a mangle. He bought a cow for £10 and learned not only how to milk but also to separate the cream. He was leaning to that other side of his soul—the India side—the part that made him paint his toenails pink and seek out the raw and the untamed.

At night he would ponder this invisible other world as he worked on his dissertation. He had already read every word of Plato, and now he wanted to view Plato through Wittgenstein. How would Plato's attempt to understand a thing by defining it properly merge with Wittgenstein's insistence that language fails the world of facts? Derek wanted to find out, and he knew that it was an unexplored area—just the gap in academic knowledge for which a budding scholar looks. So he wrote at a wooden table in the farmhouse using the volumes of Plato and Koine Greek he had brought with him. Every week

---

* Not real name

or so he would, reluctantly, mount a bicycle and ride the three miles into Dundalk to take his work to a typist.

It was on one of these trips that he nearly killed himself. He usually rode to Dundalk balancing his briefcase over the handlebars. On this nearly fatal occasion, the briefcase somehow got wedged between his knee and the handlebars, throwing him from the bike. He landed on his head and shoulder, slicing both open. He was stunned and bleeding but managed to ride the remaining miles into Dundalk. He didn't know how badly he was hurt until he heard the ladies on the street crying out, "Mother of God, have mercy on us, have mercy on us." The truth is that he was a mess, covered with blood and dirt from head to toe. When he reached his typist's home, she cleaned him up and got him to a doctor. Despite the doctor's stitches, the cuts didn't heal well and left notable scars for the rest of his life.

The risks of the ride to Dundalk may have been worth it, though, for Derek sent his dissertation off to Cambridge and received in return an offer of a fellowship. This was more than what Americans know as an academic fellowship. He was being invited to join the governing body of Cambridge and, if his fellowship was renewed twice, to enjoy the privileges of Cambridge academia for the rest of his life. He would have a salary, lodging, and privileges throughout the school. Derek accepted the offer. Then, Cambridge hesitated.

The reason for Cambridge's near reversal had to do with the coming of the war. The year was 1939, and it was obvious that Britain was about to go to war against Germany. Hitler was on the move, blitzkrieg was being perfected on the Continent, and Neville Chamberlain's policy of appeasement was showing itself a failure. What came to be known as the Battle of Britain was not far off.

Derek knew that he was going to be "called up," to be summoned into the armed forces. In fact, he already knew that he was due to enlist late in the summer. He also knew he had a decision to make and that he was putting it off. Cambridge may have begun asking the same question Derek was asking himself: "Is Derek Prince staying in Ireland to dodge the draft, or will he return to Cambridge to assume his duties?" If Derek was dodging the draft, Cambridge would not offer him a fellowship. In fact, if Derek was staying in Ireland to avoid the war, he would no longer be a British citizen. What Cambridge could not know was that Derek himself was unsure.

It was one of the most difficult decisions Derek had ever faced. He knew that his family expected him to go into the army. In fact, most of his friends at Cambridge, caught up in the patriotic fervor of the times, expected him to do the same. But Derek had serious reservations. He was in sympathy with the pacifism of Charles Raven. The two had discussed the matter many times late into the night. Moreover, his reading of Plato led him to believe that war accomplished little and that the philosopher should rise above the violent urges of the mob and petty rulers. He had to decide: Should he stay in Ireland, dodge the draft, and lose his citizenship? Should he return to England, refuse to serve, and go to jail? Or should he serve as a noncombatant, which still meant that he was supporting the war effort? What he knew without doubt was that any option shy of carrying a gun meant that he was "flying in the face of family tradition." If he didn't choose the right path, he wasn't sure his family would ever talk to him again.

He was offered a way out of his dilemma, and it says a great deal about his character that he did not take it. The British government began offering positions in the intelligence services to those with advanced standing at the universities. Their linguistic and analytical skills made them invaluable in deciphering codes and transforming data into useful information. Many of Derek's friends took this option since it offered them an officer's commission and the likelihood of a posting in England rather than near the fighting. Derek thought about this opportunity and decided it was the coward's way. He wasn't afraid to fight or die; he simply believed that war was wrong. He could not produce intelligence that sent others into battle if he believed the battle itself was immoral. So he turned down a role in the intelligence services, and the decision is a monument to his character at the time.

Derek remained in Ireland until the spring of 1940. He took long walks, smoked his pipe, and wrestled with his conscience. But the army was not the sole cause of his turmoil. There was another matter that would not let him rest.

Sean and Clare Riley were an unusual couple. Sean was simple, loving, and, by all accounts, a terrible farmer. He did what must be done to feed his family, but he had little imagination, little ingenuity, and even less ambition. Clare, on the other hand, was a woman with a keen mind who was bored with her husband, bored with Irish farm life, and driven to despair when she looked ahead to the probable course of her life. She loved her five children, but she sensed that they formed part of the unbearable prison of her life.

Derek was a welcome diversion for Clare. He was handsome and intelligent. He talked about ideas and not just the business of the day. He was humorous and helpful, always grateful for every meal and every peaceful moment with the family. For Derek, Clare was a fascination. She was bright, energetic, and warm. Her laugh was infectious, and her body was an intriguing mixture of farm-wife strong with an almost bawdy buxomness. Derek had never known anyone like her.

The two grew increasingly close. Derek was drawn to this motherly, feminine, sensual creature as though a force had grasped him against his will. Clare had begun to see a life with Derek as an escape from her dreary life. The two began finding ways to be alone together and, in time, they became sexually intimate. Not once but a number of times they possessed each other while Sean was away. And Clare became pregnant.

Now Derek was faced with two crises: Would he go into the army or stay in Ireland, and what would he do about Clare? He couldn't sleep and couldn't concentrate. The warm hearth of the Riley home became a cold slab of betrayal and pain. He knew he had to leave. The two talked and decided. Clare would tell Sean the child was his—easily done in an age before medical tests could confirm the truth—and Derek would return to England. Ireland was a haven no more.

❋

Things began to move quickly for Derek. He returned to his lonely room at Cambridge and soon after had to appear before a tribunal to declare his willingness to bear arms. He had decided he could not. He appeared before the tribunal and found that the vice provost of King's College was among them. He prepared himself for humiliation. Asked if he would bear arms, he affirmed that he would not and then made a case largely from the works of Plato. The tribunal sat patiently. Derek finished. Then they asked him if he would "serve without arms," meaning would he join the army and take a noncombatant role. Derek said he would, and then it was all over. The next day, the school magazine printed an article about

Derek's appearance under the headline "Prince Pleads Plato." The editor of the magazine, who hated Derek for once stealing his girlfriend, had written the venomous article.

Though embarrassing, the article had little effect on the course of Derek's life. He would go into the army. At least that was decided. But Derek was still burdened. He was ashamed of his betrayal of Sean, and he wondered what Clare must be going through. He worried through sleepless nights and disorienting days. In his weakened condition, he contracted a severe earache after swimming in a public pool. He could barely move for the pain. John Raven dropped by to see him and insisted that they call for the doctor. A doctor appeared soon after, but just as he entered the doorway, the first air raid sirens sounded. The Germans were bombing England for the first time. The doctor left immediately but told Derek to go to the hospital, which Derek did with John's help.

In the hospital, Derek was put in a bed among severe cases. People horribly wounded by German bombs were filling up the wards, and Derek felt silly to be among them with an earache. Thankfully, the hospital had begun testing some new drugs for infections, and they gave Derek the medication and dismissed him. The earache soon cleared up, but the drugs made him terribly depressed. While he was lying in his hospital bed, a group of Plymouth Brethren walked through the ward. An elderly member of the group approached Derek and said simply, "God is, God is love, and God loves you." Had the man lingered, Derek would have argued with him. Instead, the man just walked away, his words left behind to seize upon Derek's mind.

He went to his parents' home in Somerset and tried to stabilize. He took long walks and often paused to sleep in the grass. He was miserable, depressed, and worried. He later said he was "mentally swimming." For some reason his mind turned to India, and he began meditating and attempting yoga to soothe himself. During his Cambridge years he had practiced both yoga and voodoo, but none of it worked for him. He even revisited what he knew about Buddhism and tried to put himself in that mind-set. This didn't work either. He was void, spiritually empty, and physically tormented. Finally, the drugs killed his infection, and he stopped taking them. This improved his emotional state, but he was still swimming, searching, and ashamed.

As his mind cleared, he became aware of the exceptional kindness of his father. All his life Paul Prince had dreamed of a son who might achieve military glory. Yet now, with war erupting on the Continent and the first Nazi bombs falling on his beloved England, his only son refused to bear arms in the service of his country. Had Paul flown into a rage and refused to ever speak to Derek again, many of his time would have understood. Yet, he had not responded angrily. Instead, he was astonishingly kind and understanding. "You must do what you believe is right for yourself," he had insisted to Derek's relief. Paul held this compassionate view despite the fact that Derek's mother had become unusually quiet, and Derek sensed her disapproval. It was painful, but his father's gentleness softened the blow of his mother's disappointment and became a monument in his memory to the love of his father.

Derek also began to focus on Clare and the mess he left in Ireland. Should he go back to her? Should he come clean with Sean? How could he do such a thing? Yet he remembered her, and, in a way his shame could not drive away, he wanted her again. He was tormented, but he could not discern if he was tormented by a longing to have her in his arms again or by the horror of his sin. And, yes, it was sin, if there was such a thing. Even if there were no God, he had sinned against honor, sinned even against his own pagan moral code. The wrong he had done pressed him against his own sense of himself, against the fading image of the man he hoped to be. His sense of superiority was dissolving in an inescapable sense of his own vileness.

✖

His torment was interrupted only by the army. On September 12, 1940, Derek reported for duty at Boyce Barracks in Crookham, Hampshire. These decades later, the scene brings a smile at the ironies and the clash of cultures. Derek was probably not so amused at the time.

His enlistment forms tell the story. He arrived, was quickly interviewed, and herded into a medical exam. He looked to be in good shape. The orderly recorded that he was 6 feet tall and 150 pounds. His chest was 36 inches. He was thin, perhaps a bit gaunt. A doctor looked him over closely. He noted a scar between the left nipple and the shoulder joint. Derek explained that this was from his bicycle accident in Ireland. When he spoke, his breeding and education were immediately evident in a way that is unique to the British dominions. To the doctor, Derek sounded like a fellow university man, which made him wonder why Derek was enlisting at the lowest rank. Surely this man should have been an officer. To the orderlies and sergeants who corral the new enlistees, Derek sounded like snobbish trouble.

The doctor noticed that Derek's back and arms were scarred by acne. Perhaps this new recruit seemed to his new handlers as the pimply, scholarly type. The doctor noted, too, that Derek's pulse was 100. This was high, signaling that Derek was nervous, perhaps more from the shouting sergeants than the strain of the exam.

Following the medical exam, Derek was taken to yet another sergeant at yet another table to answer yet another series of questions. This sergeant had a heavy accent that rolled broadly from the top of his mouth. He was a cockney, and he and Derek strained to understand each other. He asked Derek what his trade classification was. Derek did not understand. "What do you do for a livin', sweetheart?" the man barked. Derek replied evenly that he was a "college don," a term often used for Cambridge scholars. The man did not understand. He asked again. Derek had no other words to explain. They repeated the exchange. Finally, the man wrote as Derek's profession that he was a "Don Colleger" and this morphed into Derek's nickname while in basic training: "Don College." Another sergeant, trying to get a better answer, asked Derek what he spent his days doing. Derek replied that he spent his time studying Plato. The orderly wrote down that Derek had spent his life "researching the philosophy of Plato." Disgusted, they waved the new recruit on.

Derek settled uneasily into barracks life. It was evident to all that he was well-educated, upper class, and aloof. Though he performed well in his duties and in the physical disciplines of military life, his fellow soldiers thought him odd and arrogant. On duty, he performed with confidence and precision. Off duty, he wandered the nearby canals aimlessly, walking for hours as though lost in another world.

He was confusing. He drank whiskey like other soldiers, and he swore with a command that impressed them. But then there were the hours he spent poring over the Bible. What was that all about? How could a man who could outdrink most everyone else in the barracks then pull away from his mates to read the Bible by the hour? What kind of strange cad was this?

What his fellow soldiers could not have known was that Derek was reading the Bible as an intellectual exercise. Before enlisting in the army he had realized that he would not have much room in his kit for books. He must think of one large, engaging volume—preferably on philosophy—that he had never read before. It must last him for months, perhaps even inviting him, thankfully, to a second read, and it must make him a better philosopher in the end.

He settled on the Bible. Surely no one could be thought educated in the Western world who had not read the Bible. His decision made, he walked to the nearest bookstore and bought himself a large, black, King James Bible, the first one he had ever owned. And he began reading it where all books should be started, at the beginning. This meant that while he was suffering in his soul over Clare and facing the noisy upheaval of an army recruit's life, he was reading of Abraham and Moses, of sons laid upon the altar, and of sacrifices made to an all-knowing God.

These themes fed into the meditations of his heart. He walked the canals, thought about his life, and held himself against the lives of the ancient patriarchs. Perhaps he took comfort in their failings and found conviction in their nobility. When he wearied of these inner exercises, he thought hard about how to relate to his fellow soldiers. He knew he was a strange bird to them, but he wanted to fit in, to understand their world. So, scholar that he was, he thought and he planned and he reasoned.

❈

When he completed the army's basic training, he was assigned to the No. 1 Lightfield Ambulance Unit of the Royal Army Medical Corps. This was a typical assignment for men who were conscientious objectors but who agreed to "serve without arms." It meant that Derek began to learn about bandages and medicines, about treating wounded men in battle and about the logistics of an army field hospital. His fellow trainees, knowing that they would soon use their new skills in battle, were excited and threw themselves into their studies with anxious devotion. Derek, typically, was bored.

What took others seven or eight tries to accomplish Derek completed in the first attempt. What others learned with difficulty and then recited aloud through the night to master, Derek absorbed effortlessly. In his boredom, he grew more aloof and depressed, his thoughts turning to Clare, to the Jewish patriarchs, and to their commandment-giving God.

Despite his distractions, Derek must have impressed his superiors, because in April 1941 he was selected to attend a noncommissioned officer's course in Scarborough, Yorkshire. He had been promoted to the rank of corporal. No one found this more ironic than Derek. Military life made absolutely no sense to him at all. The senseless routines and the mind-numbing duties all left him with a sense of absurdity that reminded him of the works of Swift and Dante. A captain approached him one day and asked him how the cooking was going. Derek wasn't a cook but knew better than to act like anything was strange. Somewhere, from some erroneous notation on a scribbled record, this captain had gotten it in his head that Derek was a cook. Derek didn't dare correct him. "Just fine, sir," he replied smartly. The next day, this same captain approached Derek, addressed him as "Corporal Prince," and so gave Derek the first notion that he had been promoted. Two days later he was on a train for Scarborough. In the British army, it was best not to ask any questions.

Throughout his life, Derek's primary impression of Scarborough was the warmth and kindness of the Yorkshire people. In the patriotic fervor of the time, families routinely welcomed young soldiers into their homes for a meal, and it was not uncommon for men in uniform to be kissed and celebrated on the street. Derek had never seen anything like it, and though he struggled to understand the Yorkshire dialect, he found the open, generous manner of these working-class northerners beginning to thaw his wintry heart.

In Scarborough, Derek studied leadership, medicine, and military theory. He also continued his reading of the Bible. Through Leviticus and Deuteronomy he slogged, refusing to admit defeat before the tedium of the sacrificial system and Jewish law. He was exercising a scholar's discipline, but there was something more. He was hoping for meaning, something true and personal that might reach to his inner emptiness.

We should reflect on Derek's mind-set at this moment in his life. Though having achieved dizzying heights in his academic career, he has also failed himself. He has bedded and impregnated his cousin's wife. He has then refused to bear arms in defense of his country, thus flying in the face of family tradition. He finds himself, now, a heavy-drinking, Bible-reading corporal among working-class soldiers. The officers who command him ought to be his peers, but army policy prevents him from associating with them. He is lonely, he is disgusted with himself, he fears he has embarrassed his parents, and he is bewildered by the irrational, mindlessly boring ways of the army. So, he drinks, he reads his Bible, and he walks alone.

The only man who took some notice of him in the barracks was a soldier who had some peculiar views about religion. Seeing that Derek read the Bible, the man engaged him in religious discussion. Derek knew the type: the religious extremist, the zealot, the kind of man who won't change his mind but can't change the subject. Derek was put off by the man's harsh ways and by his British-Israelism, the view that Israel has been replaced by the British as the chosen people of God. Derek found the idea as strange as the man but tried to be kind. The two men talked from time to time, though Derek often excused himself from the man's company to contemplate his misery.

One day this same man approached Derek and announced, "I've found a place." He meant that he had found a local church and had begun to attend it. He invited Derek to join him. Derek replied that he had no interest in religion, but that he had nothing else to do on Sundays, so he would go along. It was sheer boredom, then, that moved Derek to make one of the most momentous decisions of his life.

Derek went about his usual business through the end of the week: he attended his medical classes, read his Bible, stayed largely to himself, and drank his beloved whiskey. Then Sunday came, a cool, sunny day in May. Derek rose, dressed his trim frame in his khaki uniform, and walked the fifteen minutes to church accompanied by his unusual and ever-chattering friend.

Throughout his life, Derek had worshiped in some of the most beautiful monuments of faith in England. His parents had taken him to Westminster and St. Paul's in London, of course, but he had also spent hours in the glorious College Chapel at Eton and in the soaring King's College Chapel at Cambridge. He knew what the architecture of pure devotion looked like. On this Scarborough Sunday, though, Derek found himself entering a building that appeared from the front like any shop on the high street. But inside, he had never seen anything like it. Within was a single room with rows of wooden benches separated in the middle to create a center aisle. At the front of this room was a rough wooden podium, a clearly unusable piano pressed against the wall, and a small table.

Derek and his soldier companion were conspicuous by virtue of their uniforms and by virtue of their age. They were clearly the youngest of the near forty people in attendance that day. They were greeted warmly, though, and gestured kindly to their seats just before the service began.

What followed was unlike anything Derek had experienced in the Anglican church. The service was opened with a prayer that was both more personal and more passionate than any prayer Derek had ever heard. People encouraged the man praying with their amens and nodded their agreement. Some raised their hands into the air as though reaching to an unseen God. Then the singing began. Taking their red hymnbooks in hand, the congregation opened to the announced page and sang to the encouragement of an amazingly energetic song leader. To Derek's bewildered amusement, the congregation sang the first song through and then sang it a second time. When the second song was announced, it too was sung through twice.

Not long after the preacher rose to speak. Derek, trained in logic and textual criticism, was eager to apply his skills to the pastor's words. The text for the day came from the first few verses of Isaiah 6. In this passage, Isaiah sees a vision of the Lord seated upon His throne and is overwhelmed by the experience. "Woe is me!" Isaiah cries, "for I am undone; because I am a man of unclean lips and I dwell in the midst of a people of unclean lips."

Derek had not been expecting to hear anything from the speaker that might apply to his life. After all, the man had until recently been a taxi driver. What could he teach a Cambridge don? Yet when Derek heard Isaiah's words upon seeing his God, Derek said to himself, "There could be no better words to describe me than a man of unclean lips among a people of unclean lips." The preacher had Derek's attention. Even though the man rambled from theme to theme, scripture to scripture, Derek could not help but feel that despite the lack of intellectual content, the sermon was for him.

While Derek entertained these thoughts, the preacher came to his closing point. He was attempting to illustrate the fact that Saul was a tall man. What this had to do with his sermon Derek did not know. But to make the point, the excited preacher jumped up on a bench to illustrate Saul's height. Yet, when the man landed on the bench, it snapped in the middle and sent the poor, startled speaker tumbling to the floor. There were muffled giggles in the room, but the man quickly regained his composure and went on with his talk.

Nearing an end, the preacher asked everyone to close their eyes and bow their heads. Derek did not quite follow all that was said, but he did catch the words "if you want this, raise your hand." Derek had never raised his hands in church before and wasn't about to do so now. Yet he knew these people had something he did not, something he desperately wanted. Still, would he be a low class fool in the name of religion?

While he wrestled with himself, he realized that his arm, quite involuntarily, was rising into the air. He was sure he had done nothing to make it so, but there it was, now straight up in the air. Derek was shocked but not altogether sorry that his hand was up. He did want whatever it was these people had, and if raising your hand was the way to get it, fine. The congregation seemed to relax, the preacher seemed satisfied that a soldier had responded in his church, and the service soon came to an end.

Before Derek and his fellow soldier could make their way to the door, a short, craggy, seemingly frail woman approached them and invited them to dinner at her house. Her name was Mrs. Shaw, and she ran a boarding house nearby, she said. She would enjoy the fellowship, and, after all, the two young men looked like they could use a good meal. The woman's kind face won them, and they followed her to her home.

Derek was immediately taken with Mrs. Shaw. Perhaps there was something in her that reminded him of his grandmother, or perhaps he simply missed the female presence. Whatever the case, he walked closely by her side as they made their way to the Shaw boarding house that sunny afternoon.

Inspired by her pastor's sermon, Mrs. Shaw began telling Derek of the miracle God had given her family. Years before, her husband had attempted to enlist in the army during World War I but was found to have tuberculosis in one lung. This not only prevented him from fighting in the war but also from working. As his condition grew worse, his family grew destitute. "I prayed for my husband every day for ten years," Mrs. Shaw said matter-of-factly. Derek was astonished. He could not conceive of anyone ever praying for another human being for ten years.

Derek was amazed but assumed that was the end of the story. Mrs. Shaw had prayed, showing herself a dutiful wife and Christian, but naturally nothing had happened. But Derek was wrong. "At the end of ten years," Mrs. Shaw continued, "I was praying alone in a room. My husband was in the bedroom, sitting up in bed, propped up on the pillows, coughing up blood. As I was praying for his healing, an audible voice spoke to me and said, 'Claim it!' I answered out loud, 'Lord, I claim it now!'"

What Mrs. Shaw told Derek next was almost more than he could believe. She said that when she claimed what she had prayed, her husband was immediately healed. When Mr. Shaw later returned to his doctor, the man told him that the lung that had been affected by tuberculosis was now stronger than the lung that had never been affected!

Derek listened with complete concentration to everything Mrs. Shaw said. Her words stirred him to the core of his being. He sensed a question being posed from within, as though his own soul was rising in search of an answer. Words formed in his mind: *Is this what you've been looking for? Maybe it is*, Derek thought to himself, *maybe it is*.

These matters swirled in Derek's mind as he entered the Shaw's house. It was a small but cozy affair that radiated warmth—a warmth that must have reminded him of an Irish farmhouse he once knew. After being introduced to the other guests, he was seated at the table and was just eyeing the food with the eagerness of an underfed soldier when Mr. Shaw—obviously now in perfect health—led the gathering in prayer. Derek had never eaten a meal at which someone offered thanks to God for the food. Typically, he had the fleeting thought that perhaps such practices were common of the working class. Then he lost the matter in the joy of food.

When the meal was done, everyone remained at the table, and there was another time of prayer, this time with each person at the table praying in turn. Derek had only just heard his first blessing of the food. He had never in his life prayed aloud, and soon it would be his turn. His mind was blank, and he was a bit nervous. He simply had nothing to say. When it came his turn, though, he found himself crying out, "Lord, I believe; help thou my unbelief." His mouth snapped shut, and he could say nothing more. He sat in astonishment while the rest of the guests voiced their thanks.

Years later, Derek would look back on this moment in his life and express deep gratitude for the good that was done him in the Anglican church. Though as a child he had bemoaned all his many hours in religious services, as a man he realized that vast portions of the Word of God were embedded in his soul whether he intended them to be or not. The constant repetition, the public reading of Scripture, and the constant catechizing in Christian truth may have bored him at the time, but they clearly planted the early seeds of a faith that would shape the course of his life. Derek's prayer at the Shaws' table would not be the last time that he spoke the words of a scripture that he did not know lived in him. (See Mark 9:24.)

Before Derek and the other soldier returned to their barracks, the Shaws told them that a nearby Assemblies of God church was holding a revival service on the following Tuesday and invited the soldiers to go with them. Derek neither knew what the Assemblies of God were or what a revival was, but he eagerly agreed to attend. "If this is part of the whole thing," he said aloud—to himself as much as to the Shaws, "I'm for it."

Throughout the rest of that Sunday and all day Monday, Derek pondered what he had experienced. He had agreed to attend church with his argumentative bunkmate only because he had nothing better to do. When he arrived at the church, he found little in common with the hymns they had sung and even less in common with the preacher's sermon. But he could not deny that these people, all of them, had something in their lives—something that radiated from their souls—that he did not have and that he no longer wanted to live without. And Mrs. Shaw! What a woman of faith she was, and what a story she had to tell of the goodness of God. Derek was still surprised at his after-dinner prayer, but now, upon reflection, he was not sorry he had prayed it. *Lord, I do believe,* he thought, *or at least I want to believe. Help me!*

Tuesday night arrived, and Derek, again clad in his khaki army uniform, accompanied the Shaws to the Assemblies of God meeting. Again, there was the energetic opening prayer. Again, there were two songs from the hymnbook, each sung twice. And again, there was a dramatic sermon, illustrated by the theatrics of a sincere but rambling preacher. This time, the sermon had something to do with how Enoch was taken away by the Lord, and the preacher used the illustration of the British government's Criminal Investigation Department using dogs to find an escapee. Derek understood that the dogs lost the scent at the point where Enoch was "taken away," but that was about all that Derek understood from the "many themes" of the sermon.

Then it came. "Every eye closed, every head bowed," the preacher said. And again, the sense of the moment seemed to be "If you want this, raise your hand." Derek pondered and felt largely unmoved. Then it struck him that in the last meeting his hand had been put up for him. Now, he sensed, he must put it up himself. So, he raised his hand and again the congregation seemed to relax and again the preacher closed his message.

Derek felt nothing and was nearing disappointment when he met the preacher shaking hands at the exit. The pastor remembered Derek from the service and wanted to make sure that the young soldier's commitment was clear. "Do you realize that you are a sinner?" the man asked boldly.

"Yes," Derek replied cautiously.

"Do you believe that Jesus Christ died for your sins?" the pastor asked.

Always the man for logical honesty, Derek shot back, "To tell the truth, I can't see what the death of Jesus two thousand years ago has to do with the sins of my life," and then walked out into the night.

Derek passed several days in frustration. He later said, "I had stepped out of my old life but hadn't quite stepped into a new one." He wanted what he saw in the lives of these godly Yorkshire people. Yet, it seemed that he could not have it. When he asked the Shaws and their friends to explain their spiritual experiences, he could barely understand what they said. A confusing combination of lower class English, Yorkshire accent, and church jargon understandable only by the initiated prevented him from following their path. It did not help that his systematic, front-to-back study of the Bible had now landed him in the Book of Job. Derek found Job, his friends, and their angry God of little help. He was tempted to dismiss this whole matter of religion as merely a condition of psychology and social class—a view popular among wags at Cambridge.

Still, he could not deny what he told the preacher: "I am a sinner." If Derek had ever known he was a weak, immoral, unclean man, it was now. He also could not deny what he saw in the Shaws and the people at church.

They too admitted they were sinners and, in many cases, worse sinners than Derek had ever considered being. Yet, they said they felt clean now, and they looked it. Their faces beamed, their speech was like pure water, and they seemed—what was the right word?—innocent! Yes, that was it. No matter their prior lives they now seemed to possess an endearing innocence. What Derek would have given to have his innocence back, to rid himself of the hardened cynicism that filled his soul.

After days of this inner wrestling, Derek was worn out. He had exhausted himself with evaluating and analyzing. He could not reason his way to the reality he sought. But perhaps there was a way. The Shaws and their pastor friends had not proposed a truth to be analyzed. They offered a relationship with a person. Derek could analyze all he wished, but he knew he could not enter a relationship just by thinking about it. Perhaps this Jesus was real, and perhaps, if He was real, He might just make Himself known if Derek invited Him. It was worth a try, anyway.

Derek knew what he wanted to do. He waited until late one night when everyone in the barracks would be asleep. It was particularly important that Derek's roommate, Donald Smee, should be asleep. He was Jewish, and Derek didn't think he would appreciate any messing about with this Jesus person in his room.

When all was quiet, Derek pulled a canvas, army-issue stool in front of the large window on the east wall of his room. It had been a stroke of good fortune that this window looked directly out onto the North Sea, and Derek had spent many hours feeding his soul on the breathtaking view from this very spot. Now it was night, and while he could only dimly see the reflection of the moon on the waters below, he could hear the rhythmic beating of the waves against the rocky shore of Scarborough.

We should picture him at this very moment: He is wearing only a T-shirt and boxer shorts. He pulls the canvas stool to the window and tries to pray. No words come: no miraculous scripture sounding itself through his lips as happened at the Shaw's table. He waits and tries to pray again but doesn't know how. Then a flock of seagulls float on a seaside breeze just outside of his window. They begin to screech, and it distracts him. Those who have been to the place know that the screech of the Scarborough seagull is deafening. Derek gets up from his stool in frustration and waits. Five, ten minutes pass, and then the seagulls move on. Derek feels a bit foolish, distracted from God by a bunch of stupid birds. Still in his underwear, still on the stool, still at the moonlit window, he tries to pray again.

But he cannot. For more than an hour he tries, but there is nothing. He is frustrated nearly to tears.

And then it happens.

He feels it first in his arms. They rise toward the ceiling, his palms turned upward.

Why palms upward? he wonders nearly aloud.

A voice sounds in his soul. *It is power from on high.*

This power—this electric, radiating force—moves from his hands, up his arms, and through his torso to his legs. It is circulating through him like an electrical current, or perhaps it is washing over him like the waves of the sea he hears outside his window. He cannot tell, and he does not care. He wants it never to stop.

Words form on his lips. Again, they are words from the Bible he does not know he knows. "Unless You bless me, I will not let You go!" But he cannot stop. "I will not let You go," he repeats. "I will not let You go. I will not let You go."

Over and again he says the words. As he does, this power intensifies and begins to push him back. His hands are raised, and he is still seated on the stool, but just barely. He is falling back, and yet he is not falling. He is yielding. And now he is aware that this is not just some spiritual electricity he is feeling. It is the presence of a person, a person who he senses is the answer for his life.

"I will not let You go. I will not let You go. I will not let You go."

Derek falls, almost floats backwards from the stool to the floor, his hands raised, his lips never ceasing to offer the cry of his soul.

Then the words change. Realizing he is in the presence of the one whom he has sought, he begins to cry, "Make me love You more and more. Make me love You more and more."

He repeats this over and over as he lies on his back in his underwear, his palms raised to the ceiling, his eyes filled with tears.

"Make me love You more and more. Make me love You more and more."

He is weeping and praying. He cannot help himself, and he cannot help waking up his roommate Donald Smee.

It is the wee hours of the morning now, and Corporal Smee awakes to find his normally staid roommate on his back weeping and praying with his hands raised. He tries to talk to Derek, but Derek does not hear. He realizes the man on the floor is in an altered state.

In disgust, Smee says to Derek, "I don't know what to do. I suppose it's no good pouring water on you." Derek hears him but also hears that inner voice: *Water can't put this out.*

Smee goes back to bed, and Derek continues sobbing. Soon this sobbing turns to laughing. Then, the inner voice again: *Men must not blaspheme the Holy Spirit.* Immediately it enters Derek's mind that this must be the Holy Spirit. He thinks this while his body continues to respond with laughing, sobbing, and pleas for the third person in the room never to leave him.

Then he can take no more. Laughing and sobbing, he crawls to what passes for his bed, a straw mattress on the floor. Still unable to control his words or his mood, he curls up on the mattress to gain some bodily control and continues mumbling, "Help me love You. Help me love You."

Time condenses, and Derek continues in this fetal position of prayer for what might be hours or minutes. Then, he falls asleep—the window open, the waves crashing, and the person he has just met still near.

The next morning, Derek Prince awoke as though in another man's skin and another man's soul. He was different, new, changed. He was in the same room with the same open window and the same canvas stool. Yet as he pulled on his trousers he realized that he was almost involuntarily talking to God. The night before he had not known how to pray. Now, he could not stop. Scriptures he had never intentionally learned formed themselves into prayers and moved through his lips involuntarily. He could not drink a cup of water without giving thanks when he had once been unable to offer thanks for a feast.

He went out into his day and began his duties. He kept telling himself that he was still Derek Prince in the army in Scarborough. This he knew, but nothing else seemed normal. Usually his sentences were punctuated with graphic swearing and sexual references. Now, without giving a thought to it, he not only did not swear but also had no desire to do so.

Moreover, the weeping and laughing of the night before had quieted a bit but were still just beneath the surface. Tears formed as he felt afresh that presence, this time not in a room with him but inside him. Then, without choosing to do so, the gentle crying would form itself into giggles and of a kind that seemed to free his soul with every sound. All day long he made excuses to pull aside—into the men's room, off to his barracks—to find a private place to give vent to what felt like a new stream of cool, happy water pouring from inside him.

The evening came, and he followed habit to the local pub to enjoy his evening sherry. He was an innocent, unaware of what had happened to him or what it might mean to his manner of living. He was in the grip of an experience he could not deny, could not interpret, and could not ever wish to escape. Distractedly, he approached the door of the pub, and when he did, his feet stopped working. He simply could not command his legs to walk through the door. Becoming used to the unusual, he simply turned from the door and walked back to his barracks.

He knew he was changed, but he had no way of knowing just how. Sitting on his canvas stool, he opened his Bible to read again from the Book of Job, and his eyes fell instead on Psalm 126:1–2.

> When the LORD turned again the captivity of Zion, we were like them that dream. Then was our mouth filled with laughter, and our tongue with singing: then said they among the heathen, The LORD hath done great things for them.

For the first time in his life, Derek read in the pages of Scripture an exact description of something he was experiencing. He was amazed: that people in the past knew what he knew, that the Bible could be contemporary, that he was living the life of a freed captive.

As soon as he could, Derek made his way to the Shaws' home to tell them of his experience. They tearfully laughed with him and prayed their thanksgiving aloud. They had asked God to intervene in the life of their young soldier friend, and He had done so. Now, the profane, hard-drinking soldier who could not see a connection between the life of Jesus Christ and the problem of his own sin was laughing uncontrollably in the Shaw's parlor at the feeling of being free.

Over the following weeks, the Shaws met with Derek as often as possible. They taught him what they knew of Scripture and helped him understand the passages that described salvation and the powerful presence of their God. It was Jesus who had appeared to him, they explained. This same Jesus who died for Derek's sins had come into Derek's room that night to cleanse his sin and enter his heart forever. Now, he was born again, saved, delivered from the kingdom of darkness. He had entered the kingdom of God now, and the Bible would be his guide. Derek went back to church with them and told the story of that night on the canvas stool where God met him in his underwear. He never got through the tale without the same laughter and tears flooding him again. The congregation celebrated with him and took him as one of their own.

One evening, the Shaws sat Derek down after a meal and told him of their experience with the Holy Spirit. "This being is God in spirit form," they said, "and when a person has been freed as you have been freed, when he is saved, there is another work that God does to give that person power. It is what the apostles received on the Day of Pentecost, and it is what God wants all of His people to have." Derek listened intently and yet uncritically. As much as he had sharpened his critical faculties through the years, they barely functioned now. He read the scriptures the Shaws showed him about this "baptism" that the Holy Spirit gives, and though he did not fully understand them, he wanted whatever the Shaws had.

When he agreed to welcome anything God wanted to do, the Shaws stood around him and prayed with their hands pressed gently about Derek's shoulders and head. Phrase by phrase, they led him in a prayer asking God for His Holy Spirit and asking for any language that Spirit might give. Derek felt again what he had felt in the barracks on that night. This time it moved from the top of his head down his body to his feet. When this radiating force covered him completely, he suddenly realized that the prayers he had been mumbling quietly in English while the others prayed now had turned to a language he did not know. Derek knew that it was indeed a language, one with structure and interconnection. He knew a half a dozen languages already and could discern the pattern of a language when he heard one. This one was rising, without his telling it to do so, from his deepest soul, through his mouth, and toward the heavens. He prayed in this new language for some time while the Shaws thanked God aloud that Derek now "had the Spirit and spoke in tongues."

Derek was now a man gloriously in conflict with himself. All of his breeding, education, and culture had flowed behind him like a river, moving him in its currents toward a preset destination. Now, though, Derek had something living in him, coursing through him that made his former river seem a shallow, muddy trickle in comparison. He did not know what it would mean, but he knew the life he had been positioned to live since birth would never be his again. What he had found was more than an experience; it was a world, beneath and beyond the one he had known, and he had chosen to make that world his home.

5

Discipled in the Desert:
Lessons of a Lifetime

"So you became a Christian, Derek, but what about Clare? Did you lose contact with her during the war?

"No, she continued to write me while I was at Boyce Barracks and Scarborough. She wasn't too repentant about what we had done, and her letters more than hinted at me returning to her."

"How did you feel about the whole matter after you became a Christian?"

"I felt horribly, of course, and not long after my salvation I received a letter from her asking me what the child should be named. I knew then that I had to deal with the matter. So I got permission to go on leave to Ireland. This was no small achievement because Ireland wasn't in the war and wasn't part of the Union. People went to Ireland to escape the draft in those days the same way some Americans went to Canada to escape the Vietnam War. My commander, Colonel Dan McVicker, wasn't sure about my request at first but then decided to risk letting me go."

"So you went back to the Riley's farm in Dundalk? What happened?"

"After I greeted everyone I told Sean we had to talk. He and Clare sat with me in the parlor, and I told him that the child was mine. There were tears and a bit of anger, but he was very gracious. Before the conversation was over, Sean forgave me and agreed to adopt the child as his own. I don't think Clare was too happy with me for telling Sean."

"Did you hold the child, Derek?"

"Yes, I held him. He was a rather handsome baby. In fact, I attended his baptism while I was there. They named him Gavin David Montrose Riley."

"How did it feel to hold your son?"

"My feelings were of relief, mainly, and I was happy about the child having a good home. Of course, I felt more than a twinge of guilt at what I had done, and Clare's brazen, somewhat bitter attitude only made the situation more uncomfortable. Still, there is something about holding your own child…"

"You know, Derek, it strikes me that those moments Gavin was in your arms are the only time in your life you have ever held a child that was your own flesh and blood.

"Yes, that is true, I suppose. Although God gave me such wonderful daughters that I never felt it a loss."

"You showed a lot of character going back to Ireland to confess to Sean."

"I never thought of it that way, but whatever I had that made me do it was from God. I hadn't been a Christian very long, but I knew one thing: I knew that if I didn't deal with the situation righteously, my life would never amount to anything."

✠

When Derek Prince met Jesus and was baptized by the Holy Spirit in 1941, he joined, perhaps unwittingly, a movement that had been sweeping the world for decades. Some called it "the Renewal" and some called it "Pentecost," but no matter its name, it was even then redefining the Christian church in a manner few movements ever had.

After the followers of Jesus first received the gift of the Holy Spirit on that celebrated day in Jerusalem sometime around A.D. 30, supernatural phenomena became commonplace in the early church. Understanding this Holy Spirit as the power to continue the miraculous ministry of Jesus Christ on earth, the early church raised the dead, healed the sick, drove demonic spirits out of human flesh, spoke in spiritual languages, and received revelations from God. In other words, they did what Jesus had done, and the astonishing growth of the early church was due in large part to the miraculous works of believers in confirmation of their spoken gospel.

After the early centuries of Christianity, these supernatural phenomena seemed to decrease. Some Christians have suggested that miracles were only given by God to help the church in its infancy. Once the Bible was written, they contend, believers had a written record to confirm their message and no longer needed "signs and wonders." Others contend that the Christian church became so corrupted under Constantine and the domination of the state that a grieved Holy Spirit ceased to operate through a tainted people.

Whatever the reason for their infrequency, the truth is that miraculous works never fully died out in church history. In almost every generation, at least a remnant continued to experience the same "power from on high" the apostles had first known on the Day of Pentecost. Church fathers like Irenaeus, Tertullian, Novatian, and Anthony, who lived well after the first apostles had passed from this world, all claimed victorious confrontations with demons. Ambrose told of believers speaking in tongues and being healed through prayer in his day. Augustine recounted dozens of healings in *The City of God,* and men as diverse as St. Francis of Assisi, Ignatius of Loyola, and Martin Luther wrote unashamedly of divine healing, the miracles of the Holy Spirit, and the power of the gospel to destroy demonic forces. During the Scottish Reformation of the sixteenth century, John Knox issued prophecies that were confirmed time and again, in one case even correctly predicting the destruction of an entire unrepentant town.

Somewhat later in history, the revivals that swept England and America under the preaching of John Wesley and George Whitefield had an overtly supernatural character to them. Not uncommonly, the ground would shake during their preaching, sinners would think themselves on fire when no flame was visible, and healings, though rare, occurred as well.

These revivals under the leadership of Wesley and Whitefield, often called "the Great Awakening," created streams of renewal that continued to flow through the church. Men like Charles Finney and Dwight Moody in America and Charles Spurgeon and Andrew Murray in the British dominions led revivals for decades during the 1800s, rivers of refreshing that they understood flowed from the pioneering preachers of the Great Awakening.

Supernatural phenomena attended the ministries of each of these men.

Though Pentecostal phenomena clearly continued through the ages, nothing that the church had experienced since the days of the apostles could have prepared it for the great crashing waves of revival that announced the dawn of the twentieth century. The sweeping supernatural movement that Derek Prince joined in 1941 was unlike anything Christian believers had ever known.

It is hard to know exactly when it all began. Most scholars agree that there were early pinpricks of light among the Wesleyan renewals and brush arbor meetings of the late 1800s. There were also smaller revivals to be found in parts of Africa and Asia. The beginning of the new Pentecost, though, seems to have occurred just as the new century was born and in a place few could have expected: in an old mansion called Stone's Folly in Topeka, Kansas.

Some years before, an evangelist named Charles Parham had begun a school in Stone's Folly to train ministers. Though never large in atten-dance, the school made up for its meager size with spiritual passion. Par-ham used only the Bible as a textbook, and he expected every student to spend hours in prayer and fasting as well as share their faith publicly as often as possible.

In December 1900, Parham gave his students an assignment to complete while he was away on business. Their task was to determine what the Bible says about the biblical evidence for the baptism of the Holy Spirit. After studying the matter, all the students agreed that the answer was speaking in tongues. Several days later, on New Year's Eve, the students were conducting a "Watch Night Service," an all-night prayer meeting designed to discern the will of God for the new year. At 11:00 p.m., a thirty-year-old student named Agnes Ozman asked the students to lay hands on her as the early apostles did so that she could speak in tongues. Just as the clock in the school's hallway struck in the new year, Ozman began speaking in tongues. She continued for three days, apparently unable to speak English. Other students soon received the same gift, as did Parham. News of the phenomena spread quickly, and soon similar episodes were occurring around the world.

In 1903, a Pentecostal-style revival in Wales proved so transforming that the entire nation took notice. Conversions were widespread, prayer meetings and song services sprang up spontaneously, and an emphasis on personal holiness and purity changed entire industries. During the revival, mining officials noted that production in the mines had dropped dramatically. Investigations as to the cause revealed that miners caught up in the national revival were no longer willing to swear as they once had, a happy trend except that the mules they commanded couldn't understand the miners' wishes without the use of foul language. Policemen, bored by the low crime rate and empty jails, formed singing groups and roamed the land spreading the revival message.

In 1905, a work of similar impact sprang up in America at Azusa Street in Los Angeles. Led by a legally blind black man named William Seymour, this storefront revival was known for such displays of power that people merely walking down the street during the meetings were knocked down unconscious and rose to find themselves permanently changed, much as Derek Prince would be years later. The revival lasted for three years and drew huge crowds. Many who attended the revival from other nations returned home to give birth to Pentecostalism in their native lands.

The Pentecostal movement was marked by the belief that the Holy Spirit was continuing to do in the new century exactly what the Book of Acts described Him doing in the first century. Among Pentecostals, a sense of the Holy Spirit's presence in their lives and their meetings was common. Those who were willing received the baptism of the Holy Spirit, a special application of power to minister to others, and spoke in tongues as a divine aid to their prayer life. Gifts of the Spirit were practiced as well, so that healing, prophecy, and special discernment about spirits became tools employed by the faithful to strengthen their corporate life and help liberate lives bound by sin and religious superstition.

Though the Pentecostals quickly grew in strength and influence, they were seldom accepted by the established churches. They seemed too fanatical, their services too unstructured and excessive. Pentecostal preachers were rarely well educated, their sermons often amounting to ecstatic exhortations that no mainline churchman could understand or respect. It did not help that Pentecostals quickly descended into strict codes of behavior that seemed silly to the watching world. Movies, radio, higher education, dancing, and alcohol were all deemed sinful. Women were expected to wear their hair in a high, tight bun and leave no skin below the chin exposed other than the hands. Makeup was thought harlotry, so Pentecostal women often pinched their cheeks to gain color. All of this brought howls of laughter from outsiders who already found Pentecostal worship services—with their dancing, rolling on the floor, hand raising, and shouting—delightfully foolish enough.

When Derek Prince joined the Shaws' Pentecostal church in the opening months of World War II, there had already been a dozen new denominations formed to foster the movement: the Assemblies of God, the Nazarenes, the Church of God, the Pentecostal Church of God, and Aimee Semple McPherson's Church of the Foursquare Gospel to name a few. The movement was still growing by 1941 but was held in disrepute by mainstream society, viewed largely as an extreme form of religious emotionalism among the lower classes.

The spiritual mentoring that Derek received from the Shaws in the months following his conversion was sweet to his soul. In simple, endearing Yorkshire terms, they taught him what they knew of Christ and His ways. Yet Derek knew that his time with the Shaws would soon end. The thundering war on the Continent called, and he understood that he must soon play his part in it.

In September of 1941, Derek learned that his unit was being shipped to northern Africa as part of the No. 1 Armoured Division. The war had not been going well for Britain since she first joined the hostilities on September 3, 1939. The incessant bombing of London by Nazi planes, the costly "Battle of the Atlantic," and the humiliating evacuation of Dunkirk had all taken their toll. Only the emergence of Winston Churchill as prime minister and the defeat of the Italians in Ethiopia brought encouragement to the British people. Now, the discerning realized that northern Africa would soon be the stage for some of the most decisive battles of the war. Derek was about to be in the thick of it all.

It took months for his troopship—ironically named *The City of Paris*—to make its way to Suez where Derek was to begin his African adventures. To avoid Nazi submarines, the ship steamed across the Atlantic nearly to the coast of the United States before turning southward to round the Cape of Good Hope. For a brief time, the ship put in at Durban, on the coast of South Africa, and this occasioned two memorable moments in Derek's life.

While the ship was in port, Derek had the unusual experience of playing interpreter during a rebellion. Aboard his ship were 305 members of the French Free Navy. Not known for their military discipline, these French sailors found the conditions aboard ship deplorable and decided to mutiny. They succeeded in occupying the upper deck of the ship before they were checked by the British naval guard. A standoff ensued, made worse by the fact that the ship's captain spoke no French and the mutineers spoke no English. Someone told the captain that Prince could help, and Derek soon found himself trying to help both sides understand each other. At one point in the negotiations, the captain threatened to imprison Derek for the insulting things he was saying. Derek gently reminded the officer that he was merely interpreting the French sailor's words. The mutineers were soon talked into surrendering, and Derek received the gratitude of all.

When Derek left the ship to walk the streets of Durban, he fell in among a group of Christian soldiers who decided to hold an evangelistic street meeting. More than a few of them were surprised to find that Derek was a believer. Though they had been on ship together for two months, Derek apparently stayed to himself so much that the other believers had taken no notice of him. "I'm surprised to see you here," one fellow soldier told him before inviting him to share his testimony at the meeting. When Derek's time came to speak, he told of his experience at the Scarborough barracks and of the change that came in his life. The crowd was so moved that a group of Plymouth Brethren missionaries invited him to share in their open-air meeting, as well. Several Africans committed to Jesus after Derek spoke in this second meeting, and together these two informal gatherings mark the first time Derek ever spoke of the gospel in a foreign country, a foreshadowing of much that was to come.

Derek arrived at Suez on December 9, just in time to hear the news of the Japanese attack on Pearl Harbor. He did not have long to ponder it. After processing, the 1st Lightfield Ambulance Unit was confined just outside of Alexandria, and Derek quickly began learning the ways of the desert. He became skilled at digging a three-foot-deep square hole in the desert floor and then erecting his tent over it. This allowed for a cooler, less sandy existence below the reach of the harsh, dry wind. He learned to make his tea with as little sand added as possible, and he learned to protect his skin from the blistering sun. He also became accustomed to the rumors, the loneliness, the crude humor, and the alternating fear and boredom of a battlefield camp.

Perhaps because he was lonely or perhaps because she plied him with letters, Derek spent more than a few hours writing to Clare. It seems an odd inconsistency. He had understood his relationship with her as sin and confessed as much to his cousin, Sean. But now, in the howling emptiness of Egypt, he poured his heart out to her. His letters were filled with scriptures and with his reflections on life in the Spirit. He asked her if she was born again and she said she was, though he sensed she was simply trying to win him with the right answer. It is not hard to imagine that his thoughts turned to the cool green vistas of Ireland and the homey pleasures of the Riley's farmhouse. It is also not hard to imagine that in his loneliness Derek fought off memories of Clare herself and of the time they had shared together.

There is an Arab proverb that says the desert contains as much life as the deepest ocean, but one must simply know how to find it. Whatever the British army intended for Derek's experience in northern Africa, it is likely that Derek's God intended to teach him to find life beyond the parched surface of this world. In the nearly three years that Derek would spend in desert places, he would learn to sustain a vital spiritual existence without the aid of a church, a pastor, close Christian friends, or any of the supports that most Christians know. He would thrive, though, and learn the lessons of faith that would not only sustain him but also the many millions who would feed from his experience in the years to come. In essence, he was digging wells of refreshing for his generation.

Derek joined the British forces in northern Africa at a critical moment in history. From the beginning of the war, both sides of the conflict had realized that control of northern Africa meant control of the Suez Canal, the vast oil reserves of the Middle East, and access to what Churchill called the "soft underbelly of Europe." Initially, Italian forces had poured into Africa through Libya with the intent of containing the British in Egypt. The Italians had quickly been defeated, though, and Hitler lost no time sending troops in hopes of conquering the region. His chosen commander for the task was the brilliant strategist Erwin Rommel. The British attempt to defeat Rommel would not only determine much of Derek's life in northern Africa but also lead to one of the most critical battles of the war.

Derek's division remained in Suez for only two or three weeks before moving westward. For more than four months, British forces pursued Rommel's "desert rats" across northern Africa, to a place call El Algheila in Tripoli. Busy at the rear of the advance, Derek seldom knew what was happening at the front. His responsibility was to oversee a team of men who had jovially named themselves "Prince's Pioneers." There were ten of them, eight stretcher bearers and two drivers, whose job it was to collect the wounded men from near the front and tend them as best possible while transporting them to the field hospital. It was far from a cushy billet at the rear. There were landmines, sinkholes, and even unexploded shells embedded in the bodies of the wounded. Derek saw the horrors of war in a way few men do, yet his grace and wisdom caused his men to rally to him and trust him. Already he was showing himself an exceptional leader of men.

Every four or five days the division would move forward. Derek's men would rise early on these days and quickly fix their breakfast. This might be a bit of tea and a little bread. If they had bartered wisely with the local tribesmen, there might be some bananas or currant jelly. They would check their equipment, fill their kit bags with the proper medicines and bandages, roll their blankets around their utensils, and mount the truck. All the while, Derek would be shouting warnings and instructions: about sand in the equipment, about scorpions in their boots, about the fueling and repair of the truck. Then, as they made their way along the bone-breaking, near lunar surface, Derek would start up conversations to lift the spirits of the men. He once asked them all to describe their favorite meal back in England. Each man told his mouth-watering fantasy, and then they all insisted Derek tell his. He described, with the most agonizing care, a September morning breakfast on the terrace of a country house. His men lived on the image for weeks.

Their daily duties centered around the simple matters of survival in the desert: water, food, shelter, and transportation. Comforts they had thoughtlessly enjoyed in England now became issues of life and death. Each day they made sure they had water. There was rarely enough. When they were fortunate, they passed a natural well and filled up every container available.

Some days they had only a cup or two of water, and these days inspired fear. Would there be any water at all tomorrow? Food was meager, even with the best intentions of the quartermaster, and each man quickly became a gaunt, brown—near skeletal—version of the man he was in England. Shelter proved less of a problem except that when it was erected badly, the men froze at night, could blister under the sun even in the first few hours of the morning, and might also draw any variety of desert creatures. More than one night's sleep was interrupted by the scream of a man bitten painfully by some unidentified spider or snake.

The matter of transportation was less an issue because of their truck, but even this presented a challenge. Their three-ton lorry was often trapped in the sand or in need of repair. When this happened, the men risked being lost or left behind. On one occasion, Derek's crew was ordered to go find water. They drove over a hill toward a well, and when they turned to what they thought was the way back to camp, they realized that they had become disoriented and did not know where they were. At this moment, Derek shined. He uttered a prayer, considered the angle of the sun, and led the men back to safety. Episodes like this endeared him to his men, for they knew that many men had died horrible deaths in the desert for far less grievous errors.

In May 1942, Rommel counterattacked and began driving the British forces back toward the east. This began the longest retreat in British history, stretching over seven hundred miles of burning sand. It was miserable going. There was little water and less food. The army neared chaos at times, and fear riddled the troops. To make matters worse, Derek's truck rolled over a mine, and though no one inside was hurt, the truck was completely destroyed. This meant that Derek's men had to walk, carrying their food, water, medical gear, and personal possessions by hand across the blistering desert floor.

Derek was sustained in times like these by the disciplines he had developed since arriving in Africa. He had read enough of the Scriptures and sensed enough from the Holy Spirit to perceive that God intended to strip him and rebuild him in the desert. Barren places were often the workshop of God, he understood. No one of consequence has escaped the wilderness season. Derek welcomed it and leaned into the lessons his heavenly Father pressed upon him.

In a land of meager food and water, Derek learned to draw sustenance from the Bible. He understood the concept of manna, that what the ancient Israelites had received in natural form in their desert experience now men could find in the written Word of God. The Bible wasn't like human literature. Its words were filled with God's Spirit and were alive, radiating the meaning and power of God in the human heart as no human words could. Derek gave every moment he could to the Bible and found himself changed, cleansed, and strengthened in a way that made the deprivations of the desert less biting.

Derek also began discerning the will of the Holy Spirit. He had often heard men speak of hearing God's voice, and it made him uncomfortable. Even when the Shaws spoke of the "leading of God," he was unsure of their meaning. But now, in the desert, with little sound but the howling barrenness and the company of his own thoughts, Derek sensed another consciousness pressing itself into his mind. It wasn't a voice but it was more than a feeling, as though there was a separate mind attempting to make itself known in his thoughts. It began as an awareness of a will, something like an unformed idea. Then, words grew from the impression of this will until he had understanding of a specific idea, a thought that someone outside himself had communicated as though he were inside him. He soon came to understand that this was the voice—the will, the thoughts, the impressions—of the Holy Spirit.

He started attending to this "Voice," and when he did, he found himself entering into a kind of relationship. While he read Scripture, this Voice would remind him of another passage or raise a question. Sometimes he felt the strong impression to read the Bible in a certain place, and later in the day he would find that what he had read applied perfectly to the situation he was in or some conversation he was having. Sometimes the Voice was instant and urgent. He once had a strong sense of urgency about where he was about to put his foot. He obeyed the impression, stopped walking, and looked down only to see the raised edge of a land mine. This practical nature of the Holy Spirit impressed him, and he realized that life is meant to be lived under the constant tutelage of this Voice, the expressed will of the Holy Spirit.

In essence, Derek had entered into a school of this Holy Spirit. Between the instruction of Scripture and the moment-by-moment guidance of the Holy Spirit, he found himself positioned for the lessons God wished to teach him through the mundane of his life. There was the night, for example, that

God used blankets to teach him about the spiritual death of the believer. Every soldier was issued four blankets as insurance against the numbing cold of the desert night. One of Derek's blankets was a huge, thick affair, twice the size of the usual army issue blanket.

Each night, Derek would lay the blankets carefully on the sandy ground and enfold himself carefully into the layers. One night, Derek lay in this manner, but his mind was troubled. Why did he have to stay in the army? Why had God left him in this miserable desert? Couldn't he do more good elsewhere? These questions, and the feelings of irritation they produced, washed over him. Suddenly, he felt/heard the Voice. He realized that below the heavy press of his blankets, he was in the position of the crucified Jesus: arms outstretched, feet together, head stretched above his shoulders.

The Voice surfaced Galatians 2:20, a scripture he had recently read: "I am crucified with Christ: nevertheless I live; yet not I, but Christ liveth in me: and the life which I now live in the flesh I live by the faith of the Son of God, who loved me, and gave himself for me." Derek understood immediately the meaning of God: "Dead people don't complain. Be quiet and live the life of a new creature." Derek repented, relaxed, and slept.

On another night, he experienced a similar lesson as he lay down to sleep. He again found himself under the press of his blankets, but this time he was wrapped tight, his arms pinned at his sides. He seemed unable to move and felt as though a supernatural force held him fast. He struggled to get free and then felt/heard the Voice again. He realized he was in the exact position of a man being carried out for burial. Then came the scripture as it had before: "Buried with him in baptism, wherein also ye are risen with him through the faith of the operation of God, who hath raised him from the dead" (Col. 2:12). Again, the lesson: "You gave up your life when you took on the life of Jesus. You're mine now. I'll do with you as I will."

To press the message of death to self into his heart, he began to fast regularly. Every Wednesday he would do without food. The men of Prince's Pioneers began to call Wednesday "Ramadan," after the Muslim month of fasting. The men found it strange that a man already living on slim rations in the desert would choose to eat even less, but they grew to respect Derek. He lived what he believed and did so in a simple, unpretentious manner. As most men have, Prince's Pioneers had seen empty religious show. There were even men in their camps who talked religion all the time but whose lives never measured up. Derek's quiet devotion, intelligence, and firm grasp on the natural world won their respect. Every evening, when they planted their handmade flag with the words "Prince's Pioneers" on it into the sand as a joke, they realized the pride they increasingly felt in their unusual leader.

Derek's fasting moved him more deeply into the things of the Holy Spirit. He found himself praying in tongues more constantly. In fact, his prayer in tongues or "in the Spirit" became a constant stream of expression. Though Derek didn't understand the sounds he made, he knew they came from deep within him, that he hadn't formed the syllables in his mind, and that he had received this stream of indiscernible language when the Shaws laid hands on him. Not long after his first experience with tongues, he realized that sometimes he understood what he was saying. It was just as though someone was speaking French or German, both languages he understood. Upon occasion, he would be praying in tongues and an understanding of the sounds came to him.

The first time this had happened it was as he sat in the Pentecostal church in Scarborough. A twelve-year-old girl behind him was praying in tongues, and Derek, new to the experience, listened carefully. After a few moments, he realized that he could understand what she was saying. He began saying the words aloud in English: "Amen, Lord Jesus, come quickly. Come quickly, Lord Jesus, come quickly." He turned to look at the girl, and when their eyes met, he saw that she knew he had been saying in English what she had said in an unknown language.

There were other times that this interpretation of spiritual language happened, and one in particular would prove to be of huge importance to the course of his life. He was getting ready for bed one night when his prayer language—a very clear, fluent, powerful, rhythmic language—arose from his heart into his mouth. He began to speak the syllables aloud, and very soon after he began to understand what he was saying.

> It shall be like a little stream,
> The stream shall become a river,
> The river shall become a great river,
> The great river shall become a sea,
> The sea shall become a mighty ocean,
> And it shall be through thee;
> But how, thou must not know,

Thou canst not know,
Thou shalt not know.

Derek was unsure of what it meant, but he had a sense that the words pertained to his destiny, to what he would later describe as the "calling" of his life. He knew too that the words had been given in the form God normally used with him—Elizabethan English. Derek preferred it, for it was clearer, more precise than modern English. Scholar that he was, he liked knowing that "ye" pertained to a group but "thou" pertained to an individual. Each time he interpreted his prayer language, he heard it in the Shakespearean style he so loved.

Now, in the desert of Africa, Derek learned to pray in tongues and interpret himself as a normal part of his Christian life. Because praying in tongues required nothing of his mind, he could do it quietly while he worked. Days would go by with Derek praying for hours and hours in tongues beyond his concentrated prayer times in English. Then, suddenly, it would happen. He would become aware that a meaning was forming itself in his mind, framed by the syllables he had been streaming in a near whisper, perhaps while packing supplies or servicing the truck. It was God speaking to him through his own words. On one occasion, God would explain a passage of Scripture. On another, God would warn Derek about some practical matter such as the need to rest for a day or to notice a hole in the water tanks. With time, Derek learned to listen and obey, always scanning the silence for the "entrance" of the Voice.

Sometimes that Voice came in comforting tones of instruction, and sometimes it came in rebuke. On one occasion, Derek had been complaining in prayer: "God, why aren't You near to me? Why must I continue in this monotonous, wearisome life in this desert?"

Then came the Voice of God in response: "Why have you not thanked Me? Why have you not praised Me?"

Derek knew that in his complaining he had given rise to an unthankful heart, one that was sure to blind him to God's goodness and block the good things God intended for him. Derek began to be thankful, singing songs and praying prayers focused on God's goodness. As he later said, "I adjusted my life, and I learned the discipline of giving thanks and praising God in every situation and circumstance. Do you know what I discovered? My circumstances did not change, but I did! When I changed, then my view of my circumstances became different, too."

Walking east across the barrens of northern Africa with a discouraged army in retreat, Derek strained to keep his thoughts on the scriptures he had learned, on the words the Holy Spirit had spoken to him, and on the lessons he had learned from his discipling in the desert. He knew too that there was more than just his own well-being at hand. His Pioneers were staying unusually close to him. They knew he had some source of strength from another world, and they needed it now more than ever. They had little confidence in their other commanders, but this Corporal Prince had shown that he was made of different stuff. At the most desperate times of their retreat, a soldier would turn to Derek from time to time and say, "Corporal Prince, I'm glad you are here." He was their touchstone. For some, he was like a good luck charm. For others, he was the first example of a godly man they had ever known, and they needed him.

Finally, the great retreat ended at a point 150 miles west of Cairo, in a nondescript little town called El Alamein. Though he could not have known it at the time, Derek was about to play witness to one of the most decisive military battles in history. The victor in this conflict would control the Suez Canal, the back door to Europe, the course of the Middle East, and the well-being of a sliver of land called Israel. Those few among Allied leadership who knew what was happening in the labor camps of Germany also knew that if the Nazis won the battle then taking shape at El Alamein, the Jews of Israel would be wiped from the face of the earth.

Astonishingly, it was at this tense moment in the war that Derek was granted leave. He was finally to get a rest after an exhausting year in the desert. And there was more. He would take that leave in Palestine. The army had determined that he would rest from his military duties in the one place he most longed to go. So after months of sand, sweat, and hardship, Derek found himself living in a Jerusalem hotel, sleeping late, eating well, and walking the ancient streets. As a relatively new believer who was only just beginning to understand the connection between his faith and the land of the Jews, it was an opportunity for refreshing and learning that seemed to fall from heaven.

While Derek roamed Jerusalem, he came upon a band of Assemblies of God missionaries. One of them, an Assyrian, pressed him about his baptism.

Derek admitted he had never been baptized and, frankly, hadn't seen the need. Truthfully, he felt a little overwhelmed by all that he had been experiencing, and that during a war. But the Assyrian, Saleem Farhood Haddad, wouldn't let the matter die and showed Derek in the Scriptures how baptism was commanded of all Jesus' disciples. Once Derek saw the meaning of baptism from the pages of Scripture, he agreed. It was an added draw that the men offered to baptize him in the Jordan River. On August 23, 1942, Derek—donning a black baptism robe and standing in inches of ancient mud—was baptized by Pastor Saul Benjamin, the leader of the missionary band. In his typically droll fashion, Derek would ever afterward report, "Lots of people would get excited about that. I didn't enjoy it at all." The words wring a smile these years later, but Derek remembered that while baptism was a holy thing to be done because Jesus commanded it, he had felt nothing. Ever afterward, he would not necessarily expect good feelings to accompany the doing of God's will. It was a lesson that would see him in good stead.

Once Derek returned to northern Africa, he discovered that the British situation there had grown even more desperate. Rommel had shown unprecedented brilliance in driving the British back into their Egyptian lair. The men who marched in retreat with Derek feared and respected Rommel. Their British general, Claude Auchinleck, commanded little respect among his troops. He was a small, vain man who had made a mess of the recent campaign. One order that he issued during the retreat tells the tale. Knowing that the troops had made a near mythological figure out of Rommel, Auchinleck wrote to his commanders, "You must dispel by all possible means the idea that Rommel represents anything other than the ordinary German general...P.S. I'm not jealous of Rommel."

Morale was almost nonexistent among the British troops. Derek thought he knew why. He was descended from a long line of military commanders, and he had some sense of what an officer ought to be. He ought to be a model of courage and self-sacrifice. He ought to see to the needs of his men before his own comforts. He ought to believe in the fight before him, inspire his men to their best, and throw himself into battle at the head of his troops. This was the kind of commander his father, his uncle, and his grandfather had been.

Yet, Derek saw that few of the officers around him were men of consequence. They wrapped themselves in comfort at the rear of the line and left their men to suffer. The troops were constantly lectured about preserv-ing water, yet the officers often drank more water with their whiskey than the average soldier received in a day. The troops were constantly harangued about preserving gasoline. Yet when one officer contracted malaria, a com-mon malady in northern Africa, he commandeered a four-berth ambulance and a one-and-a-half-ton truck to carry his belongings to Cairo. Then he was flown home to England, a move completely unnecessary for a mere case of malaria. Weeks later, Derek and his men listened to their radio while this same officer described the horrors of combat in the desert from a studio in London. Such cowardice and devotion to personal comfort drained away what little respect the men had left for their officers.

Derek was troubled by what he saw. With a major battle looming and so much in the balance, he knew that disaster awaited the Allies if matters continued as they were. During the retreat, he kept sensing that the Spirit's voice was urging him to pray for the British forces in the desert and for the whole situation in the Middle East. He resisted though, for in the black-and-white thinking of a young believer he could not see how a holy God could work through a leadership that was so unworthy and inefficient. Still, the Voice pressed, and soon he gave in and asked his heavenly Father what prayer he should be praying for the army's dilemma. He sensed that the Holy Spirit gave him this prayer: "Lord, give us leaders such that it will be for Your glory to give us victory through them." Day after day, he prayed these words, hoping to see the situation change.

Not long after, he learned that Auchinleck was to be replaced by Lieuten-ant General W. H. E. Gott. It would not have been lost on Derek that *Gott* was the German name for "God." *Perhaps*, Derek thought, *Gott is God's man to right this mess.* He continued to pray the prayer the Spirit had given him and continued to hope that he was seeing his answer unfold. Several weeks later, on August 7, he heard on the radio that Gott had died horribly when his plane was shot down near Heliopolis.

Derek was crushed. Winston Churchill was frantic. He knew morale among the troops was in a desperate state, he was facing a vote of no con-fidence in the House of Commons, and what promised to be the deciding battle of the northern African campaign was looming just ahead. Acting on his own authority, Churchill ordered a relatively unknown general to take command. His name was General Bernard Montgomery.

The son of an evangelical Anglican clergyman, General Montgomery—or "Monty," as his troops would affectionately call him—was a bit of an outcast among his fellow officers both because of his arrogance and because of his devotion to a new brand of warfare. Monty believed in a new military doctrine based on a strategy of advance, overwhelming force, and the power of mobile artillery, particularly the tank. He seemed to Churchill the perfect man for the challenge of El Alamein.

Positioned at a bottleneck between the Mediterranean Sea and the Qattara Depression to the south, El Alamein was the perfect site for a British stand. Rommel had overwhelmed the Allies on the battlefield largely because of his favorite tactic: sweeping into the enemy from the rear. But the geography of El Alamein would not allow such freewheeling movement. The British could close the bottleneck and seize the initiative by first bombarding and then attacking their attackers.

Monty saw the matter clearly and took control. In his first order as commander, he proclaimed, "There will be no more bellyaching and no more retreats." By use of deception, diversion, and round-the-clock preparation—not to mention the arrival of three hundred Sherman tanks—Monty prepared the Eighth Army for battle. On the eve of battle, Monty sent a message to all the men in his army: "Everyone must be imbued with the desire to kill Germans, even the padres—one for weekdays and two on Sundays."

The men loved such irreverent bravado. Though they could barely stomach the usual sort of officer, this Monty loved his troops and wanted to win. His fighting spirit moved out into the battle lines, and when the first bombardment began on October 23, his men were as ready for battle as any British unit had been since the start of the war.

The battle lasted until November 4 before Rommel started his retreat. It was a bloody, torturous fight. Monty's Eighth Army lost some thirteen thousand men while inflicting twice that number of casualties on Rommel's smaller forces. It was a stunning victory, one that protected the Middle East from Nazism and earned Monty the lasting title, "Montgomery of El Alamein."

Derek knew little of the details of the battle. He was busy in the rear tending the wounded and the dying. All the while he had seen the transformation of the army under Monty, but he still wondered if this new, brash general was the answer to his prayer.

Several days after the battle ended, Derek was listening to a radio when a BBC commentator began describing the scene at Montgomery's headquarters as it had been on the eve of the battle. Monty had issued a statement to his men that Derek had never heard. It read, "Let us ask the Lord, mighty in battle, to give us the victory." When Derek heard these words over the radio, the radiating presence he had first felt in the Scarborough barracks descended on the top of his head and moved through his body to the bottom of his feet. At that moment, the Voice said very clearly, "That is the answer to your prayer." Derek wept, overwhelmed that the Creator of the universe was willing to change the course of history in answer to the prayers of a lowly soldier in the wilderness of Africa.

El Alamein was the turning point in the war for England. As Churchill later said, before El Alamein the British failed to win a single battle against the German armies; afterward, they were never again to taste defeat. The battle represented a critical turning point for Derek, as well, but for a far different reason. He came to understand that the course of nations could be shaped by the prayers of God's people. What an astonishing revelation it was. Derek had known little of Christians in his time, having only had a matter of months with the Shaws and their church before leaving for Africa. He could not judge with certainty, but most of the prayers he had heard were for personal needs and the salvation of individuals. This was certainly God's will, but now he saw that there was more. Perhaps God intended that His will on earth should be executed by the prayers of believing people. Perhaps the Ruler of Nations unleashed His purposes for the nations of men through the intercession of those who had a vision for something more than just the individual. These new ideas circulated in Derek's soul and fed into his reading of Scripture. His concept of God expanded. He began to see history, and not just biblical history, in a new light. More than ever, he burned with a sense of destiny, with a message he knew the people of God in his generation needed to hear.

Almost immediately after El Alamein, Derek developed a painful skin condition on his feet. His doctors struggled to reach a diagnosis and suggested increasingly complex-sounding diseases until they finally settled on chronic eczema. The heat, the sand, the lack of bathing, and the miles of walking all conspired to nearly cripple Derek. He tried to continue his duties knowing that his officers valued him and desperately needed his skills. In time, though, they reluctantly saw that if he was ever to heal, he would have to be in a hospital.

Derek returned to the hospital in Cairo, but because his condition was not critical, doctors quickly moved him to a secondary facility at El Ballah. Now, far from his men, his duties, and any sense of purpose, Derek met his old nemesis again: the smothering loneliness that fed a black depression. It reached to him through the sickening smells of an army hospital. It took voice in the agonizing moans of wounded men. It lashed at him through the cold, impersonal manner of the overworked hospital staff. "You are alone," his enemy told him, "and you always will be." Derek was tempted to agree.

Just as the blackness threatened to enfold him, she appeared. Clad in a black bonnet affixed to her head by a large bow and wrapped in a sweeping black frock, her name was Mrs. Ross, and she was not to be denied. She had been the wife of a Salvation Army brigadier general in Cairo when he had unexpectedly died. According to tradition, she took her husband's rank, and now, in her seventies, she had become a juggernaut, unfettered by human opinion, undaunted by convention, and with that burning sense of mission that widowed women often find in their latter years.

What set Mrs. Ross apart was not just her abrupt, commanding manner, but her complete devotion to the baptism of the Holy Spirit and the value of speaking in tongues. She was an oddity among her Salvation Army cohorts, many of whom would not have agreed that Spirit baptism and tongues had survived the apostles. Clearly, Mrs. Ross didn't care what they thought and preached the need for spiritual power and a divine prayer language the way most her fellow soldiers for Christ preached salvation.

Somehow, this one-woman crusade in black heard about a young soldier ailing alone in an El Ballah hospital and decided to go to him. Never mind that nearly fifty miles of desert road lay between The Salvation Army head-quarters in Cairo and the young man's bed. Her decision made, she miracu-lously found a car, a driver from New Zealand, and a young American woman from Oklahoma who also served in The Salvation Army. Fueled as much by Mrs. Ross's indomitable will as they were by gasoline, the three covered the miles to El Ballah, found the hospital Derek was in, and nearly kicked in the door. Before Derek knew what was happening, Mrs. Ross announced she had come for Corporal Prince, got him up, dressed, and out the door before anyone of authority could object.

The four of them—Derek, Mrs. Ross, the driver, and the American woman—sat together, squeezed tightly into the tiny car. Mrs. Ross announced that they had come to pray for Derek. The young American woman also said some things, but Derek couldn't make out her Oklahoma accent and never understood a word she said. No matter. Mrs. Ross commanded everyone to prayer. Derek tried to focus, still unsteady from the pace of recent events, and soon realized that the American woman was vibrating: not shaking in a way she might have chosen, but vibrating in a way beyond her control. Then Derek began vibrating, as did Mrs. Ross and the unsuspecting driver. The car itself vibrated violently though the engine was turned off. Mrs. Ross began to pray, as did the American woman. Then the three who could, with the driver surely in shock, began to pray in tongues. After a few moments, Derek and Mrs. Ross stopped, but the American woman continued, and Derek soon realized that he could understand what she was saying in a heavenly language. He never forgot the words: "Consider the work of Calvary, a perfect work, perfect in every respect, and perfect in every aspect."

Soon after, the prayer meeting ended. Derek returned to his bed, and Mrs. Ross and her two companions returned to Cairo. As he pondered the meaning of it all, Derek realized that something new was living inside him. It was an idea, but an idea that seemed to pulsate with potential power. He thought about the words he had understood from the American woman's prayer and realized what God was trying to show him: healing is part of Jesus' work on the cross. God did not just send Jesus to the cross to give men salvation, but to make them whole as well.

The thought thrilled Derek and then seemed to crash him to the floor. *If God has provided healing,* he reflected, *then why am I not healed? Perhaps I don't believe as I should. Perhaps I don't have faith.* And on the wings of these thoughts, the blackness began creeping in at the edge of his consciousness.

It was as this battle wore on in his soul that he happened onto the words of Romans 10:17: "Faith cometh by hearing, and hearing by the word of God." The first two words captured him. *Faith cometh.* He read them again. *Faith can come,* he thought. *Faith can arrive where it wasn't originally. If a man doesn't have faith, it can come to him.* He was starting to hope. Newborn though it was, it pressed back against the encroaching blackness.

Then Derek, ever the questioning scholar, asked the critical question: "But how does faith come?" He returned to the sentences in the Book of Romans: "Faith cometh by hearing, and hearing by the word of God." Then he saw it. Faith grows from the seeds of God's words planted in the human heart. Faith grows. It arises, and it does so from a man's hearing of the Word of God.

Derek knew what he had to do. He had to devour God's Word, and he had to focus on the passages that gave faith for what he needed—healing. So he decided to start at the beginning of the Bible with a blue pencil in hand and mark all the passages that pertained to healing. As he would delight in saying for the rest of his life, "Of course, I ended up with a blue Bible. God's provision of healing leapt from every page of Scripture."

But there was a problem. When Derek heard the word *healing*, he thought of the healing of the soul, but never the healing of the body. He was wrestling with his knowledge of Plato. Spiritual things were otherworldly, non-physical, Plato had taught. Truth lay in the invisible realm of the ideal but never in the natural world of the form. Derek would struggle against a Platonic mysticism his whole life, but, on this occasion, God gave him a clear correction. He came upon Proverbs 4:20–22. For the man who gave himself to God's Word, the passage promised "health to all [his] flesh." Derek knew there was no confusing flesh with soul, and more, the translation of the word *health* in the margin of his Bible suggested medicine might be the meaning. So, Derek thought, *the Word of God is medicine for the human body. Not just general nourishment for the soul, but healing specifically for the body.*

The subject of medicine activated Derek's training. *How is medicine taken?* he asked himself. The answer: three times daily, after meals. So, he decided to take the Word of God like medicine after every meal. For months, he paused after every meal and absorbed the words of Scripture with the mindset of a man taking an antidote on a precise schedule. At first, there was no change. Derek continued undaunted. Then, his doctor noted a change: the eczema was subsiding. Derek, encouraged, began taking bigger doses of Bible. Within months, his condition had largely disappeared. Finally, the doctor told him that while he was not fully healed, he could be released on his own responsibility. The next day, Derek walked out of the hospital, his home for more than a year.

The combination of his healing through Scripture and the deliverance of British troops largely through prayer at the battle of El Alamein was working a deep change in Derek's heart. His three years of Christian life had been a wonderful season of learning how to love Jesus and live in harmony with the Holy Spirit. Now, the lessons were changing. God had begun teaching him how to walk in power, how to apply the victory of Jesus on the cross to the condition of mankind. Derek sensed that these lessons were not meant for him alone, and he leaned into them, sensing that each experience was a spiritual well he would draw from again and again.

✖

It was good that he was thinking of his life as the classroom of the Holy Spirit, because just days after leaving the hospital he got orders for Sudan. If Egypt was bad, Sudan was worse, but the news didn't have the depressive effect on Derek that it might have on another man. He had become intrigued with life as the university of God, and he sensed, somehow, that Sudan was merely the next course in the curriculum.

He traveled by boat from Cairo to the Aswan Dam and then took a train to Khartoum. It was the most desert place he had ever seen, and he had seen many. He was assigned to a medical pool and found his life tightly regimented—his food meager and his duties extensive. Still, he continued to practice the lessons God had pressed into his life: the discipline of fasting, the power of Scripture, the necessity of thanksgiving, the impact of prayer, and the leadership of the Holy Spirit.

He was not in Khartoum long before he received orders to Atbarah, a medical reception station to the north. Though he was happy to escape the regimentation of life in Khartoum, he knew that Atbarah was a remote, backwater place that might even be worse. Still he gave thanks; still he prayed.

He was confused, at first, with what he found at his new posting. It was a small medical facility with clean rooms, straw beds, and ready linens and supplies. But there were no patients. It looked as though the sick never made it to Atbarah, but the supply trucks did. Derek didn't mind a bit. He had been sleeping in sand or in rough field hospitals for three years. In this new remote outpost, he cleaned himself, put on a freshly laundered nightgown, and slept on a real bed—or at least the closest thing to it in Sudan. He was humbled by the luxury, surely a gift from God. He rested as he had not in years, read his Bible, and waited for the next lesson of God.

It came one night shortly after he went to bed. For some time he had been feeling an inner heaviness of compassion for the Sudanese people. It wasn't just their poverty; it was the emptiness of their Muslim faith that moved him. He knew enough about Islam to know that it offered no real salvation, no real connection to the true God, and no real healing for the heart or the body. He was grieved, and in time he realized that he was feeling more than his own soul's tenderness. It was as though a more compassionate heart was sharing its burden with his.

These feelings grew so strong on this night that he rose from his bed and began praying for the Sudanese people. Tears flowed as he asked his God, the same God who intervened at El Alamein, to intervene for these dear people who lived under such horrible oppression. As Derek prayed, he sensed a familiar presence in the room, one he first met those years ago in his Scarborough barracks. He kept praying, and soon he noticed that his white hospital gown began to glow. The more he prayed, the brighter it got, and Derek came to understand that God was giving him an external sign of an invisible reality. He was being given an anointing, an application of power or spiritual ability to pray for Muslims.

This experience introduced him to a deeper level of spiritual warfare than he had ever known before. He found himself constantly battling in prayer for the Muslim world, wrestling in his soul before God. This intensity was particularly severe during Ramadan, the thirty-day period each year when Muslims fast during daylight hours and await the kind of revelations Muhammad first had in the sixth century. During this time, Derek found his prayer life hindered by an intense heaviness. He came to conclude that he was working against the spiritual darkness assigned against Muslims world-wide during Ramadan. It all became clear to him. Islam was born in the revelation of an evil spirit to Muhammad. It was only logical that this same spirit would oppress those who welcomed it during the holiest month in Islam. Derek realized that only through aggressive, concerted prayer could this Islamic spirit of deception be broken. It was a lesson that profoundly shaped his life.

It is not hard from this vantage point to envision the importance of what Derek was experiencing. He was then in the middle of an Islamic stronghold.

If he could have looked down the corridor of time, he would have seen the rise of a militant Islam on the very ground he was walking. He would have seen a resurgence of slavery and the death of millions through tribal conflict. He would have seen starvation and pain and the radicalizing of some of the world's most heinous terrorists, men like Osama bin Laden. And he would have seen that the rise of angry Islam in Sudan would join its like throughout the nations to become the most serious challenge to Christianity and free-dom the twentieth century would ever know. That Derek was walking the land of Sudan in the 1940s, tearfully interceding for Muslims and pioneering intercession against the looming anti-Christian force of resurgent Islam, is surely in retrospect among the more strategically prophetic acts of his life.

✕

But the university of God moved on. Derek was soon transferred to Jubayt where he worked in a small hospital that tended Italian prisoners of war. It was Derek's job to oversee the staff, which meant that he was put in charge of a small group of Sudanese workers. This is what brought him into contact with Ali Dawir Adroub.

It is a testament to Derek's character that he ever made room in his life for friendship with a Sudanese man. The British had done much good wherever their flag had flown in the world, but friendship with the natives was not among their legacies. Derek had arrived in Jubayt on a train that did not allow *wogs*—the derisive term for the dark-skinned men England ruled—in the passenger section. He had been taught not to eat with these *wogs*, not to trust them, not to allow them into his quarter, and not to be manipulated by them. They were basically stupid, lazy, and primitive, the army orientation insisted, and only through British industry would they ever thrive.

It is likely that Derek remembered similar opinions about the Indians he knew in the land of his birth. Fortunately, he had not absorbed them, largely because his father was an exceptional man. Captain Paul Prince had preferred the company of his Indian engineers to his fellow British officers and said so publicly. Derek learned from him and saw through the blinding cultural racism. At Eton, he caused a row when he asked why a white man couldn't have lunch with an Indian. Such traditions died hard in England, but Derek, thanks to his father, was ahead of his time.

From the beginning, Ali had impressed Derek as a smart, friendly, capable man. He was, as Derek later said, "an enjoyable rogue" who spoke only "soldier's English" but used facial expressions and hand gestures to ingeniously make his meaning known. He made his fellow Sudanese workers kick back portions of salary to him by insisting, "I got you your job." Still, he was charming and endeared himself to the English hospital staff who viewed him as a cute member of the untouchable class.

Derek had found no connection with Ali despite their weekly meetings until Ali happened to reveal that he believed in Satan, one of the points of doctrines Muslims share with Christians. Derek said that he believed in Satan also, and this impressed Ali. Englishmen rarely spoke of their faith, but this tall one was clearly different. Nothing more was said though, and the two resumed their routine.

A few weeks later, Ali showed up late for his regular meeting with Derek and explained that he had been at the clinic to have a wounded leg examined. Derek had an impression. He had never prayed for anyone to be healed before, but the phrase "lay hands on the sick and they will recover" went through his mind, and he knew what he must do. He asked Ali if he wanted him to pray for healing. Ali said he did, and Derek very gingerly placed his hands on the man "as though he was a bomb likely to explode" and prayed a very formal prayer. Derek felt nothing, Ali showed no response, and they went about their business. The next week, though, Ali returned to say that his leg had been completely healed. Derek was as amazed as Ali but acted as though such things happened all the time among Christians.

The healing broke the ice, and the two men began to meet every day. Derek read to Ali from John's Gospel, rephrasing the words into simpler terms. Ali was fascinated. He not only couldn't read—meaning that he had never read the Quran of his own faith—but he certainly had never heard the words of Jesus so clearly.

In keeping with the hospitality of his culture, Ali wanted to honor Derek for his kindness. Derek had said he would like to learn how to ride a camel, so Ali showed up one day with two camels in tow and was delighted to find that within minutes Derek was running his animal like an expert. Next, Ali suggested a picnic. Since Derek was in charge of the rations, he provided the food, and Ali, again, brought the camels. The two men went half a day's ride into the wild, but as they settled down to eat they realized they had no water. Nearby was a stream of the kind that a Sudanese would drink from but whites wouldn't go near. Ali pointed to the stream and apologized that there was nothing else to drink. Derek instantly remembered the scripture that said nothing that you drink will by any means hurt you and decided that if Ali could drink the water, so could he. (See Mark 16:18.)

Ali was amazed. Here was a white man who not only prayed with power but also broke convention to befriend a black man and even drank with him from the same stream. "Why are you different from other white people?" Ali asked.

"Because I am born again," Derek explained, and on the ride home he told Ali what this meant.

When they arrived back at the station, Derek asked Ali if he wanted to be born again. Ali said he did, and Derek instructed him to ask God to save him that evening at sunset when he returned to his hut. Derek said he would pray as well.

The next morning, Derek asked Ali what had happened. Ali's downcast face told the story, and Derek, sensing the Spirit reminding him that Ali was a Muslim, asked, "Did you pray in the name of Jesus?" Ali said he hadn't. "All right, when you go to your hut tonight at sunset," Derek insisted, "pray in the name of Jesus to be born again."

The next morning, when Ali returned, Derek knew what had happened. "You got it!" he proclaimed, for Ali's smile said it all.

The change in Ali quickly became evident to everyone at the station, and people flocked to Derek to ask what had happened. The station commander even sent for Derek to ask, "What has happened to Ali?" Derek delighted to explain the new birth to the officer and could not help expressing his deep gratitude for the privilege of reaching his first convert.

Not long after, Derek baptized Ali in a swimming pool with both English and Sudanese hospital staff looking on. The change in Ali made others hungry for the same, and over the following weeks Derek prayed with and baptized both black and white seekers alike. Derek was overwhelmed that God had honored him in such a way, and he sensed that something lasting had begun. Teaching the gospel to others, praying for their needs, helping them grow in Christ—this might well be his life's work. He felt as though he was born for it, and this gave rise to a sense of design and destiny he had never before known.

As honored as he was to be a tool in the hands of God, Derek was also weary. He was nearing four years of hard service in desert regions and backwater stations. He needed a break, and he knew it. He put in for leave anywhere near water and away from fighting and hospitals. His request was granted but with an expected twist: he would go on leave to Palestine. Again his gracious God allowed him to take leave from his duties in the land of his Lord's birth, and within days he found himself resting in the hills of Jerusalem and recovering from his African hardships. He had been to Palestine once before on leave, but this time it felt different. There was a magnetic pull, a force that emanated from the land and seemed to envelop him. Did he, somehow, belong here? Was this the next step in the path of God's will?

On his last few days in Jerusalem, he told an older Christian lady what he felt about the pull of the Holy Land. Perhaps, he said, he would come back to Jerusalem one day. Maybe after the war he would choose to live here. The woman had lived in this ancient land for many years and knew something Derek did not, something that would become, in time, a banner over his life. "Oh, young man," she said, "you do not choose Jerusalem. Jerusalem chooses you."

6

Palestine:
Land of Love and Longing

"DEREK, WHEN DID you first see Lydia?"

"It was in 1944 while I was working at a medical supply depot at Kiriat Motzkin, a small village just north of Haifa. In Sudan, a Christian soldier who had been to Palestine told me, 'If you want a real spiritual blessing, there's a little children's home in Palestine, just north of Jerusalem that you need to visit. It's run by a Danish lady. Soldiers are going there from all over the Middle East, and God is meeting them in a wonderful way.' Since my duties at the supply depot didn't keep me very busy, I not only had more time for prayer but found opportunity to make my way to Lydia."

"What was your first impression of her?"

"My first impression wasn't of her but of the atmosphere in her home. There was nearly a visible presence all about the house. It felt like dew descended upon you when you entered. It was refreshing, an instant feeling of peace and faith. A spirit of prayer, really. I can only describe it as 'holiness.' Once I felt it, I never ceased to long for it."

"But what about her? Were you attracted to her immediately?"

"Yes, but not in a romantic way. After so many years in the desert without a woman about, I was certainly drawn to the home life of a woman with daughters. But I was drawn more to her manner. She was blue-eyed, blonde, and buxom as Scandinavian women tend to be. She radiated deep faith and love for Jesus. That is what first drew me."

"Did you feel one with her in a spiritual sense before anything romantic happened?"

"Yes. From the moment I first told her about my years in the desert, alone and living on the Word of God, I felt she understood. She had been alone with God in a hostile land, too, and we found in each other—I suppose the phrase used today would be—soul mates."

"When did you start feeling something more than friendship for her?"

"I can't truly recall. I remember telling her that I thought the Lord wanted us to work together. When I first met her, I felt compassion for her as a lady alone in the ministry. I determined to pray for her, and when I did, I felt God said, "I have joined you together under the same yolk and in the same harness." Probably foolishly, I told her this and said that I thought God wanted us to work together. That's when she famously said, "Well, God will have to work on both ends of the chain.""

"But, Derek, did you want her then as a man wants a woman?"

"Do you mean sexually?"

"No, that would have been inappropriate. I mean romantically."

"I think I felt it first just after the Lord told me we were to be yoked."

"So, it was as though your manly feelings for her came along with the word of the Lord."

"Yes, very much so."

"Did you find her age daunting at all?"

"No, I knew she was older, of course, but it didn't seem to matter."

"Older? She was older than your mother, nearly three decades older than you!"

"Yes, but it just didn't weigh upon my mind."

"You know what psychologists would say today: you were marrying her to work out issues with your mother."

"I know. I've heard it all. But it truly was a pure, holy work of the Lord."

"OK, let me be a nosy American for a moment. Did you kiss her or hold her hand before you were married?"

"Yes, we held hands, and I think I kissed her several times."

"And what was that like?"

"It was wonderful, but I think I will keep those memories to myself."

"Fair enough. But Derek, when I take into account the age difference between the two of you and the fact that you were acting on the word of the Lord when you proposed to her, I wonder if you desired her. I mean, did you want her physically when you married her?"

"Yes, I did. Very much. Very much indeed."

In 1915—the year that Derek Prince was born, that fateful year when a violent new world was rising from the wreckage of the old—there was a twenty-five-year-old woman in Denmark just then beginning her work as a teacher. Her name was Lydia Camilla Agnete Christensen. Though she would not meet Derek Prince for another three decades, she was just launching out upon the torturous journey of faith that would place her at his side until the end of her life.

She was the daughter of a wealthy factory owner named Jens Christensen, and his prosperity had assured her the comforts of the Danish upper class. Tended by servants and lacking for nothing, she had graduated from the best schools, excelled in sports and music, and become a darling of her social set. Far from the spoiled dilettante she might have become, her advantages had instead fashioned her into an exceptional woman. She was hardworking, intelligent, and driven; intent upon making her mark in the world and enjoying the good life along the way.

For the first fifteen years of her career, she did just that. She became an expert in domestic science—now called home economics—then a rising field in the schools of Europe and quickly emerged as one of the most respected educators in Denmark. Most every school in the land wished to establish a domestic science program, and for Lydia this meant prestige and prosperity in return for her expertise. Her quick mind and commanding manner served her well. So stellar were her contributions to her field that the king of Denmark took note and awarded her a medal along with her nation's gratitude.

As she entered her late thirties, she should have been content. All the success, esteem, and fulfillment that she had ever envisioned were hers. But there was something wrong. She was agonizingly unfulfilled. At first her discontent was but a haunting sense of emptiness. It nagged at the edges of her mind but only occasionally. In time, it became an obsession. She seemed unable to enjoy her pleasures as she once had, and though she performed her duties well, she no longer felt joy in her work. The death of her father in 1925 turned her thoughts to spiritual matters and forced her to confront her inner emptiness. "Surely," she insisted to a friend, "there is something more to life than just a career and an apartment, nice furniture, and a pension at the end of it all."

This question and others like it drove her to matters of the Spirit. She had grown up in the Danish state church like most everyone else she knew. Her family prayed the prayers and sang the songs, but it all left her feeling that she had fulfilled a duty without engaging anything real. Desperate, she began to read her Bible, and as she did so one day, she saw Jesus in front of her. He sat in her room silently and looked at her with an other-worldly tenderness. She melted at His feet and felt her heart rising to Him as though it would fly out of her chest. He remained only a moment, but it was long enough for Lydia to see His face, feel His power, and be forever changed by His radiating love.

Her life now concentrated completely upon this man. She started to believe it, all of it: that He was the Son of God, that He was born on earth to a virgin named Mary, that He taught men how to know His Father, and that He died a cruel death, which in some way removed the cancer of sin for those who believed He had done it. He now was her Lord, her Savior, her Master, her King, and her Lover. His ways, His truth, and His plan became her consuming passion.

Searching for a people who would understand her experience, she fell in among Pentecostals, a tribe she had once regarded as backward and dull. Soon she was filled with the Holy Spirit, spoke in other tongues, and was baptized in water in her pastor's kitchen. She also began to have visions, to see images that were real but weren't physical. One in particular held her fascination. A woman, dressed in what she later learned was Jewish dress, danced before her. Somehow she sensed that the vision signaled a new path for her life, and before long she knew what she must do: leave Denmark and serve God in the Holy Land.

What ensued certainly ranks among the great tales of missionary women. In 1928, Lydia traveled with difficulty to the Holy Land and lived, at first,

as the guest of welcoming Christians. Then she rented a small room in the basement of a friend's house. With little money and no knowledge of Arabic or Hebrew, she lived by faith, trusting God for everything she needed. Though God never left her destitute, her circumstances—living alone in a dank basement on prayer and a Bible promise—were a far cry from the comforts she had known in Denmark.

She had taken up residence in a troubled land, marked by economic turmoil, Arab riots, British mismanagement, and religious division. She was a woman alone but undaunted. Her saving grace was that she learned quickly. Creating her own version of the local language, she soon discovered how to barter for food, how not to hang her laundry on the Sabbath, how not to expect European manners from Arab men, and how to live a life of complete reliance on God's provision. Most of all, she learned how to know the will of her Master.

It was this will that led her into the life of Tikva. One day a man named Cohen, owner of a small restaurant on Jaffa Road, appeared before her and asked her to take his dying baby. Lydia had no intention of agreeing until, again, her Master called. Relenting, she took the girl in, prayed for her healing, saw her become as healthy as any child, and made young Tikva her own. Tikva—it meant "hope" in Hebrew. Lydia came to understand that her Tikva was a living symbol of the hope she had in God.

Soon she would have more symbols than she had ever dreamed. After a move to the conservative Jewish area of Jerusalem called Mahaneh Yehuda, which means "Camp of Judah"—Lydia realized that God had not sent her to the Holy Land to stay for a few years. Instead, she had been sent to make the land her own: to be a "watchman on the walls," an intercessor for the city of Jerusalem and a witness to God's love for the Jewish people. Once she embraced her purpose, God began to give her sons and daughters.

It started when Lydia discovered that Tikva had sisters, and that they needed a home. Soon Peninah and Ruhammah joined Lydia's little family, but their Mahaneh Yehuda apartment quickly proved too cramped for the four of them. They needed a house, and after a careful search she moved the girls to an Arab village just north of Jerusalem called Ramallah. It would be from this unlikely place that the story of Lydia's life and love would go to the far reaches of the world.

In time, other children came to her. Some would stay for a short

until their parents could care for them again. Some would come, stay for a while, and die in Lydia's arms of horrible diseases and deformities. Others would come and live with her permanently. Soon her house became known as the Danish Children's Home. She had, quite without intending to do so, become the head of an orphanage.

Yet it was for her ministry as much as for her willingness to take in unwanted children that she ultimately became known. She was a woman who listened to the voice of the Holy Spirit and who loved prayer, the Scriptures, and the grace that God often poured through her for others. An Arab woman might come to the door to deliver some oil that Lydia had ordered, but before the woman turned to go, Lydia had explained the gospel of Jesus Christ and prayed for her to be healed. A Jewish mason might rework the stones on Lydia's steps while the impassioned Dane prayed aloud for a blessing on his business. Miracles happened, and Lydia sometimes had supernatural insights into people's needs and problems. Soon there was a constant stream of Arab villagers who came to see the European lady who heard from God.

Then there were the soldiers. As the clouds of war gathered over the Middle East in the late 1930s, weary, lonely soldiers began coming to the house in Ramallah. They came at first because they found a kind, older woman and a hot cup of tea waiting for them. In time, they came because they knew their souls were in need. Lydia was a one-woman church. She taught her eager young soldiers of the Scriptures, prayed for them to be devoted to Jesus, assigned them studies in the Bible, and put them to work. She led meetings for worship and intercession, prayed for the sick and the empty, rebuked the immoral, and challenged the lazy. Always she urged her charges to be filled with the Spirit, live by faith, and share the gospel with others. For men far from home who were facing death in the barrenness of Africa and the Middle East, the Danish lady's house became an oasis of refreshing for body and soul. By war's end, hundreds of men from dozens of nations had passed through Lydia's home, fed on her life in Christ, and either died in battle assured of their salvation or returned home to live for the glory of God.

It was as one of these war-weary soldiers that Derek Prince first entered the home of Lydia Christensen. Though the story of their meeting and

eventual marriage would transform into legend with the passing years, there is another story line that must also be inserted to make the drama complete: the story of the daughters. Always in the background of the Prince story are the eight daughters who lived with Lydia in Ramallah. Their individual journeys into Lydia's home, their varying personalities, and the shifting tide of their memories through the years are central to the Derek Prince story and to the meaning that story has for generations yet to come.

The daughter who has received the most attention throughout the years is Tikva, the child of whom Lydia wrote in her partial autobiography, *Appointment in Jerusalem*. Tikva was the miracle child—the first among Lydia's adopted family—the one who nearly died, was healed, and became the symbol of God's affirming grace in Lydia's early ministry.

She was the daughter of Eliezer and Hadassa Cohen, orthodox Jews who owned a Jerusalem restaurant but seldom had a peaceful marital moment. Choosing to keep their sons, Eliezer and Zvi, rather than their sickly daughter, they gave Tikva into Lydia's care. Then they changed their minds and kidnapped the girl time and again until they finally settled the matter in their hearts and gave her up for good. Even then they often brought toys or tried to take Tikva away to meet other family members. Lydia finally put a stop to it all, and the Cohens eventually walked out of their daughter's life forever.

Tikva would always be the pretty, outgoing daughter, the one some suspected drew the soldiers to the house in Ramallah as much as Lydia's ministry. Pictures of the family in the early days show Tikva ever at her mother's side. She had raven black hair that cascaded thickly to her shoulders, long enough to draw attention but not so long that a Pentecostal might think her unchaste. Her eyes were dark, alluring pools, and she had a full, strongly feminine figure that must have kept more than one visiting soldier mesmerized. Yet she was also deeply intelligent, passionately devoted to Jesus, and more her mother's confidante than any other until Derek arrived on the scene. Indeed, Tikva was so attractive and mature for her age that Lydia's daughters suspected that Derek kept coming around because he had designs on this beautiful Hebrew girl.

In time, Tikva's two sisters, Peninah and Ruhammah, came under Lydia's roof as well. They were of vastly different personalities. Sweet and gentle,

Peninah had often been thought slow in her early years because she had bad eyesight and painfully underdeveloped language skills. As a result, she had been kept out of school for years at a time and often treated with impatience. She was, though, the sensitive one, the one whose impressionable soul retained well into her later years an almost poetic sense of Jewish life in those early days. Like many of the other girls, she was deeply mystical and had astonishing spiritual experiences that impressed the many visitors who came to the Christensen home.

By contrast, Ruhammah was fiery, precocious, bold, and defiant. She often pressed Lydia to the end of herself, for the fact is the two were very much alike. There were differences, though. Lydia was stern, and Ruhammah was mischievous. Lydia was devoted to the household routines that one might expect of a domestic science expert. Ruhammah was devoted to the thrill of outwitting Lydia. Upon one occasion, when one of the other girls was sick, Ruhammah took note that every day the ailing girl received a generous portion of ice cream. The next day, Ruhammah snuck into the sick girl's bed and opened wide in hopes that Lydia might mistake her mouth for her sister's. This was Ruhammah's way, one that could alternatively enrage or delight Lydia through the years.

After the three Cohen girls came to her, Lydia welcomed little Johanne into her growing family. Johanne's parents were two young lovers who were prevented from marrying largely by the boy's uncle, a wealthy pharmacy owner. Desperate to be together, the two decided to conceive a child in the hopes that this would win them permission to marry. It was not to be, though, and the pregnant girl found herself alone, despised, and facing the care of a child. In a way that has been lost to history, Lydia entered the story and insisted that the girl have the baby in Jaffa Hospital. Apparently there was some conversation about putting the baby up for adoption, but when the child was born and Lydia went to the hospital to see her, she was smitten. As she later told that child, "I went to see you, and I fell in love with you. I looked at your face and saw those beautiful green eyes. I could not let you go."

Lydia loved Johanne, as she clearly did all her daughters and perfected the art of assuring them that they were as dear to her as if they had come from her own body. Once a young Johanne fretted at the thought of her life without Lydia. "What might have happened if I had never been given to you?" she asked her mother tearfully.

"Don't think about it," Lydia assured. "It was ordained before the beginning of time. I may not have borne you in my womb, but it was under my heart where I carried you."

Soon, there were more girls for Lydia to love as tenderly. Magdalene was next, the daughter of a Tel Aviv rabbi named Katz. She was quite literally placed on Lydia's doorstep in the hope that the Danish missionary would take her in. Lydia refused at first and told the family so in forceful terms. Magdalene's sweetness melted her, though, and Lydia soon found herself making a place for the girl. Of all of Lydia's girls, the one the others speak of with reverence and respect is Magdalene. She absorbed both Lydia's willing generosity and the hospitality of her Middle Eastern culture. It made her one of the kindest people any of the Christensen girls would ever know. Her life would not be easy, but along her often-troubled journey she would leave both altars of devotion and wells of refreshing for the many she loved so deeply.

The only Arab among Lydia's girls joined the family not long after. Young Kirsten's mother had died of a hemorrhage while giving birth to her. Though her father came from a good family—he was the mayor of her hometown of El Bireh, and his brother was an attorney—he had trouble caring for the girl and asked Lydia to take her in. Kirsten would grow up straddling two worlds—Lydia's European culture and the Arab world of her native family. In the press between the two, she absorbed the best of both worlds into her gentle, gracious soul.

As a girl, Kirsten would often have to leave Lydia's house and her adoptive mother's Western ways to visit her first family. Her father, Bajees Faraj, lived with his own family in the single room of a house carved into the side of a hill. Farm animals lolled on the floor just below. After a few weeks of immersion in Arab village life, Kirsten would return to Lydia and become a European again. This arrangement continued until Bajees Faraj attempted during one of his daughter's visits to arrange a marriage for the girl. Kirsten was twelve years old at the time, though, and Lydia soon decided that the visits with her father should stop. She would remain a European.

Kirsten's memories of life in Ramallah are among the clearest and most endearing of all the girls—evidence of her poetic, Arab soul. She was able to recall even late in life, for example, watching the Catholic girls in the village make their way to their confirmation. With childish envy Kirsten saw her schoolmates march through the streets in their immaculate dresses, and she longed to be Catholic herself. It was not too much of a stretch. Lydia got along well with the nuns in Ramallah and often commented that she thought they were truly born again. Kirsten's soul yearned to belong to this mysterious, ornate religion and yearned most for the white gloves and rites of passage her Catholic schoolmates enjoyed.

Kirsten also recalled throughout her life the beauty of Christmas as Lydia created it. The Scandinavians are known for their love of Christmas, and Lydia was no exception to her countrymen. Kirsten recalled all her days that the Christmas tree was adorned with little Danish flags and pretty white candles, a vision certain to impress the soul of a child. She also remembered the impatience she felt when she was barred along with her sisters from the living room while Tikva and Lydia wrapped presents, usually heart-shaped bags filled with sweets. Then all the family would stand around the tree and sing "O Christmas Tree" in Arabic. It was a tender scene, sweetly remembered by an orphaned Arab child.

Kirsten would have the closest relationship of all the girls with Lydia's maid, Jameela. Blind in one eye and rejected for this deformity by her Arab peers, Jameela attached herself to Lydia and her growing band of girls. Her father owned the house where Lydia lived in Ramallah. In fact, Jameela lived in the flat just below Lydia's and was therefore an ever-present force in the girls' lives. She was also a constant source of entertainment. She irritated Lydia by flirting with the village men, lying without remorse, and using what she learned of the gospel in novel ways. She was afraid of cats, and when a particularly black one crossed the road one day, she courageously protected the girls with her by shouting, "I stretch out my hand in Jesus' name." She had heard the words in one of Lydia's sermons and was sure the cat would instantly disappear as she spoke them.

Jameela would always feel an affinity for Kirsten because they were both Arab. She saw it as her duty to make sure that the bright-eyed child wasn't neglected among the other Jewish and European girls. It was not uncommon for Kirsten to find a piece of candy or one of her favorite foods held in reserve for her and for her clothes to receive special attention from an ever-vigilant Jameela. It was to Kirsten that Jameela would turn with her stream of light-hearted complaints about Lydia, to Kirsten that she would teach Arab lore, and to Kirsten that she would look, even in old age, for understanding of puzzling Western ways.

Lydia was busy raising five little Jews and one Arab, then, when two tiny Europeans entered her life. The first of these, Anna, came to her when she was just ten days old. A sixteen-year-old German Jew had become pregnant and knew she was in no condition to care for a child. She gave the newborn to the Danish woman at the children's home and went off to join the Haganah, the budding Jewish defense force. Anna was blonde, hazel-eyed, and precocious. Often described by her sisters as "a bundle of joy," she was ever the darling of the neighboring Arabs who were fascinated with her Germanic features and gregarious ways.

It was not long after Anna joined the family that Lydia received a call from Nazareth. It was from a Scottish nurse named Lockhart. She had become entangled in an affair with a British officer and planned to marry him until she discovered that he was already married. Then she discovered she was pregnant. Devastated, she decided to give birth to the child and put it up for adoption. Thus the call to Lydia, who immediately took Tikva and Johanne with her to the hospital in Nazareth to meet the newest addition to their family—a baby girl named Elisabeth. The newborn became the darling of the Christensen household, a cute, blonde, sweet-tempered child whom the other girls loved to entertain.

These, then, were the faces and the stories that met Derek Prince when he began his regular visits to Lydia's home in Ramallah in 1945. Every moment he spent with this unusual woman and her amazing daughters was like immersion in a completely different universe. Derek had grown up the only child of a British army officer who was in turn married to the daughter of a British army officer. He had spent most of his youth away at school: Hawtrey's, Eton, and then Cambridge. His time with women had been minimal except when he was being immoral, and his time with children was virtually nonexistent. Now he spent almost every spare moment with nine women ranging in age from one to fifty-five, and he loved it. He also loved how it was changing him.

He would arrive at the home in the late afternoons, and almost immediately someone would put him to work. There were floors to clean, meals to prepare, and even clothes to wash. Routinely, baby Elisabeth would find Derek and crawl up his leg until she stood wobbling with a death grip on his trousers. But he had seldom been around children, and he did not know what to do. The girls, half in disgust and half in amusement, would shout for him to pick her up. He did but held her as if she were a smelly cat. One of the girls would inevitably reposition Elisabeth on Derek's shoulder and show him how to support her back. Immediately, the child would begin reaching for Derek's prominent nose or pulling on his lips to see his teeth.

Derek was used to relative quiet broken only by the good-natured chatter of men. He now found himself in a swirling world of feminine noise. Tikva and Johanne might be practicing the piano. Jameela and Lydia might be having a spirited debate in the kitchen about the proper way to cook the lamb. Kirsten could be chattering away in Arabic with a neighborhood child, both excited about the plums they had gathered from the tree in the front yard. Anna and Elisabeth might be screaming for attention. The other girls—Magdalene, Peninah, and Ruhammah—would almost certainly be calling to each other about how best to do the next chore. And it would be nothing unusual for all of this commotion to take place alongside a full-volume soldiers' prayer meeting in the parlor.

There were slips and bras hanging on laundry lines and the smells of girls' ointments and perfumes throughout the house. Tension between two girls would be attended with a kind of screaming and tears that Derek associated with a German assault. He marveled at the dinnertime chatter. He noted with interest the emerging womanhood in the older girls. He was fascinated by Lydia's descriptions of her relationship with Jesus, realizing as he listened that a woman experiences spiritual things in a different way than a man does. He was learning to see the world through feminine eyes. It was an education his past had seldom provided but that his future would urgently demand.

If Derek's frequent visits to Lydia's home were changing him in pleasant ways, they were also setting him in greater tension with his life in the military. During working hours, he was still a medical orderly at Kiriat Motzkin supply depot, and he was still chafing under the restrictions of army life. In fact, matters had recently grown worse. His commanding officer at the depot had begun to resent the Bible reading that Derek enjoyed during his breaks. The officer chastised Derek for his "religious extremism" and did everything in his power to disrupt Derek's routine. When Derek had finally had enough of this man's haranguing, he decided to ask for a transfer to the British hospital in Jerusalem. This would not only end his unbearable situation with the officer but also put him closer to Lydia as well. The transfer was granted, landing Derek in the last assignment of his army career. He would serve at No. 16 British General Hospital on the Mount of Olives, a facility that was once a guesthouse of the German kaiser.

Before Derek left Kiriat Motzkin, though, he received one of the most important revelations of his life. Moved by Lydia's ministry and devotion to God, he had begun contemplating more fully his own life's purpose, the reason for all he had experienced, and all of the hopes that burned so fiercely in his heart. As he held these dreams before his God, he found himself praying in tongues, and, as often happened, the meaning of what he prayed formed itself in his mind. The words were clear, and Derek never forgot them: "I have called thee to be a teacher of the Scriptures, in truth and faith and love, which are in Christ Jesus—for many."

Derek rolled the words over and over in his mind, drawing from them the understanding that he would spend his life teaching God's truth to others. Perhaps this was why he had walked such a winding path—through the best schools in England, through the betrayal in Ireland, through the years in the desert, and now in the land of his Lord's birth. He was beginning to understand. He had been in school for his calling. But he wondered, now, when that calling would begin. Derek was in the crucible that all great men endure. He was pressed between a driving inner sense of purpose and an outer life that kept this purpose bound. So he did what he must do: the next thing at hand. He performed his duties at the British hospital on the Mount of Olives, and, when those duties were done, he boarded the bus that carried him to Ramallah.

The months that Derek came and went from Lydia's home were transforming for him. He and Lydia shared the Scriptures together and prayed constantly. And they talked by the hour. She was surely enjoying the company of an educated European whose passion for God matched her own. He was learning some of the lessons his Bible college in the desert had not covered. He learned, for example, of the kind of faith that looks to God for every need. Lydia had been forced to trust God to meet the kind of needs Derek had rarely even thought about. When food was scarce, Lydia and her girls would pray. Without fail, a basket of eggs would appear on the doorstep or a shopkeeper would send food that he could not find room for on his shelves. Lydia and her girls lived in expectation of the miraculous. This included miraculous healing as well. Time and again, one of the girls would develop an ailment, and Lydia would gather her family for prayer. The ailment would disappear, sometimes instantly. This was Lydia's world—a world in which spiritual things were normal—and Derek eagerly drank from the well of her battle-tested faith.

As Lydia and Derek grew closer, they began talking about their dreams and their future hopes. Derek found he could say things to Lydia that he had never felt free to say to anyone else. In a sense, he was unpacking his soul to another human being for the first time. Lydia felt it, too, and was moved when Derek told her of the words he had received from God, of how he was called to be a teacher, and how his teaching was meant to reach the world. He knew sharing such things might make him sound boastful, but Lydia seemed to understand and treated these treasures of his heart with tenderness.

It was during one of their intimate talks that Derek told Lydia of Clare. Lydia had already suspected something. On the few occasions when Derek stayed too late to catch the last bus back to Jerusalem, he slept on the sweeping veranda of Lydia's home. Each time he did, he put the picture of a baby boy by his bed. Lydia wondered who the child was and suspected that Derek had a difficult story to tell. When he told her of Clare, of his confession to Sean, and of the correspondence he'd had with Clare over the years, Lydia was moved but warned him about his ongoing contact with Clare. It was unclean, she said, and he should end it. They had sinned together, and though they had confessed, they must follow up repentance with obedience. It was wrong for Derek to maintain a correspondence with another man's wife, particularly one with whom he had immorally conceived a child. Derek saw the wisdom of her words and wrote Clare soon afterward to tell her that their relationship must end. Reluctantly, she agreed, and the two never saw or heard from each other again.

This conversation about Clare was more than just a soldier seeking counsel from an older woman. Derek and Lydia were surfacing the subjects that men and women do when they are approaching marriage. Derek felt the need to come clean about Clare because he was beginning to fall in love with Lydia. She, on the other hand, gave Derek solid spiritual counsel but later confessed to Tikva that the tale of Clare made her jealous and that she had trouble getting it out of her mind. She too was nurturing a growing affection for Derek, and in a way that must have surprised her fifty-five-year-old soul.

Lydia's girls sensed that something was happening between their mother and the handsome young soldier, but they did not know what it was. Often in the evenings, Derek and Lydia would sit beside each other in the large, ornate parlor of the Christensen home and talk intimately, sometimes even holding hands as they did. The girls would often sneak out of bed and watch their mother's strange behavior through the windows of the large French doors that separated the parlor from the rest of the house. Then, amazed and giggling, they would run back down the hall to their beds before their mother found them out.

It was not long before all mysteries were revealed. Lydia sat all eight girls upon her bed one evening and told them that Derek had asked her to marry him. The Christensen girls couldn't believe their ears. All this time they thought Derek was pursuing Tikva. Now their mother was telling them that this handsome young soldier was actually interested in their fifty-five-year-old mother. And he wanted to marry her, for heaven's sake!

The girls barely knew what to say and, in the way of the young, objected to how the marriage would disrupt their own lives. "Mommy," Tikva appealed, "you can't have a man in this house." She was thinking of a home filled with nine women and how a man would mean always having to be fully clothed or always keeping doors closed. And what of the bathroom and the laundry? Can a man be included in these things?

Lydia was patient but explained herself in words that betray more than just her feelings about Derek. "I am going to get older, and you girls won't be there," she said tenderly, "but I need a bit of happiness. With Derek, I will have it." The girls protested, but Lydia was resolved. Her words, though, are revealing. She had been serving her God in Palestine for nearly twenty years, and though she believed that doing her spiritual duty was its own reward, she was clearly unfulfilled as a woman. Perhaps she had tried to put her womanly needs on an altar of sacrifice. Perhaps she had even tried to envision herself single and alone until the end of her days and all to the glory of God. Clearly, the picture disturbed her, and she knew that she was, in some deep and unspoken way, unhappy. When she told her children that she needed a "bit of happiness," she gave them a rare glimpse into her heart, the heart of a spiritual woman who was nevertheless fully a woman—with all the need for love and protection that even a strong woman craves. Knowing herself, then, and knowing her feelings for Derek, when he asked her to marry him she said yes.

He had asked rather clumsily, though. The two had been sitting in the parlor one evening when Derek got up, walked across the room, and asked Lydia if she would be his wife. She said yes, and then the two just stared at each other, neither sure of what ought to come next. Derek took her hands, kissed them, and then sat beside her. Almost immediately, the two discussed their age differences. Then they discussed telling the girls. And then it was done. Derek returned to the Mount of Olives, and Lydia began planning her chat with her daughters. Both Derek and Lydia found themselves giggling at the oddness of their relationship and, in the way of lovers, at their excitement about each other.

In a manner common to expatriates, Derek and Lydia had two wedding ceremonies. The first was an informal one led by a Jewish believer in the home of Mrs. Radford, a Christian missionary woman who had befriended Lydia when she first landed in Palestine. The ceremony had very nearly been canceled. Though the date for the wedding had been set for weeks, Lydia arose on the much-anticipated day and saw that it was snowing. Announcing to her girls that it was "too cold to get married," she decided to postpone the wedding. This was clearly a case of bridal nerves, endearing in a woman of Lydia's age. Her daughters prevailed, though, and the simple ceremony took place. It might have been a happier occasion. The older Christensen girls sat in the back during the ceremony and cried, not for the beauty of the moment but because they feared they were losing their mother to this British stranger.

Derek and Lydia consummated their marriage that night, but this left Derek with surprising feelings of guilt. He had not told his commanding officer of his wedding, and he wondered if the union was legal—or even moral, for that matter. It did not help that after several days of sharing Lydia's bed, Derek had to return to his billet at the hospital. For weeks, either he commuted to Ramallah or Lydia took the bus to Jerusalem to meet her new husband at their appointed spot: in front of Barclay's Bank near the Damascus Gate of the Old City. The arrangement began to feel a bit seedy to Derek, and he wondered if he was living in sin.

This continued for more than a month until the marriage was finally solemnized by the British District Commissioner on April 17, 1946. Derek's *pakkah*-trained British soul was set at ease: he was legally married. The marriage certificate issued by that commissioner is revealing. Derek is listed as a thirty-year-old Englishman serving as corporal in the Royal Army Medical Corps. Lydia is listed as a fifty-six-year-old Danish "spinster missionary." Tikva Cohen, Lydia's eighteen-year-old Jewish daughter, is recorded as the witness to the marriage. Clearly, an unusual family entered the British record on that spring day in 1946.

Apparently, the strangeness of the situation occurred to Derek's father, too. When Derek wrote him about the marriage, Paul wrote back asking about Lydia's age. Derek replied that a proper gentleman does not inquire about a woman's age. Paul then apologized and offered his blessing, though the exchange must have left him wondering.

It was not long afterward that Derek decided to leave the army. He had been contemplating the move for some time. The war had ended the year before, and Derek had watched many of his fellow soldiers return to civilian life. Moreover, he had proven so skilled at his work that the British army, typically, had given him the responsibilities of a sergeant yet with the pay of a corporal. He had a family now and needed the additional money. He appealed for a promotion but was denied.

He took this as a sign from God. He had long sensed that he and Lydia were brought together for ministry as much as for love, and the ministry he envisioned was impossible as long as he was in the army. He was willing to stay, though, until he found that the army wouldn't pay him for the work he was doing. It was time to get out. But whom should he tell? He looked around, considered the matter carefully, and realized that the person responsible for processing discharges was—Corporal Derek Prince. So he filed his own papers and on June 6, 1946, was discharged from the British army.

Almost immediately, Derek developed a crisis of conscience about the three pounds a week he was receiving as a fellow at King's College, Cambridge. He wasn't doing any work for the money, and this bothered him. It says much about his character at the time. He wrote King's to ask them to stop sending the money, but they refused. This was the way of things, they explained. Derek was disturbed but then remembered that King's College had been founded by Henry VI, who wanted to propagate true religion. Derek realized that now, with Lydia, this was exactly what he would be doing. His conscience clear, he happily spent the money on his new family.

Derek now entered the life of a newly married man, a father of eight, and a missionary. Whereas his days had once been filled with wounded men, military order, and the clerical responsibilities of a British hospital abroad, he found himself attempting sanity in the swirling world of Lydia's home. He rose in the morning to a new wife, children that ranged over seventeen years in age, and a home that was more ministry center than refuge. The barracks gave way to a house filled with hanging feminine garments. Dressing the wounds of war gave way to changing the diapers of children. The frustrating routine of the British army gave way to the rigid and long-established routine of Lydia Prince. It was not an easy transition. Derek gave it his best. He learned to clean to Lydia's standards and to tend the youngest children without being too present in the bedrooms of the older girls. He cooked, he washed, he tended, and he bargained in the shops of Ramallah. With time he became a dutiful husband, father, and friend.

He also became a teacher. Before his arrival, the girls' home life was largely a matter of Bible reading, praying, and singing. Derek added to this by encouraging the girls to memorize the Bible, but he took things even further. He made the Bible live in their imaginations by telling them the age-old stories with drama and fire. Once he awakened their imaginations, he introduced them to the writings of Charles Dickens and then to the classics. The older girls began to read broadly, a luxury often eschewed by Pentecostals. Derek could not have known that some Christians disdained great literature as carnal. No one so narrow was there in his desert seminary to tell him. So he read and taught and opened the girls' minds to literary wonders they had never known. More than one of the Prince daughters remembers Dickens read aloud in Derek's Cambridge diction as among the great pleasures of their lives.

The girls also delighted when Derek and Lydia danced together. They already knew that Lydia had long loved music. There was a wind-up gramophone in the house, and Handel's *Messiah*—Lydia's favorite piece—often blared from it. What some of her girls did not know until Derek arrived was that Lydia also loved to dance, something a good Pentecostal almost never did other than in church. But Lydia had learned to enjoy dancing years before in Denmark, and she never lost the passion. Amazingly light on her feet for a full-figured woman, she could move with astonishing grace on a dance floor, and her girls shrieked with glee when she and Derek danced to a bit of the jazz sometimes aired on the BBC. It was not just the dancing that delighted the girls, though. It was the change in their mother's spirit, the new lightness in her step as well as her heart.

The girls also delighted in Derek's manly ways. His morning shave fascinated them, and they called each other to the open bathroom door to watch him smear a white substance on his face and then scrape it off again. Derek let them smear their faces with the same substance and even let them scrape his face with the sharp little device he used. Everything about him intrigued them, from his physical strength to the hair on his chest to his calming control of a crisis. They had never known a stable father before, and he changed them with his masculine ways as much as they changed him with their sweetness and love.

We should freeze this moment in Derek's life. It is, in a sense, the calm before the storm. He has left a lonely childhood, a wintry academic career, and the immorality of his Christless years behind. He has endured the furnace of the African desert and the anvil of God's disciplining school, only to end both his army career and his life as a single man in a small village just outside of the city that gave faith to the world. He is now husband to a woman nearly twice his age, father to eight adopted daughters, and minister to all who make their way to his home. It would not be hard to imagine that he is content, or perhaps content for the moment. For he knows that he is made for something more, that the word of the Lord and his own sense of destiny prod him, stir him, so that he can never fully settle until the stream of revelation that has poured into his heart pours in turn through his life to a needy world. The word of the Lord has told him he will go to the nations. But the word of the Lord has also told him he will not know how or when. He is still, then. Patient. He loves, he teaches, he prays, and he waits—waits for a promised day of destiny.

Major R. E.
Vaughan—Derek's
uncle

Paul and Gwendolyn—
Derek's parents

Grandfather's commission—the last thing Queen
Victoria signed with her own hand

Derek's parents' wedding picture

Derek with his mother at his christening, six weeks old

Derek in baby carriage, eight months old

Derek in
Indian clothing,
two years old

Portrait of
Derek, age
two, India,
1917

Off to boarding
school, age nine, 1924

Derek at Eton, sixteen
years old, 1931

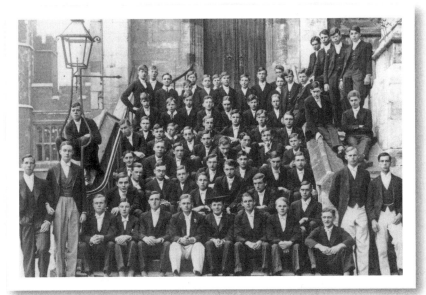

Eton College—upperclassmen

Portrait, sixteen years old

Eton College schoolyard showing chapel and Lupton's tower

Cambridge University, 1930s

Portrait of Derek, in his early twenties

Derek in army
uniform, World
War II, 1942

Derek in Sudan with
truck, early 1940s

In the Sudan,
early 1940s

Derek, Lydia,
and girls in
Ramallah, 1946

Derek and Lydia
in Ramallah

Derek and Lydia
in Denmark

Members
of Derek's
church in
London

Preaching in
Hyde Park
Speakers'
Corner,
1950

Preaching in Hyde Park; Magdalene and
Ruhammah in background

Derek in Kenya with
African baby

Baptizing
a young
Kenyan boy

Villagers by typical Kenyan hut

Derek, Lydia, and Joska, 1960

Lydia and Joska—photo taken by
Canadian newspaper for article, 1962

The Ft. Lauderdale Five (left to right): Ern Baxter, Derek Prince, Charles Simpson, Don Basham, Bob Mumford, early 1970s

Preaching at
Westminster
Chapel,
London,
1970s

Preaching at
Cornerstone
Church, San
Antonio, 1974

Zimbabwe,
late 1970s

Derek and Ruth, 1985

Teaching, 1980s

Teaching in Europe, 1980s

Lublin, Poland,
1996

DPM Retreat in
Blowing Rock, NC,
1999

Walking in
Jerusalem,
2001

7

Eretz Israel:
Present at the Creation

EREK PEERED INTENTLY into the distance, his eyes misty but searching as he scanned the Judean wilderness that seemed to lie just outside our window. Perhaps he was mentally roaming the streets of postwar Ramallah or perhaps he was remembering those first years with Lydia. It was hard to tell, but it was clear he needed a quiet moment, and I gave it to him.

As he sipped his ever-present tea and let the memories flow, I thought about the point to which we had come in his story. I was fascinated by what he must have been thinking in those early years. What was it like to be a thirty-year-old man with eight daughters and a wife twice your age living in the backwaters of Palestine? What about all the dreams, the hopes, the manly ambitions? Was he frustrated? Was he disappointed or tempted? Did he wish for something more?

I gave him his moment to reflect, and then I asked, "Derek, around the time you married and got out of the army, can you remember ever stopping to contemplate your life? Can you remember lifting your head from the press of the immediate and taking stock of where you were going?"

Derek's face looked the way it always did when I pressed him to talk about his feelings. There was a flash of confusion that betrayed itself mostly in his eyes before a quiet, pained look washed over him as he dug into his soul. Then it came: that calm sense of satisfaction that registered largely around his mouth. It was the look of a teacher who knew his text. I think Derek loved this moment—the announcement, the proclamation, the new perspective on an old experience.

"Yes, I do," he said. "In fact, I have described it in one of my books."

"Really," I replied, amazed. I couldn't remember anything so introspective in the books he had written. "Do you remember which book?"

He thought for a moment and said, "No, I can't. But I remember describing an evening on the Mount of Olives."

Then it came to me. "You mean the night on the Mount of Olives you described in *The Last Word on the Middle East*? The time you saw into the meaning of Israel?"

"Yes, that's it."

I reached for a copy of the book nearby and scanned the section Derek mentioned. But then I grew suspicious. I didn't think Derek would tell me something untrue, but I did think he might send me to a story he had told over and again rather than speak from the heart. I wanted the meaning not the sermon, and so I pressed.

"Derek, can you remember that night in terms you haven't used in a sermon or a book? Can you tell me about it as though it happened last night?"

He looked at me with a slight air of exasperation, but then seemed resigned and closed his eyes. "It was on a fine night in April of 1946, and I stood on a saddle of land..."

"Derek," I interrupted. "You're giving me the book. Can you take a moment and see that night in your mind's eye? I know it is hard since you've told this so many times, but I'm hoping to see it through the eyes of a thirty-year-old soldier rather than a nearly ninety-year-old minister."

Derek then opened his eyes and stared down at the cup in his hands. Just when I thought he was going to tell me he couldn't remember more than he wrote, he said, "I was thinking about what was next, not just in my life or the life of the girls, but in the world. It felt to me like the great cataclysm of the war had just ended and all the world was returning to normal. But I had a sense that something was about to happen, and I was thinking about what it all might mean. The course of the world seemed to be flooding through me that night."

"Where were you as you thought these things?" I asked.

"I was standing high above Jerusalem on a little landing just in front of the Augusta Victoria Hospital. This was the name for the hospital I had served in, No. 16 British Hospital, during the war. The whole area appears like the large, curved edge of a mountain. The hospital sat in that saddle of land I mentioned between Mount Scopus on the north end and the Mount of Olives on the south. The view from there was magnificent. The Old City spread out before me, and I felt how dearly I loved it. I remember specifically how brightly the moon reflected off the Dome of the Rock and the silver dome of the Mosque of Al Aksa."

"Tell me what you were thinking, Derek."

"Well, as I said, I was thinking about the future when it felt to me as though I stopped thinking in linear time and I thought only in the dimensions of Jerusalem. It was as though my thoughts about history and our times dissolved into the geography that lay before me. Bible verses began to flood through my mind about Israel and the specific features of Jerusalem. Passage after passage seemed no longer descriptive of an ancient land but of present realities, as though I was reading a travel guide for modern Israel out of the pages of the Bible. I've described all this in the book, though."

"I know, Derek, but tell me what it meant to you that night."

"I had this deep feeling that world history and my life were bound together through the geography that lay before me. I don't know if I can explain it. It was as though I was trying to think about the future, and my spirit was telling me that the future was here, in this place. It seemed that the Bible, history, and the course of my life were all overlaid on the geography of Israel, that they all became one. I knew then that my life was intertwined with Israel and that Israel, in some sense, determined the history of the world."

"Can you remember if you concluded anything when you walked off that landing?"

"Yes, I remember feeling that whatever was next for the world, the nations would have to deal with the land of Israel. And I remember feeling how thankful I was to be there, how I wasn't at all removed from the flow of history, but I was at that moment in the middle of biblical prophecy and at the focal point of the times."

"To use the words of Esther, did you feel that you had 'come to the kingdom for such a time as this'?"

"Yes, and it seemed to settle me. No matter the promises about my life that God had given me, they would come to pass only in connection with this land."

"In a sense, then, you and the land of Israel were one?"

"Yes, my destiny, I knew, was tied to the destiny of Israel."

<hr>

When Derek and Lydia Prince began their new lives together in the quiet Arab village of Ramallah in 1946, they could not have known how their world would soon change and change violently. History was converging upon them, a history they would spend the rest of their lives trying to fully understand. They were not alone. Few in the world at that time knew much about the Middle East, and even fewer understood the journey of the Jews through history or what that journey might mean for their age. It was a failure that would have tragic results for the plans of the world's statesmen but which would ultimately lead to the birth of modern Israel.

The Israel that played the stage to the ministry of Jesus Christ ceased to exist in A.D. 70 when Roman armies answered a Jewish rebellion by destroying Jerusalem. The ancient Temple of Solomon was dismantled, the holy city was burned, and the Jewish people began their centuries of global wandering. Thus ended the kingdom whose history had provided the vehicle of biblical revelation: the rise of a people under patriarchs, the fashioning of a kingdom under misbehaving kings, the cruel captivities by Assyrian and Babylonian armies, the restoration to the land under Persians, and the domination by both Greece and Rome. Their heritage destroyed, the Jews moved out into the nations of the world and began to live their faith divorced from their land.

This was called the "Diaspora," the "dispersion," and no one welcomed it more than the Christians. For centuries after the Jewish nation was no more, Christian priests and bishops preached that the Jews had crucified God in human form and thus had come under a curse. In fact, the church taught that the Jews bore the mark of Cain: they would always be rootless wanderers, despised upon the earth. The Jews, then, should be hated and betrayed and all to the glory of the Jewish Son of God.

So it was for centuries. In the Middle Ages, for example, tortured theology joined with superstition to assure the devastation of a race. If disease ravaged a village, it must mean that God was displeased with the Jews. If a baby was missing, it was surely because the Jews had stolen the child to drink its blood. In some regions the law counted it nothing to rape a Jewish woman, take a Jewish life, or raze a Jewish village. Indeed, these crimes were often transformed into virtues, particularly if practiced by a crusading European army on the march to retake Jerusalem for its God. And, later on, if the Jews refused to believe the Christian gospel, Christians were urged to attack them and make them converts. Hadn't that priest Martin Luther said it should be done? Hadn't their Catholic majesties of Castile and Aragon, Ferdinand and Isabella, ordered it before driving the Jews from their land? Weren't these Jews the Christ-killers, the vermin who polluted the world?

In fairness, not all Christians believed such things. From time to time Christian voices would arise in protest. The Jews are still God's people, they would proclaim. Didn't Paul say in the Book of Romans that he hoped for the redemption of Israel? Aren't Christians grafted into a Jewish tree? Might it be that God intends to restore the Jews to their land as He seemed to promise in the ancient writings? But these voices were quickly silenced. They were too much a challenge to the prevailing theologies, too much an indictment of the history of the church.

It fell, then, to a Muslim empire to grant the Jews the first lasting protection they had enjoyed since the fall of Jerusalem. The Ottoman Empire, which ruled the Middle East for more than four hundred years, treated the Jews more kindly than the Christian dominions ever had. This was because the sultans who ruled the Ottoman Empire from Constantinople were Muslims who revered the Quran, the holy book of Islam, which teaches that Christians and Jews are to be honored as a "people of the book"—meaning a people who revered the Bible, a book Muslims also esteem. So the Ottoman Jews lived in relative peace from the fifteenth until the twentieth century, a privilege routinely denied their European kin.

The Ottoman Empire came to an end, though, in the bloodletting of World War I. The sultans who once ruled became the fiefdoms of European powers. Though the Arab peoples were promised autonomy by the Europeans as a reward for throwing off the Ottoman yoke, they found at the end of the war that they had been duped. A secret treaty called the Sykes-Picot Agreement had quietly granted Arab lands to the victorious European powers. The Middle East would never be the same. The old League of Nations granted the British and the French "mandates," or temporary colonial administration, over former Ottoman domains, and immediately the two powers took their pens and created three new Arab countries—Iraq, Syria, and Lebanon.

Then the British took an area known as "southern Syria" and created what it officially called "Palestine" in English, "Falastin" in Arabic, and "Palestine Al" in Hebrew. The portion to the east of the Jordan River was split to form an autonomous emirate then known as Transjordan, later renamed the Kingdom of Jordan. As Winston Churchill once famously said, "I created Transjordan with a stroke of a pen on a Sunday afternoon in Cairo." The area to the west of the Jordan River—with the holy city of Jerusalem at its heart—became the focus for all who yearned for a Jewish homeland: for secular Jews in the mold of Theodor Herzl who tired of Europe's oppression, for British Restorationists who dreamed of a messianic Israel in the land of their Lord, for weary Jews of every kind who dreamed of a land of their own.

All these found hope in the words of what came to be known as the Balfour Declaration, a simple document that had passed between Lord Balfour, the British Foreign Secretary, and Lord Walter Rothschild, the head of a famed Jewish family, in 1917. The document contained a promise: "His Majesty's Government view with favor the establishment in Palestine of a national home for the Jewish people." At the end of the First World War, Jews and their supporters around the world thrilled at the thought that the ancient land of Israel was in the hands of a government that intended to grant the Jews a homeland.

But it was not to be. The idea of a Jewish homeland enraged the Arab majority west of the Jordan River. In 1922, at the time the British mandate came into effect, there were more than 589,000 Arabs but less than 84,000 Jews in the land. Nevertheless, the Arabs feared Jewish immigration might cost them their control of the region. Riots broke out, first in 1921 and then in 1929. Jews were killed by the dozens, as were British soldiers. By 1939, the British were so weary of policing the region that they issued the MacDonald White Paper, severely restricting Jewish immigration. This merely emboldened the Arabs, sent Zionist groups underground, and left many world leaders believing that separate homelands for Jews and Arabs were the only real solution.

Then came World War II and Hitler's "Final Solution of the Jewish Question" (*Endlösung der Judenfrage*). More than six million Jewish lives were snuffed out by Nazi hands, and several million more were left homeless and destitute by war's end. Jewish eyes turned again to the ancient land of Israel. Surely now it was time for the persecuted wanderers to have a home of their own. Surely these people had won the right for a homeland in places like Auschwitz and Dachau. Who would dare deny them after so much suffering?

The answer came quickly: the Arabs. During the war years and just after, many Arab nations had emerged from colonial rule and, with British prompting, formed the Arab League to coordinate policy between their states. This league was vehemently opposed to a Jewish homeland and lobbied in the capitals of the world against it. When talk failed, violence prevailed, and swirling clouds of war began to form just as the frustrated British asked the United Nations (UN) to decide the fate of the Jewish people.

The mounting tensions between Arabs and Jews were felt in each village and house of Palestine. Men whose grandparents had often supped together began eyeing each other with suspicion. Women who had taken food to each other's homes when children were sick or relatives died were soon unwilling to speak. It was a heartrending, disorienting time, but it was nothing compared to the devastation that came soon after. In time, tension gave way to bloodshed, and the children of ancient friends began gunning each other down in the streets without remorse.

⁂

In the latter part of 1946, the Prince family was living a largely Arab life in the little village of Ramallah. To their credit, they had refused to isolate themselves from the surrounding culture, as missionaries sometimes do, and instead felt a strong connection to their neighbors and to the traditions of the local people. This was not only because Lydia and her girls had lived in Ramallah for more than a decade, but also because the people of Ramallah were largely Greek Orthodox Christians. The Princes and their neighbors, then, shared a common faith, celebrated the same holy days, and believed many of the same doctrines. They also shared an admiration for the beautiful cathedral that stood in the center of Ramallah, a symbol of the ancient faith of the land. Kirsten remembered sitting in this cathedral for hours, rapt in admiration of the beautiful stained glass windows, particularly the one depicting Abraham's sacrifice of Isaac.

The Prince family felt very much at peace in their Arab world. The girls played with Arab children, Lydia shopped in the Arab market, and Derek did his best to pass time with the neighboring Arab men. Gifts were exchanged with their Arab neighbors on holy days, and the gracious rules of Arab hospitality were observed. Derek even delighted throughout his life to recall the very simple Middle Eastern diet that the family enjoyed in those early days: "coarse bread, olive oil, powdered hyssop, milk, eggs, and, for a treat, a sack of oranges which could be had for two shillings." On special occasions and when money allowed, there might even be a meal of lamb. Clearly, the Prince family felt very much at home both in Arab culture and with their friends in the Christian village of Ramallah.

It was not long after Derek and Lydia married, though, that they began to notice a change. Ramallah began to feel less friendly. The once welcoming smiles were harder to find. Groups of men who had once greeted Derek warmly on the street remained closed and gave him little more than an over-the-shoulder glance. Shopkeepers Lydia had known for years seemed chilly and businesslike at best. Derek and Lydia discussed this change and quickly realized what was happening. It was the same thing that was happening all throughout Palestine. Arabs were beginning to resent the Jews, sensing that world events might mean a Jewish homeland where Arabs had lived for centuries. And here were the Princes, a family with six Jewish girls, living in an Arab village.

Just as Derek and Lydia were pondering how to respond, a near tragedy made their direction clear. On July 22, 1946, Tikva tried to board a crowded bus that was bound for Jerusalem. The driver turned her away because there was no room. A few hours later, she and her family learned that this same bus was sitting in front of the King David Hotel, headquarters of the British forces in Jerusalem, when a bomb exploded. A guerrilla faction known as the Irgun, led by Menachem Begin, had set off the bomb in hopes of driving the British out of Palestine. More than ninety Arabs, Jews, and Britons were killed in the bombing, including many who were on the bus. Had Tikva been aboard, she might have been killed.

There were other dark omens. The Irgun killed two British sergeants and then booby-trapped their dead bodies to inflict even more damage. The news of this shocked the Western world and filled the villages of Palestine with fear. There were more bombings and assassinations. Both Arabs and Jews seemed to be gearing up for some immense, unnamed conflict that lay just ahead. Certainly, the peaceful life the Prince family had known was coming to an end. Derek and Lydia knew what they had to do: they must move the girls into the safety of Jerusalem.

Derek began searching immediately and made repeated trips into the city to find a new home. Each time he returned empty-handed. The girls would pray even harder, Derek would voyage out again, and still there was nothing. Everyone grew concerned. The tension was heightening in the streets. Finally, Lydia felt a jolt of faith fill her heart. "Let's believe God will send people to our door," she urged. So the family prayed that news of a home in Jerusalem would come to their door. Two short hours later, an Assyrian builder appeared on their doorstep. He had heard the Princes were looking for a house, and he had just built one in Jerusalem that they could rent. The family rejoiced at the news and shared their astonishment at how rapidly God had answered.

Then a harsh reality set in. It was common in those days for a new renter to have to pay two years' rent—or key money—in advance. Derek was troubled by the need. Where would they get the money? Not long after, he had a dream in which a man paid the key money. He took comfort from this but still waited eagerly for God to provide. He soon realized that he had an insurance policy from his army days that he no longer needed. Cashing it in would provide just the money the family needed. So, Derek cashed in the policy and moved his family into a new home in Upper Bakaa at 90 Hebron Road.

The house was much grander than any they had known before. The family occupied the top two floors, which were filled with large, spacious rooms and new furniture. On the floor below lived a kind Jewish family and an Arab boy who kept the house for the builder. The two floors the Princes occupied were more than they needed, and after they dedicated their new home to God, they put a sign over the front that read "Swedish Bible and Children's Home" in honor of the Swedish church that provided most of their financial support.

The Prince home quickly became a center of ministry just as it had been in Ramallah. The new neighbors heard the gospel from the moment they met Lydia on the streets and heard the Prince prayer meetings sounding from the windows on the second floor. Each Sunday morning, a small congregation of Arabs gathered for a kind of informal church the Princes conducted in their living room. While the other girls ran a Sunday school for neighborhood children, Tikva or Johanne played piano before Derek preached. He would stand before a small table with an Arab woman's shawl draped over it and expound the Word of God as though preaching to thousands. On one morning, he was talking about the Holy Spirit when a dove landed on the table. Everyone there took this as a sign of the Spirit's presence, as a blessing both on the house and on the spreading of God's Word.

Despite the heightening tension in the city, the months the Princes lived in this house were happy ones. The girls went to a larger, more modern school than they had known in Ramallah. There were music lessons, hours of playing with Toby, the family dog, in the spacious new yard, and always the delights of Jerusalem. Derek and Lydia found an ever-widening circle of people who needed their ministry, and they stayed busy praying for the sick, sharing biblical truth with the lost, and praying about the events that were announced over the BBC on the family radio.

This relative happiness continued until fall of 1947 when, on November 29, the UN approved a plan that partitioned the British Mandate of Palestine into two states: one Jewish and one Arab. In the words of Larry Collins and Dominique Lapierre in their masterful *O Jerusalem!*, the decision was "a mapmaker's nightmare . . . at best, a possible compromise; at worst, an abomination. It gave fifty-seven percent of Palestine to the Jewish people despite the fact that two thirds of its population and more than half its land was Arab."[15] The fear and the hatred that had been steadily rising in Palestine since the end of the Second World War now exploded into the streets.

The impact of the United Nation's decision upon Jerusalem was immediate. Neighborhoods that were purely Arab or Jewish locked down into armed camps. Neighborhoods that were mixed, that contained both Jewish and Arab homes, were immediately thrown into crisis. Everyone expected violence, and no one wanted to live next to their enemy. In neighborhoods with a majority of Jews, the Arabs simply packed up their belongings and fled. The reverse occurred where Arabs were dominant. The city was in turmoil, and the British seemed powerless to bring order.

One by one, Derek and Lydia watched their largely Jewish neighbors gather a few belongings and steal away in the night to avoid the snipers who quickly began to rule the streets. Naïvely, perhaps, the Princes had decided that this conflict between Arab and Jew wouldn't affect them. They were Christians, after all, and their family included both Jews and Arabs. Who would want to harm them?

The answer came on December 12. That morning, as Derek and Lydia began their day with prayer in their bedroom, Lydia began to speak in an unknown tongue, which sounded like the word "urgent." Derek received an interpretation from God, the sense of which was that the urgency had to do with the safety of the family but that "none shall be lost or scattered." The two were somewhat alarmed but took comfort in the promise of God and went on with their day.

That afternoon an Australian policeman from the Palestine Police Force visited the house. He asked about the address of an Australian lady who was connected to The Salvation Army, and rather than give out the lady's address in such troubled times, Derek and Lydia sent one of the girls to see if the woman could drop by. When the lady arrived, the four had prayer together, and the policeman—who had been a member of The Salvation Army but had fallen away—dedicated his life to his faith again. When they resumed praying, Derek felt that God was placing a Scripture verse into his mind: "I have delivered thee from the snare of the fowler"—words from Psalm 91:3.

Just as the prayer meeting ended, Johanne burst into the room, pale and trembling.

While Derek and Lydia had been praying that afternoon, Johanne was making her way home from her music lessons. She had been delayed and quickly realized it was already getting dark. As she approached the house, she noticed a truck filled with soldiers of the Arab Legion. This was unusual, but even more unusual was that the Arab boy who lived on the lower level of the Prince's house was talking to the man in charge of the soldiers. Sensing danger, Johanne ran around to the back of the house and went up to the second floor. At the front of the house on this floor was a veranda with a low, stone wall. By crawling on her hands and knees, she could work her way to the front edge of the veranda where she would be just above the heads of the boy and the legionnaire.

Johanne was frightened by what she heard. The boy was giving the commander details about the Prince family: who lived in the house, how many were there, how many were girls, and what kind of things the Princes owned. Then the legionnaire asked about the patrols in the area. Routinely, a patrol would include one British soldier, one Jewish soldier, and an Arab legionnaire. They didn't do much good, but they did prevent the lesser crimes and they might serve as witnesses. The boy said that the patrols ended at midnight, and there would be no security on the road thereafter. Promising to return, the legionnaires drove away.

It was just as Derek, Lydia, the policeman, and the Australian Salvation Army lady were finishing their prayer time—the one in which Derek sensed the words "I have delivered thee from the snare of the fowler"—that Johanne burst into the room and told her tale. Everyone was immediately alarmed. Knowing how enraged the Arabs had become and how Jews had been assaulted and even murdered in their homes, the Princes knew they were in danger. Immediately, the policeman escorted the Australian lady home and then went to the nearest police station to ask for help. He returned dejected. The police could send little more than a small patrol, and that would do no good against an entire truckload of legionnaires.

Now Derek and Lydia knew they were in dire trouble. It was very likely that the truckload of Arab soldiers would return that night to rape the Jewish girls and pillage the house. But what could they do? There were few options. With a largely abandoned neighborhood all about them and no security forces to count on they had only one choice: leave their home and their possessions for safety—and do it immediately.

Events began to move at a blurring speed. Lydia hastily prepared a meal. She could not know when her family might eat again. Derek told the girls they had to leave and then instructed them to pack their Bibles and what few things they needed in their pillowcases. The older girls helped the younger, and in two hours the family was ready to go. As Derek packed, he was thankful for two blessings. First, he was grateful that the Australian policeman had agreed to stay with them until they were safe. Derek sensed that he would be invaluable. Second, Derek was thankful for what had seemed a tragedy a few days before but now seemed a blessing. The family's beloved dog, Toby, had been run over by a truck and killed. Derek thought to himself that had the dog not died, he would now have to be abandoned, only adding to the girls' distress.

At nine o'clock, the sad procession began. Into the dark, deserted streets the Princes marched in a quiet single file. Lydia led the way, with Derek bringing up the rear and the policeman helping to carry the smaller children. The sound of rifle fire occasionally split the night silence. There was no way of knowing if a sniper had his sight trained on them. As they walked, Derek could hear a few of the girls sniffing back tears, and he wondered if they wept for what was left behind or for the unknown that lay ahead.

The trudging band made their way through the blackened emptiness of Jerusalem. Derek and Lydia had decided to seek help at an American Assemblies of God mission in the center of Jerusalem. They knew they would find help there, but first they had to enter the British security zone. This would take some doing because none of them had the proper passes. Thankfully, the policeman could go in, and he left immediately to meet with the British commander. While the family waited, the sentry took pity on Lydia and offered her and the two youngest children his seat behind the sandbagged wall of the guard house.

The irony of the moment must have crossed Derek's mind. There he stood with his Danish wife and his Arab, Jewish, and British children applying for entrance into the compound of his own country. He had just left the British army the year before, but now he had to stand outside by a sentry post waiting for an Australian to gain him access to his own country's protection.

Finally, the policeman returned, having gained permission for the family to enter. They passed through the barbed wire barricade and continued down the still streets to the door of the American mission. Their welcome was warm. A bit of food was prepared. Mattresses were spread about the floor, and the children were put to bed, weary from their night's adventure. Before they slept, Derek and Lydia thanked God that He had seen them to safety and affirmed in prayer their confidence that their lives were in His hands.

Word of the Prince's plight spread quickly in the neighborhood surrounding the mission, particularly among the Arabs. The next morning, a leader of the Christian Arabs brought a message from the Muslim forces stating that if the Jewish girls remained in the mission they would burn the whole house down. It was no idle threat. The American missionaries said they would be happy to keep Derek, Lydia, and the non-Jewish children, but that the others would have to go. But this would never do: Derek and Lydia would never split their family. The search for a new home began.

Several days later, Derek found a place for his family at a British mission on the edge of one of the purely Jewish areas of Jerusalem, near what would later be known as the Mendelbaum Gate. The family would be safe from attack there, but they would also have a front-row seat for the battles then tearing at the soul of Jerusalem. Just beyond the mission was a "no man's land," a housing area that had been vacated due to the fighting but which at night became the battlefield of opposing bands. As soon as darkness fell, the sound of gunfire and bombs erupted from the fields just outside the wall of the mission. When the shooting began, the family immediately gathered into one of the interior rooms that were safe from shrapnel and stray bullets. Derek and Lydia led the girls in singing and games to keep their minds from the unnerving concussion of the battle just outside their home. It was in this manner that the Prince family passed Christmas of 1947 and into the new year of 1948.

In mid-January, Derek received word that the Assemblies of God missionaries who had helped them on that first horrible night were returning to America. The Arabs who threatened the house before had been driven from the area by Jewish forces, and the missionaries thought their home would now be perfect for the Prince family. Derek was grateful for God's provision. Their new home was a large, sturdy affair in a section of Jerusalem called Shemaria. Its strategic location—on the southeast corner of a main intersection between George Avenue and a street leading eastward to the Jaffa Gate of the Old City—placed the Prince family at the center of the events that were just beginning to capture the attention of the world.

Derek, Lydia, and the girls now entered a phase of their lives that would be unlike any other. They were living at the heart of Jerusalem, which was in turn at the heart of a war for the birth of a nation. Armies ruled the land, roving bands ruled the neighborhoods, and snipers ruled the streets. To walk upright by an open window might mean instant death. The simple act of visiting a nearby shop meant not only navigating an ever-convoluted system of checkpoints but also the possibility of being shot for taking a wrong turn. Nights were filled with the ground-shaking thud of explosions and the ever-present crack of rifle fire. Even children learned to know the voice of battle, to know what army was firing and at what distance by the angry sounds that filled the city.

The British army tried to intervene in the mounting violence between Arab and Jew but to little avail. England had already announced her intention to leave Palestine, and Jewish guerrilla forces like the Irgun and the Stern Gang harassed British troops with bombings and assassinations to hasten the day. The British soldier was weary, and the British resolve was drained. Perhaps as important, British sympathies were strongly pro-Arab, a legacy of T. E. Lawrence—better known today as Lawrence of Arabia—the politics of oil and a centuries-old stream of anti-Semitism. England did little to stop the oncoming bloodbath.

By the end of March, the Arabs had completely cut off the vital road from Tel-Aviv to Jerusalem, the home of one-sixth of Palestine's Jews. Food became desperately scarce, and fear of starvation drove many to panic. Any edible scrap was bartered at exorbitant prices, and homes rumored to contain hidden rations were ransacked. Women tried to grow vegetables in flower-pots. By March, Jewish leaders estimated that in all of Jerusalem there was only enough food to give each resident just six slices of bread.

At the American mission in the heart of the city, Derek and Lydia kept their eyes on the God who had seen them through so many crises. They prayed, they encouraged the girls, and they waited for the next act of their merciful God. In the meantime, Lydia grew so concerned about food she once tried to catch a dove that frequented the backyard using a string, a stick, and a shoebox. Thankfully, God had something better in mind. One day Derek was rummaging through the basement when he happened upon a large locker. Curious as to what such a massive object might contain, he opened the lid to find that locker was filled with food, certainly enough to feed his family for months! Apparently the American missionaries had filled the locker against a day of trouble and then forgotten to mention it when they left. Derek and Lydia knew that, once again, their God had shown Himself faithful.

The crisis of food resolved, the Prince home once again became a center of ministry despite the war that raged just outside their walls. Late that spring, two Russian women named Irena and Sarah appeared at the Prince's front door with an amazing story to tell. They had left Russia after the war and come by ship to Palestine to live in the land of their faith. When they arrived, though, they found that the Jews were cruel to them because they were Russian. They grew angry and depressed and had agreed to commit suicide together on a designated night. As they prepared to die on the chosen night, a Russian Baptist pastor knocked at the door, told them God had sent him, and then spent the evening telling them of Jesus, the Messiah. Both women believed.

Not long after, the women heard the voice of this Jesus telling them to find Mr. Prince. They made their way to the American mission house and, through poor English, tried to explain how they needed help. Fortunately, Derek's amazing gift for languages had allowed him to absorb enough Russian to talk to them. He gave them a Russian Bible and explained the baptism of the Holy Spirit. When he prayed for them, they both received the baptism of the Holy Spirit and spoke in other tongues. Derek would always recall that one of them sang her prayer language in tones that reminded him of Bach.

Word spread that miracles happened when the Princes prayed, and people came from miles for help of every kind. A knock at the door might be an Arab maid seeking prayer or a backslidden British soldier seeking return to his faith. On one occasion, the knock came from a Jewish soldier of the Haganah named Phineas. He was polite and gracious, but he wanted to know if he could have permission to put a cannon in the family's back yard. Derek giggled at the request. He realized that their house was so strategically located that it was the perfect location for a Haganah outpost. Knowing that if he refused the Jewish authorities would commandeer the house anyway, Derek agreed.

Now, in addition to all the other people who came to them for prayer or counsel, Derek and Lydia had soldiers of the Haganah virtually living with them. This only meant more opportunity to share God's truth, a fact not lost on the younger girls. Several of them decided to play "church" in the backyard where the soldiers stood watch. At the top of their voices they sang hymns in Hebrew, and then one of them, usually Kirsten, would mount a wooden box and pound out the gospel in unmistakable terms. The soldiers were amused but—probably because they were interested more in the older girls than they were in the preaching of a ten-year-old—they listened.

Derek and Lydia also listened to these young soldiers. For quite some time the Prince family had been praying about the plight of the Jewish people in Palestine. They reminded God of His promises, that He would extend His mercy on Zion and that He would gather His people "from the ends of the earth." One day, while the family was interceding, Lydia suddenly prayed, "Lord, paralyze the Arabs!" Derek echoed the cry, and the two used the words continually over the following weeks in praying for a Jewish victory.

Some time later, during a cease-fire, the young Haganah soldiers visited with Derek and Lydia in their living room and began sharing their experiences in the recent fighting. "There's something we can't understand," one young man said. "We go into an area where the Arabs are. They outnumber us ten to one and are much better armed than we are. Yet, at times, they seem powerless to do anything against us. It's as if they are paralyzed." When the soldier used the same words that Derek and Lydia had been praying, the family felt that God was hearing their prayers, that they were playing a role through intercession in God's will for Israel.

Despite such spiritual victories, Jerusalem was increasingly a dangerous place to be. The family began to sense that God was telling them to leave. This was easier said than done. With the British abandoning Palestine and with the certainty of violence once Israel announced its birth on May 14, many thousands hoped to get out of the country. Yet to whom should they turn? The only real government in the region was about to depart, and neither the Arabs nor the Jews had sufficient strength to fill the vacuum.

Early in May, Tikva found a way for at least some of the girls to make it out of the country. She learned that the Anglican Church was offering passage to England for any Hebrew Christians who might experience persecution if they remained in Palestine. Tikva knew this meant her. Jerusalem had become a difficult place for a pretty Hebrew Christian girl with European parents and an Arab sister. Tikva had experienced constant harassment and questioning and had nearly been beaten and raped on more than one occasion. When she learned there was a way out, she went to Lydia and said, "Mummy, I've had it. Can I go?" Lydia told her she could if she would take her sisters, and on the next day Tikva applied for Ruhammah, Peninah, and Johanne to accompany her to England. And permission came.

The morning of May 7, 1948, witnessed a heartbreaking scene in the Prince home. The four girls leaving the only homeland they had ever known stood in a circle as the rest of the family tearfully prayed that God would watch over them. Then, after desperate hugs and lingering kisses, the girls climbed into the cargo holds of military trucks. Soldiers pulled canvas covers tightly over metal supports so that the girls could not be seen from the street and drove off toward the port of Haifa. Young Kirsten, crying uncontrollably, ran through the house from window to window trying desperately to keep in view the trucks that bore her sisters. But they were gone, and when Kirsten could see them no more, she collapsed in tears on the floor, convinced she would never see her sisters again.

The four girls made it safely to Haifa and then boarded a troopship called *The Georgic* that was bound for Liverpool. They were alone, they were away from home for the first time in their lives, and they were going to a country they knew little about. They were also aboard a ship for the first time, and they soon learned the agonies of seasickness. For ten days, they steamed across the Mediterranean, around the coast of Portugal, north through the Atlantic, and into Liverpool through the Irish Sea. They sensed that whatever England held for them, their lives would never again be the same.

On May 14, a British officer knocked at the Prince's door and said, "We're moving out. Tomorrow you'll be under the Jews." Derek sensed the historic importance of the words, but he had no idea what practical import they might have for his family. Later that day, he climbed to the roof of their home and looked out on Jerusalem. *Israel is now a nation*, he thought to himself. He kept rolling the words over in his mind. They were hard to believe. Not since A.D. 70 had Israel been a nation of its own, and now, with the stroke of a pen, the British were leaving and the modern state of Israel was born. *And I am here to see it*, Derek thought to himself. *What an honor to witness this moment.* He noted the date: the fifth day of the month of Iyar in the year 5708 of the Hebrew calendar.

Each day Derek would climb to the roof of his house to look out upon the city of Jerusalem. He listened to the quiet when the UN imposed a cease-fire until the sixth of June. He watched the fighting when that cease-fire ended. He had already seen the Jewish community in the Old City leave under protection of British soldiers. And he wept to think of the days of violence ahead.

The hardships the family endured in the following weeks are best captured by Lydia's own words. From the time she had first come to Palestine, Lydia had maintained a missionary's correspondence with her supporters at home. In handwritten letters, she told of her victories, her struggles, and her needs. In time, these informal letters evolved into typewritten sheets that were mimeographed for mailing to supporters all over the world: to family members, to soldiers who had met her in Ramallah and then returned home, and to churches that shared her vision for Israel and orphans. In one of her 1948 letters, she described what the family experienced after May 14.

> After the British left, open warfare broke out. The Jews gained control of almost the whole of Jerusalem outside the Old City walls, and also over many other districts of Palestine. But the main supply road leading to Jerusalem from Haifa and Tel-Aviv remained in the hands of the Arabs; and so it was not long before the food shortage became critical. Our water supply also was cut off and the small quantity of water remaining in the city was very strictly rationed. On top of this, the Arabs from their positions all round Jerusalem began to shell the city day and night. For nearly a month we all had to live together in one basement room, which had previously served as our wash-house.

This shelling by the Arab Legion announced itself to the Prince family in a startling manner. On May 17, in the middle of the afternoon, a shell landed just a few yards to the south of their home and exploded. A large fragment from the shell flew through an upstairs window of the Prince home where two of the girls were playing. The jagged piece of metal passed right between the girls and embedded itself in a wall opposite the window. When Derek examined the fragment, he discovered that the shell had been manufactured in England. That his daughters were almost killed by a bomb manufactured in his own country and employed in violation of the United Nation's decree sent him into a fury.

On June 11, Derek wrote a letter entitled "An Open Letter from Jerusalem," which described the suffering in Jerusalem, the dangers his own family had passed, and the hypocrisy of British policies in the region. His conclusion was pointed and angry. He charged the British government with prolonging the fighting, with frustrating the establishment of a Jewish state, and with sponsoring the Arab shelling of Jerusalem. "In closing," he thundered, "let me give utterance to two questions that now form themselves daily in my mind: Do the people of Britain know what is being done in their name in Palestine? If so, are they satisfied about it?"

It was a rare moment of political passion. Throughout Derek's life he had maintained a studied distance from governments and politicians. Yet when he saw his own country supporting the enemies of Israel and contributing to the deaths of so many, he could remain silent no more. By favoring the Arabs, Britain had betrayed the Jews, betrayed the UN, and betrayed her own citizens, he believed. He feared for his native land. He began to believe that if England did not repent of her treatment of the Jews, she would lose her empire and, worse, lose the blessing of God. It was a belief that would shape his theology and his ministry for the rest of his days.

The pressing need now, though, was to get his family out of Israel. He began to look for help. He'd heard that the head man for the British remaining in Israel was a Canadian and that he might help. When he arrived at the man's office, though, there was a long line of people hoping to leave the country. For some reason, Derek bypassed the line and walked into the man's office. As a Canadian, the official was put off by what he saw as Derek's British arrogance in pushing past the others who were waiting. After chastising him for jumping ahead of the line, the man told him he needed to talk to the military governor.

Derek's task now seemed overwhelming. How does one find the military governor of a besieged city in the middle of a war? For hours he searched until finally some soldiers told him where the man was hiding. Derek made his way to the man's hideout, and, speaking Hebrew, he asked for help. The man told him that the next day there was a convoy leaving from the King David Hotel, but that he would have to talk to the UN officials about it.

Wearily, Derek made his way to the UN headquarters. His mastery of languages now served him well, though. The man in charge was a Swedish colonel, and Derek told him in Swedish that he was in Israel working with a Swedish mission. This was true. Lydia's primary financial support had long come from a large Swedish church, and this is why the home was known as "the Swedish mission." Once the colonel heard that the mission was connected to his homeland, he was delighted to help. He told Derek to have his family at the King David Hotel early the next morning.

Derek returned home quickly. He told the family to prepare to leave. Once again, the Prince family would leave all behind. This time, they were happy they were going. Lydia sold the remaining food on the street to pay their fare to England, and once again the girls packed what few belongings they had into pillowcases to prepare for the journey ahead. The family slept fitfully that night. At five the next morning, they arrived at the King David Hotel. The Swedish colonel met them and loaded them onto the truck that would take them out of the city. Thus, Derek and Lydia Prince, along with their four girls, departed on the last truck of the last British convoy to leave Jerusalem in the summer of 1948.

As their truck bounced along the road to Haifa, young Kirsten reminded her mother that this was what she had seen in a vision. Lydia remembered. The family had been at prayer some weeks before when Kirsten had seen a vision of a light at the end of a passageway. There was a gate, and two figures in white came and opened the gate. Kirsten jumped up during the prayer time and said, "Mummy, Mummy, I'm going to England." Lydia was surprised: "Why do you say this?" "Because I saw it in a vision," Kirsten replied, with the confidence of a child reared on the supernatural. Now in the truck en route to England, Derek, Lydia, and the girls thanked their God that the vision had become reality.

Though the Prince family would be safely in England while it lasted, the war for the birth of Israel continued until February 1949. It was one of the most unusual conflicts in world history. Seeking to drive the newborn Israel into the sea were ten thousand Lebanese soldiers, sixty thousand Syrian soldiers, forty-five thousand Iraqi soldiers, more than fifty thousand Egyptian soldiers, and over ninety thousand Transjordanian soldiers. Israel's troops never numbered more than thirty-five thousand. Yet when the cease-fire agreements were signed with each of the Arab countries, Israel was able to draw its own borders. She had won and against all odds. She would have a place among the nations. And Derek and Lydia along with their girls had been present at the creation.

8

London to Vancouver:
The Day of Small Beginnings

"I DON'T UNDERSTAND."

"I know you don't. You are of a different generation."

"You mean that you had no driving passion, no dream for the future?"

"I had a passion, but it was to serve the Lord. You see, we thought differently then. We wanted to know the Lord and live in His ways. We believed the future would unfold through a moment-by-moment obedience."

"So, you had no ambition, no burning sense of destiny?"

"I can honestly say I had a total lack of ambition. I don't mean to say I had no hope or spiritual passion. I simply had no ambition. As for destiny, I think that word is often used today as a substitute for kingdom building or the drive for power."

"But don't you believe that men are made for a purpose?"

"Yes, but that purpose is to know the Lord. The meaning of life is a relationship. The future comes from pursuing Him, not pursuing the future."

"You realize, don't you, that the idea of destiny and of a promised future is very much the rage in Christian circles today?"

"I do. I remember reading a major Christian magazine and seeing advertisements about dynamic men and prophetic conferences and seminars to know your destiny. It felt like prostitution to me. I felt as though I needed a shower when I was finished."

"So, it was different in your day."

"Well, I did not have much contact with the organized church until I got to London, but I can say this: the hope of my heart was to know the Lord and do His will. The future, I believed, was His to fashion through my obedience."

When the Prince family left Israel in 1948, they fled to an England in crisis. Britain had won the war but was well on the way to losing the peace. It was a heartbreaking reality, for the sacrifices of the British people during the war years had been dear. More than four hundred thousand British soldiers had been lost in battle, and another sixty thousand civilians had died from the German bombing of their land. Indeed, enemy air attacks had left more than a million homes damaged or destroyed and more than four billion dollars worth of destruction in London alone.

The English people were valiant, though, and took their losses in stride. They welcomed home their soldiers, hauled away their rubble, and began to build an England equal to their sacrifices. Tragically, the times soon demanded even more. When Derek and Lydia landed in London on August 12, 1948, the country was suffering from a horrible economic depression. Prices were steep, unemployment was high, and despair filled the land. The government was in crisis. Food and gasoline were rationed just as they had been during the war, and the coal, rail, and health industries had just been nationalized. Long lines, empty shelves, mounting poverty, and national frustration became the lot of the English people.

This swirling misery made things difficult for Derek and his family. Though they were thankful to be safely out of Israel, they quickly found that the very things they needed—housing, food, and jobs—were in fearfully short supply. They were also stunned by the confusing unfamiliarity of English culture: the odd customs, the strange foods, the difficult dialects.

The first months were painful. The first four girls had arrived on May 17 and were immediately separated. Some stayed with Derek's father, and some were sent to the families of men Derek and Lydia had known during the war. This did not always work out well. The girls were often worked like maids. Some found their lodgings far below what they had known before in their lives. Johanne, for example, was sent to stay with a railway stationmaster in Loughborough. The man's house was right on the platform of the station and shook when the trains went by. There was no toilet and no indoor plumbing. One took a bath by sitting in a big tub in front of the fireplace.

Even when Derek, Lydia, and the other four girls arrived in August, it was still impossible for the family to live together. There was simply nowhere for all of them to stay. Life became an unsettling matter of living with friends and looking for a home. When their search for a place of their own yielded nothing, Derek decided to exercise his academic privileges as a Fellow of King's College and took a room at Cambridge. While there, he took courses in biblical Hebrew to prepare himself for fulfilling the dream of again preaching Christ in Israel. Lydia stayed in London with the smallest girls to continue the search. She would spend several months moving from the back rooms of friends' homes to small apartments and then back into the homes of friends again. She even lived for a time in an unheated garage. It is not hard to imagine that her first months in England reminded her of her first weeks in Palestine all those years before.

Despite the frustrations, there is a sweet image that emerges from this time. Lydia and some of the girls took the train to visit Derek at Cambridge and spent a pleasant afternoon strolling the grounds at King's. The girls were amazed by the lush, green grass that stretched out like a carpet before the ornate buildings. It was all too tempting. Several of them walked out onto the manicured lawn to see what it was like. They were used to the beige, rocky ground of Israel. This patch of deep green seemed like a piece of heaven. Just as they were reveling in the beauty, a groundskeeper looked up to see dark-complexioned girls walking on his lawn and angrily ordered them to get off. Then he saw Derek, a striking, authoritative figure in his gown and mortarboard. The groundskeeper apologized and left the girls to their joy. To taste of Derek's rank and protection must have been a healing experience indeed for Lydia and her girls, who must have felt like unwanted refugees all the months they had been in England.

By March of 1949, the family still did not have a place to live. Derek's frustration was mounting. In his newsletter of that month, he wrote, "Since I last wrote, my wife and I have continued to search for a suitable home for our large 'family.' My wife has at last obtained a small apartment of two rooms in London, and she is now living there with the three youngest children. We are, however, continuing to search for something larger, which will provide a gathering place for the whole family. We feel that if we can establish a center in London from which to work, the Lord will open a door for us amongst the large Jewish population there."

Finally, by August 1949, Lydia was able to report, "God has now given us a good house in the center of London; and praise His name, in it we found 'a large upper room furnished.'" (See Luke 22:12.) Her joy is understandable. She had found a three-story apartment that with rent controls would cost only three pounds a week. They could just manage it. Not only did Derek have his stipend from King's College, but also Lydia had made a quick trip to a large Assemblies of God church in Copenhagen, which had agreed to support them as missionaries. Money would be no obstacle. The apartment was in the center of London, not far from Hyde Park, and offered more space than they needed. What was more, as Lydia said, the top floor was furnished and just the size to allow large gatherings. Late in the summer of 1949, the Prince family moved into their new home at 77 Westbourne Grove.

Once the children were gathered from around the country, the family thanked God for His mercy and settled into their new lives. There were rooms to clean and furniture to buy. Lydia and the older girls had to learn to cook the prepackaged food of the London shops, a far cry from the raw, simple foods of Ramallah. Each day had its routine. The older girls rose first to prepare the family breakfast. Lydia usually stayed in bed and waited for her morning meal to appear, a luxury she had learned to enjoy after coming to England. Derek would routinely rise, bathe, and then kneel at a chair with a blanket over his head to commune with his God. When he finished, he studied Scripture, dealt with the family correspondence, and joined in the cleaning. It was not uncommon for him to don an apron and wash dishes or scrub the ninety-five stairs that led to the apartment. The girls learned to avoid sharing duties with Derek since his thoroughness in every task made their work take twice the usual time.

While the older girls went to school, there was more work to do for those who were left behind. Someone had to do the shopping at the nearby Portobello Market. Lydia, who loved sweets, would also send one of the girls across the street to the patisserie for what came to be known as her "morning sweet." There were bills to pay, Bible studies to prepare, and newsletters to write, mimeograph, and mail. As the day progressed, Derek and Lydia would pray together and take long walks at nearby Hyde Park to discuss God's purpose for their strategic location in this most strategic city of the world. Evening would bring its own busyness. When the older girls returned from school, there were meals to cook, homework to do, and children to hurry off to bed. In many ways, the Princes looked like any other London family. This very normal looking routine would not last long, though.

✕

It was soon after the family settled into their Westbourne lives that the path of their future ministry made itself known. One fall Sunday afternoon, Derek and Lydia were enjoying a long, conversational walk in Hyde Park when they neared the famous Speakers' Corner. Since 1872, this section of the park had been devoted to the celebration of free speech, allowing anyone to sound forth on any subject he desired. It was not uncommon, then, for passersby to witness an impassioned speaker addressing a raucous audience with the London police standing nearby. Derek and Lydia had passed Speakers' Corner many times on their walks and had begun to barely notice the almost daily commotion there.

This particular Sunday afternoon was different, though. As the two passed the notorious site, they noticed that a young girl was trying to address the gathered crowd. She was having a difficult time. While she spoke, men pulled at her hair and shouted obscenities. The crowd laughed and urged the men on. The girl was resolute, though, and continued proclaiming her message despite the abuse. The people were too distracted by the antics of the men to listen, but Derek and Lydia drew closer to hear what she was saying.

The girl pressed on with her message while the men became increasingly rude and disruptive. Finally, Derek stepped forward to stand the men down, and when he did, he realized that the girl bravely preaching to this unhearing crowd was his own daughter, Ruhammah. In broken English, she was trying to tell the crowd that they were all "selfish-ed" and that their souls were in peril. Tears filled Derek's eyes as he moved to his daughter and tenderly asked her if he could speak. Ruhammah was surely relieved both to see her parents and to have someone take her place before the threatening crowd.

Derek began to speak, and the crowd grew quiet. Immediately they recognized the Cambridge diction. They realized this was a learned man. Derek rebuked the gathering for their treatment of Ruhammah and then continued her message. The British people were indeed selfish, he assured, and lost in their sins. They needed a savior, and God had provided one. They had only to believe in the work of this Savior to be free from the evil that filled their souls. Derek finished his talk with a prayer and offered to speak with anyone who had questions. Some did, and Derek stood with Lydia and Ruhammah for a while afterwards helping those who stayed behind to understand his message and what it meant for their lives.

As Derek walked home that day, he sensed that something deeply meaningful had just happened. He was proud of Ruhammah, of course, but there was something more stirring in his soul. Soon it came to him. Perhaps this was something he was meant to do. He laughed at the thought. Months before when he and Lydia had first passed Speakers' Corner he had commented to her that he would never want to preach the gospel in such an undignified way. Now, he not only had done it, but he was also beginning to believe that God was leading him to do it again. Perhaps this was why God had placed them in the heart of London. Perhaps Ruhammah, in her guileless way, had been God's instrument to show them the way.

A few days later, Derek returned to Speakers' Corner and preached again. Once more, the crowd grew quiet, listened, and then bowed their heads as Derek finished in prayer. Once more, some lingered afterward for prayer and counsel. As Derek walked the sixteen minutes from the famous corner near Marble Arch to his home on Westbourne Grove, he was sure that God was telling him this was the way. As laughable as it was, this was God's chosen method: to reach the city of London by sending a Cambridge don to preach the gospel from the corner of a city park. Derek knew his God delighted in doing the unusual. His job was to simply obey.

And so it began. Each week—on Wednesday, Saturday, and Sunday—Derek spent time in prayer and then walked to Speakers' Corner to join the crowd. Lydia often went with him, along with some of the girls or a few believing friends. When he felt the moment was right, he stepped forward and began speaking. His themes were salvation, healing, and the baptism of the Holy Spirit. Often, he told stories of people whose lives had been changed by believing in Jesus or whose bodies had been healed through prayer. He sometimes gave his own amazing testimony and called others to follow Jesus as he did. While he spoke, Lydia and those with her prayed, sometimes fanning out into the crowd to intercede for people they sensed were particular targets of God's grace that day. As was Derek's habit, he closed in prayer and offered to speak with anyone who was willing. Some were saved, some were healed, and some were baptized in the Holy Spirit.

Some months along in this unusual work, Derek took stock of his ministry in Hyde Park. He was thrilled with what God was doing: hundreds were hearing the gospel, and many were turning to Christ. It was a more effective work than he had dared to dream. But there was something missing, and Derek quickly saw what it was: the people he was leading to Jesus needed to be taught and nurtured in the things of God. He thought about what to do. He soon realized that the small gathering of believers who met in his home on Sunday mornings—his family and a few Christian friends—were probably intended to be the beginnings of a church. He thought he saw the plan of God. He would preach at Speakers' Corner and then invite people to the meeting in his upper room. Here they could be taught and connected to other believers. This must be the way, he reasoned. He could not send these newly converted lambs to the dead churches of London. Surely God intended Derek to be their shepherd.

The next time Derek preached in Hyde Park, he stressed his usual themes: the need for salvation, the value of the baptism of the Holy Spirit, and the power of God to heal. This time, though, he also talked about the need for believers to join with those of like faith. Then, in an astonishing move, he invited the entire crowd to the meeting in his home. He told them, in words he would repeat thousands of times, to "take bus 50 or 23 to Westbourne Grove and look for the 77 address."

And people came. By April 1950, Derek told his newsletter readers:

> As we have gone forward in faith and in obedience...the Lord has continued to bless us, and to 'confirm his word with signs following.'

At first, we met only as a family in our 'upper room' every Sunday morning and held a communion service together. Then we were led out to witness and preach in the open air in the centre of the city. So many contacts were made in this way, that we felt it necessary to hold a gospel meeting on Sunday evening, to which we could invite those whom we contacted in the course of the week. It was not long before we were holding five meetings a week; and now, in addition, we are seeking ways in which the capacity of our 'upper room' may be increased.

In the same newsletter, Derek exulted:

In the space of just over six months, we estimate that between forty and fifty have sought the Lord for salvation and forgiveness of sins; nine have passed through the waters of baptism; and fifteen have been baptized in the Holy Ghost…Here in the centre of London, we meet day by day members of every class, of every creed, of every nationality; and there are daily opportunities to make spiritual contacts of which the effects may eventually be felt in the most distant corners of the earth. Amongst those who have visited us in recent months and have felt the Lord's touch for spirit, soul, or body, there have been—a Frenchman; an African and his English wife; an Indian student (formerly a Hindu, now a believer in Christ); two or three colored brothers from Jamaica; several Irish Catholics; men and women from all corners of the British Isles; and—last but not least—a number of Jewish people.

In time, the church at 77 Westbourne Grove grew to a steady fifty souls. The majority were Jamaican, with English or Scots filling out the rest. A few were Jewish believers, much to the delight of Derek and Lydia. Hundreds of others passed through over the years with some staying for a few months and some never returning again after a single visit. This may have been because the meetings were deeply Pentecostal and proved too much for the more staid English culture. Women all wore hats, and everyone addressed each other as "brother" or "sister." Each meeting began with singing, usually led by the tone-deaf Derek while Tikva or Johanne played the piano. The congregation would raise their hands in worship, shout, and sometimes break into dancing. Then Derek would preach, and a time of ministry followed, often with people sprawled out on the floor "under the Spirit" or weeping uncontrollably at the tenderness of the "Spirit's touch."

Those who stayed were often drawn by the dramatic miracles that regularly occurred. There was the Scotsman whose lung x-rays showed serious problems but who returned to his doctors after Derek prayed for him to find he had been healed. Then there was the blind German man whose eyesight was restored. Lydia was almost more amazed that a German was in her house than she was by the healing. There was also the demon-possessed man who tried to push Derek out the fifth-story window before he was set free, and the woman with a goiter that simply fell off when Lydia prayed for her.

There were humorous moments, too. A man named Mr. Poole came to the meeting one Sunday. He had heard Derek preach about the baptism of the Holy Spirit and desperately wanted to receive this gift of speaking in other tongues. Derek prayed and the man received, but he began speaking so rapidly and forcefully that his false teeth flew out of his mouth into the watching congregation. On another occasion, Derek went long in his sermon and then, in typical preacher's manner, said, "I'll close in a minute," before continuing his text. A hungry Magdalene turned to Kirsten and said, "The roast will be burned." She said this, though, more loudly than she intended. The whole congregation heard and erupted in laughter.

Because of Derek's earnest, systematic teaching of Scripture and his courageous ministry at Speakers' Corner, the church grew to a respectable size by Pentecostal standards. Soon Derek came to the attention of other pastors in the city, and this was a new experience for him. He knew that unity among Christian leaders was important, but he had quickly soured on the churches of London when he saw their ineffectiveness in helping people and the haughty style of many ministers. He was particularly disappointed with the Pentecostals, whom he believed were like the Pharisees of old—they knew the truth but diluted it in legalism and pride.

Finally, after much soul searching and more than a little urging from Lydia, Derek decided to attend a meeting of the London Pentecostal ministers association. He was greeted warmly when he arrived, but then the meeting began and the topic of discussion was announced. The subject under consideration was how to reach old Etonians for Jesus. Oddly, Derek never opened his mouth, but one wonders what good might have come from these Pentecostal ministers learning that one of their number was a born-again, Spirit-baptized old Etonian.

One of the men at the meeting was the head of an Assemblies of God Bible school. Hearing that Derek was a teacher, he asked him to speak to his students. Derek agreed. Later, though, the man learned of Derek's academic background and withdrew the invitation, citing his belief that no educated person could truly "have the Spirit." This was a common Pentecostal belief in that day. Clearly, the man thought Derek was unqualified to teach in a Pentecostal Bible school because he had studied at Eton and King's.

✕

Derek's mounting sense of holy dissatisfaction was fueled by the press of ministry, his disappointment with the state of Christianity in England, and the growing awareness that there was more to his calling than he had lived. He knew he was walking in the will of his Lord, and yet he hungered for more. He wanted to see England return to her God, and he wanted to see the churches become the fonts of living water they were supposed to be. Perhaps even more, despite how much he loved his growing little church, he could not shake the words God had given him long before in Israel: "You will be a teacher in the body of Christ." He knew this was his life's purpose, and he could not be content until it was fulfilled. There was a stirring in his soul, a hunger that never left him. Years later, he said that he felt as though he was pregnant with a purpose that would not make itself known.

As he contemplated this unrest in his soul, he decided to give himself to a season of prayer and fasting. He had always fasted one day a week and had long taught his congregation that fasting was part of fulfilling the ministry of Jesus. Now, though, he sensed that God was calling him aside for a deepening of his inner well. He told his family what he was planning and then locked himself in the upper room every day for twenty-one days to hear from his Lord. Each day Derek pleaded with God to send revival to England, to awaken the churches of the land, and to make him the teacher he was called to be. The girls were told not to disturb him. From time to time, they were sent to him with pitchers of juice or water. He would hug them at the door of the upper room and then turn to continue seeking his God.

When he finally emerged, Derek sensed that an invisible dam had broken. When he spoke, there was greater power. When he prayed, there were more instant miracles. And in his soul, he felt a welling of faith—for England, for his calling, and for the cause of the gospel worldwide—than he had ever known before. He still felt pregnant with purpose, but now he had faith that his purpose would soon be fulfilled.

It was not long after this fast that Derek began preparing with the rest of the evangelical ministers in London for a long-awaited event: the Billy Graham Crusade of 1954. He felt that this was an answer to his prayers, that God was reaching to a weary England through the words of the dynamic American evangelist. Derek threw himself into the cause. He volunteered for training and then volunteered to train others to counsel the lost at the meetings. He called his church to lengthy sessions of prayer and challenged them to believe that God intended to transform England through the preaching of His truth.

The Graham meeting was highly controversial. Many in England were suspicious of the dramatic evangelist and of the "enthusiastic" brand of American Christianity in general. An Anglican bishop predicted that Graham would return to America with his tail between his legs. A member of the House of Commons sought to prevent Graham's entrance into the country on the charge that the American was "interfering in British politics under the guise of religion." Even the start of the meetings was shaky. On the first night, only two thousand people showed up to an arena that seated eleven thousand.

Once the crusade got underway, though, Derek's deepest hopes were fulfilled. The arena was jammed night after night for more than three months. Extra meetings had to be scheduled to meet the needs of spiritually hungry Britons who sang hymns in the subways and mobbed Graham wherever he went. More than two million people attended the crusade, with tens of thousands committing their lives to Jesus Christ. Even Winston Churchill heard the evangelist. In a private meeting, he told Graham, "I do not see much hope for the future unless it is the hope you are talking about, young man. We must have a return to God." Clearly, England's return to God had begun.

As 1954 drew to a close, Derek knew that he was undergoing a dramatic change. He had already realized that the pastorate was an ill fit and that, while he was fulfilling a season of the Lord's calling, the work of a pastor could never be his for life. He had also learned something important from Billy Graham. Though Derek had preached for years at Speakers' Corner and seen many turn to Christ, he had come to believe that very few human beings were genuinely interested in the gospel. In fact, he began to believe that only a few will ever be saved, probably an extension of his experience in Hyde Park: from a crowd of a hundred, for example, maybe five or ten would respond to his messages. It did not take much to assume that this proportion would be the same wherever the gospel was preached.

Graham changed his mind. The passionate evangelist taught Derek how to draw people to a commitment to Jesus and convinced him that God was indeed able to reach large numbers of lost souls, even in a disillusioned England. This made Derek bolder and even more evangelistic, but it also made him hungry to live powerfully in the calling of a teacher just as Graham lived powerfully in the calling of an evangelist. Derek began to dream of what a teacher with Graham's kind of power could do in the world.

While he continued pastoring his home church and preaching in Hyde Park, Derek also began wrestling with some of the changes that were occurring in his own family. Not only were the girls getting older and more independent, but they were also gravitating to what Derek and Lydia condemned as the worldly ways of London. Some of the older girls began wearing makeup and dressing in the latest styles. On occasion, they attended dances. This was a serious offense in the Pentecostal world, as was watching movies. Derek and Lydia learned that some of their girls went to movies when they stepped off a London bus just as young Anna was emerging from a theater. She had sneaked into the cinema hoping her parents would never know, but, much to her chagrin, she stepped out of the theater and right into Lydia's disapproving gaze.

This struggle with worldliness highlights an intriguing progression in Derek's life. He had grown up a nonbeliever who outwardly conformed to the formal Christianity of his social class. After he met Jesus Christ in his Scarborough barracks, he was largely unchurched despite his brief association with the Pentecostal church the Shaws attended. Then there were the years in the desert with no church, no Christian community, and no spiritual leadership. There was only the voice of God. The truth is that by the time Derek arrived in Israel, he had been discipled by his Lord and by hardship, but he had never been indoctrinated into a particular church culture. He knew only what the Bible forbade or what the Bible allowed. His ethics were as broad as Scripture, then, so that when he first met Lydia and her girls, he thought nothing of taking some of the older girls to a movie in Jerusalem—the film *Tarzan* was a favorite—or reading the latest books aloud in the home.

Lydia was cut from different cloth. She was more thoroughly Pentecostal in her ethics, and it is obvious that she drew Derek in her doctrinal direction. By 1955, Derek had clearly become a hard-core Pentecostal so far as his theology and his ethics were concerned. He and Lydia both chastised the girls for using makeup and for their interest in men. Any connection to alcohol, movies, dances, smoking, or the newly popular television signaled to Derek and Lydia that their girls were sliding away from the faith. In fact, it was not uncommon for Lydia to use the word *prostitute* for a daughter who offended. The tension over these issues occasioned long harangues that played out well into the night.

The truth is that Derek and Lydia were dealing with the pain of their daughters coming of age and stepping out to lives of their own. Lydia's daughters had been her life, her ministry, and her joy. Now, they were moving out into the world, and she feared for them. She also tried to keep them close far too long. Tikva, for example, was still living at home and was required to be in by ten o'clock every night when she was twenty-two years old. She thought it too much to ask of a young adult in the mid-1950s, and, as much to escape their parents' demands as to shape their own lives, she and the other girls soon began moving away.

Peninah was the first to marry and create her own life. She remembers that Lydia offered a dismissive wave of the hand when she told her that she planned to marry a young Irish painter. It was a memory that festered throughout her life, but her recall does not seem to fit the written record. In her newsletter, Lydia reported the news with joy: "Peninah…is being married at the end of this month. We are most happy for this match. Her husband-to-be is a fine young man, saved and baptized in the Spirit, and a member of the little Pentecostal assembly which now meets regularly for worship in our 'upper room.'"

At the same time, Tikva began nurse's training with her parents' encouragement. For two years, she trained in London's Hammersmith Hospital while living at home until a problem with her feet developed and she left the program. Shortly after, she was engaged to an airman for a while and carried his picture faithfully. When he found another woman, Tikva took the picture out and stomped on it violently. It was typical of this pretty and passionate woman. Finally, she met a Welshman named John Morrissey and fell in love. The two married in August 1951. Lydia reported the marriage in her newsletter by saying that Tikva "was married to a young Welshman who had come up to London as a backslider running away from his Christian home in Wales, but was—through our open-air meetings—gloriously reclaimed and refilled with the Holy Spirit. After a honeymoon in Wales, they have begun their married life in one room near us here and are looking to the Lord to open the way for them, as He did for Peninah and her husband."

Magdalene worked as Lydia's personal assistant until Derek urged her, along with Kirsten, to pursue work as a seamstress. Magdalene thrived in this and remained a gifted seamstress all her life. During the same time, she began babysitting for a family by the name of Wyns, who also attended the Prince's church. Irvine Wyns had been raised by missionaries in Mongolia and lived in London as a tool and die maker with his pregnant wife and five children. Sadly, Irvine's wife died not long after giving birth to twins, one of whom died, and Irvine came to rely on young Magdalene to care for the children. In time, the two fell in love and married.

Lydia's announcement of the marriage in her newsletter reflects her concern for Magdalene's instant responsibilities: "We must mention that the fifth of our Jewish girls, Magdalene, is now married. Her husband, who was an active worker in our mission here, until he moved out of London, is a widower and the father of six little children. Pray for Magdalene, that she may be given grace and strength to carry the heavy burden of such a home on her young shoulders." Magdalene's "burdens" would quickly increase. She and Irvine left England for Canada while Derek and Lydia were still pastoring in London and, in time, had five more children of their own.

Johanne served both her parents and her church well. Hardly a newsletter was written without mention of her devotion to God or her skills as a minister. While she was faithfully serving the church, a young man named George Hedges began to attend. He was a cockney whose mother was Jewish and whose family had done well in the tea business. Magdalene's husband, Irvine, had met George, led him to faith in Jesus, and taken him to Derek and Lydia's church. He soon joined, became a helpful servant at Derek's side, and was smitten with the striking, energetic Johanne. The two fell in love and married in 1950, much to the joy of the family.

Ruhammah took a more tortured path. Though in 1950, Lydia was able to boast of "our eighteen-year-old evangelist" who had been the first to preach at Speakers' Corner, such favor soon lifted. Ruhammah, whom her family sometimes called Ruth, seemed to have borne the scars of Lydia's early harshness more keenly than the other girls. Once Derek assumed the preaching in Hyde Park, Ruhammah began to pull away from the family. For some unnamed transgression, she was banned from the Prince home and lived alone in a room kindly rented to her by a Mrs. Moxy, a caring woman who became Ruhammah's surrogate mother. In time, Ruhammah made her own way, but not until passing some dark and painful years.

⚜

These, then, are the challenges Derek and Lydia faced as they continued to pastor in London. It was a troubling, tumultuous time. England had not yet emerged from the disillusionment of the postwar years, the tensions with some of the older daughters continued, and the ministry demanded ever more from the family. Moreover, Derek was still wrestling with his calling. He wanted to be faithful and serve well however God chose to use him, but he felt as though he was wearing another man's clothes. The pastorate simply wasn't the best use of him, and he knew it. Still he served, still he prayed, and still he poured out his heart to Lydia.

Sensing the need for something to change, Derek and Lydia called their little congregation to devote the first Sunday of 1955 to "united prayer and fasting." In the weeks after, there seemed to be a new blessing on the life of the church. George and Johanne, who had been waiting for direction for their lives, received an invitation to "go out" to Kenya and serve amongst the Kikuyu tribe there. They left on March 25, the first missionaries sent from the church.

Miracles and conversions increased, and people from the upper classes began to attend the church. Derek reported baptizing "one of Britain's leading medical specialists, who had been coming to us to learn more of the things of God." Deliverance from demons and healing occurred with greater frequency than before. Overall, the church increased in number, and Derek began to believe that perhaps he had let his frustration get the best of him, that maybe God wanted him to remain in London and pastor until the end of his days.

With new wind in his sails, Derek went on the offensive. He rented a local movie theater and began advertising healing services. More than thirty people "received Christ," and a larger number were healed, according to Derek's newsletter report. One elderly Jew was healed of bronchitis, and another was healed of deafness. There was new movement, and not just in the London church. George and Johanne wrote from Kenya to report that seventy-three Kikuyu had been born again, along with some Europeans. It seemed that God had heard their prayers on that first day in 1955 and filled the year with grace.

Success continued, but Derek could not shake the sense that he was missing his highest mission. He fasted and prayed with Lydia, but still he felt like a caged lion. There was something more, just beyond his reach, that he yearned for, but he did not know what it was. For a long while he hoped that God would return the remaining family to Israel to minister among the Jews. God did not make a way to Israel, though, and still he waited.

In the middle of 1956, Derek and Lydia began an intense time of soul-searching and prayer. Something had to change. Derek seemed unable to be at peace, and he felt that God was stirring him in preparation for a change. Finally, by Christmas of that year, Derek's newsletter announced to their supporters that they knew the path they should take. His explanation for this new direction is worth repeating here in full.

> Perhaps you have wondered why you have had to wait so much longer than usual for news from us. The answer is that we have been passing through some months of earnest waiting upon God for guidance concerning our future, and until we had a definite answer from the Lord, we did not feel free to write to you. Now, however, we are able to write and tell you that the Lord has clearly and wonderfully opened the door for us into a new field of service. We have received an urgent request from the Pentecostal Assemblies of East Africa to go out immediately to Kenya and help them in their educational work—primarily in training African teachers for the Mission Schools in one of the main provinces of Kenya. The call has been like that

which Paul received from Macedonia: "Come over and help us." The work is so exactly in line with our qualifications and experience, as well as with the inner prompting of God's Spirit, that we have not hesitated to answer: "Yes." We expect to be in Kenya early in 1957. Anna (16) and Elisabeth (14) will be coming with us. Kirsten (20) will be remaining behind to complete her training as a nurse at a local London hospital. Later, she trusts to follow us out and to enter the Lord's service in Kenya, as a nurse.

In our new work in Kenya, we shall have passing through our hands an important proportion of the prospective leaders of the African community (by far the largest element of the population) and since these will be teachers, they will in turn be influencing and shaping the leaders of the next generation. The opportunities along this line in Kenya at present are almost without parallel in the history of mission work. There is an urgent, almost universal demand for education. Both the government and the Africans are willing—and even desirous—that this demand for education should in large measure be met through the work of Christian missions. On the other hand, if the true Christians do not meet this demand for education, the Communists, and other agents of evil, undoubtedly will. Thus the Christian church in Kenya faces one of the most challenging opportunities of its history, and we count it a great privilege to be called to play our part in meeting this challenge.

These words form a moving testament to the man Derek had become by 1956. He was forty-one when these lines were penned. In the years since his conversion he had fought in a war, married into a large missionary family, and escaped war in Israel only to build a church in London largely through street preaching. He had been a faithful man of God's Word, of prayer, of fasting, and of ministry to the needs of hurting people. Now, though, he seemed to yearn for a fight, for a mission to match his gifts and his manly energy. Kenya was the place he would find it.

Just emerging from the Mau-Mau Uprising of 1952—in which more than thirty thousand Kikuyu violently attempted to overthrow British rule—the future of Kenya was hanging in the balance. Communism was spreading, British control was weakening, and Kenyans were beginning to dream of independence. Moreover, there was a battle forming for the minds and hearts of the next generation. The British wanted teachers, good ones with solid Christian character, to shape the lives of the young. Such leaders could only be trained by wise and courageous instructors, and Derek Prince intended to be one of them.

※

The Princes must have been eager to get on with their new lives. They had only decided to leave in December 1956, but by January 30 of the next year they were already in Kisumu, Kenya, and were settled enough to produce a newsletter relaying their experience. The congregation in London had been anguished to hear their pastors were leaving. Most of them were Jamaicans and did not feel welcome in other churches. There was much weeping and pleading, but it was all to no avail. After trying to find good churches for everyone in their congregation, Derek, Lydia, Anna, and Elisabeth packed their belongings in metal containers and boarded a plane for Nairobi. Kirsten would join them when her nurse's training was done.

Once they arrived, they were immediately put to work. Derek had barely unpacked his bags before he found himself teaching classes at the Nyang'ori Teacher Training Center where seventy-five male students were preparing to teach in the Kenyan public schools. Derek's years at Eton and Cambridge had not prepared him for the three-hour class in "Woodwork" that he was asked to teach within days of his arrival. By the end of the year, he was not only expected to plan a two-year course on the contents of the Bible for students who did not own Bibles, but he was also supposed to master the school's administration well enough to become its principal.

While Derek started his work at the school, Lydia spent her first days fashioning a home at the compound of the Pentecostal Assemblies Mission Station. She cleaned, learned the local lore, and made a home away from home for her family. For a third time in her life, Lydia served her God by leaving the familiar and immersing herself in a completely foreign culture. She did not have long to contemplate her new circumstances, though, for once she had her home in order, she learned that the school needed her to teach classes that ranged from home economics to religion. Ever-engaged by a new challenge, Lydia remembered the years in which she was Denmark's leading domestic science expert and threw herself into the task at hand.

Life in Kisumu was a huge change from London. They would live just two miles north of the equator and more than a mile above sea level, an alternatively harsh and inviting climate. Though the family had a two-story brick house that was quite modern by Kenyan standards, there was no electricity and no indoor plumbing. The only bathroom was an outhouse that the locals called the "Kenyan longdrop." Drinkable water was often in short supply, and the heat could be withering. Garbage had to be handled wisely, or wild animals might wander into the yard. And always there was the threat of another uprising, another plague of violence and fear.

Despite the obstacles, Derek and Lydia fell in love with the Kenyan people. They found them warm, eager to learn, and honorable. They loved the way their students said things like, "Please, sir, I am defeated," or "Please, sir, may I release myself." Lydia particularly grew to hold the Kenyans dear, and they returned the affection. Wherever she went a small crowd of skinny, black children followed her while she joked and nipped at them with her apron.

This love—which Derek believed was a special grace from God—led him and Lydia to break from the chilly traditions of English missionaries in Kenya. For decades, English Christians serving in Kenya had believed that it was best to hold blacks at a suspicious distance. The conventional wisdom dictated that never should a black man be allowed in a missionary's home, never should a white man go in a Kenyan home, and never should an Englishman count a Kenyan as a friend. Missionaries lived in compounds that were islands of English culture and spent their spare time at the British "club," a combination of family resort and hotel. As one African politician complained, "When you go to a missionary's house, they offer you a glass of water through the window."

Derek was uniquely prepared to confront such traditions. He had learned from his father about the British disregard for *wogs*—a derisive British term for natives—and had admired Captain Paul for befriending his Indian workers. Then there was his delightful friendship with Ali in the Sudan, which taught him the beauty and grace of African ways. He learned, also, from the many races that streamed through his London church, from the gentle Jamaicans to the intriguing Asian believers. Derek knew that the British Empire was crumbling under the weight of racial arrogance, and he knew that the missionaries in Kenya were reflecting the lesser nature of their culture more than they were the example of their Christ. He set about to make a difference.

From the beginning he and Lydia began inviting Kenyans into their home and accepting invitations to visit the homes of their students. Their fellow missionaries were shocked and grumbled against them. It didn't matter. Derek and Lydia refused to limit the love of Jesus. They agreed to hold services in African villages and even began witnessing to the growing Indian community in Kenya, which most missionaries ignored. The British expatriate community was scandalized.

Derek and Lydia weren't through offending, though. When Derek became the principal of the school, he treated his students with respect and instilled in them a sense of honor for their race and their heritage. He made the school the best it could be and threw himself into his own teaching duties with a devotion that would have made him the star professor at Cambridge. He amazed his students by learning Swahili with astonishing speed and then thrilled them again when he began joking with them in a uniquely Kenyan style. Clearly, Derek pushed himself to love them beyond his natural introversion. He ate their food, joined in their banter, and attended their ceremonies. Lydia was even more outrageous in the eyes of other whites. She thought nothing of kissing the faces of black-skinned children or baking Danish delicacies for the students at the school. It was also not uncommon for her to spend an entire day in a village teaching the women how to store food or tend the sick. The other missionary women thought Lydia had "gone native." She replied, "Yes, I have gone native, and if you loved Jesus, you would, too."

Then came the most radical act of all. The mother of one of the students died, and Derek and Lydia attended the funeral. Afterward, the student, whose name was Matroba, apologetically told the Princes that she could no longer attend school because she had to care for her two small sisters. Derek and Lydia wouldn't allow it. They told Matroba, "You continue your studies, and we will care for your sisters." So into the home of the English principal with the Danish wife came two little African girls, Susanna and Mirka. Derek and Lydia knew what they were doing. Someone had to model the racial harmony of the kingdom of God if Kenya was ever to see the reality of Jesus Christ. As Derek wrote to his supporters, "I am impressed afresh with the enormous barrier of fear and racial prejudice which exists between the

Africans and the white people, and which only the power of the Holy Spirit can fully break down."

Derek's heart was tender toward the plight of Kenya's children. In his newsletter of July 1959, he recounted a touching story he hoped would touch the hearts of his readers: "I was sitting in our car outside a big African market in Kisumu, with Susanna in the back seat, and an African boy of about ten came up and looked at us both closely. After awhile he asked me in Swahili if Susanna were my daughter. I did not properly understand his questions, so I answered 'Yes.'

"He looked at us both again closely and then he said: 'But that's impossible! You are white, and she is black!'

"Being surprised that an African boy would come up and speak so freely to an Englishman, I started to ask him some questions: 'Where is your father?'

"'Dead!'

"'Where is your mother?'

"'Dead'

"'Where do you live?'

"'I just find a place to sleep.'

"'Where do you get your food?'

"He just pointed to the Market Place. I asked him if he would like to come home with us, and he said 'Yes.' So my wife and I took him home with us for a few days."

Compassion paved the way for the miraculous. Derek and Lydia had already seen healing and changed lives in their ministry to Kenyans. Soon the works of God were beyond anything they had ever witnessed. Derek told this story of one in a newsletter.

> Noah had given his heart to the Lord at a service in the Centre in March of this year, but later he became sick and had to give up his studies. It was on the 29th of July that we first visited Noah in his home in a hilly district about 20 miles north-east from here. We found him lying on a rude bed, under a shelter of banana leaves, behind an African hut. He was suffering from some infection of his kidneys, which had caused parts of his body to become bloated and swollen—particularly his left arm. He had attended two hospitals, but they had not been able to cure him.
>
> We read the Scriptures together with him and his relatives, and

we explained God's way of salvation and healing through faith in Christ's atonement. Then we laid our hands on him in the name of Jesus, and claimed the promise of Mark 16:18. My wife in particular laid her hands on his swollen arm. When we returned home quite late that evening, we were again burdened in prayer for him, and we once again claimed the promise of Mark 16:18.

On August 2, we made another journey to Noah's home and this is the story that he told us. On the evening of the day that we first prayed for him, he became extremely ill until he was quite paralyzed and unable to move or speak. Finally, he died and his spirit left his body.

At this point, two men came to him and laid their hands on those parts of his body on which we had previously laid our hands in prayer. Then they took him with them to a "wonderful place," where he spent some minutes. Then the men told him that his time had not come to die, but that he was being tested and that he was now to return to live.

Meanwhile, his family, seeing him dead, sent for the local African Christian elder. The elder came and prayed for him and he also was given the assurance that Noah was not to die at that time.

Noah then returned to life, and by the next day (Sunday) the swelling on his arm had gone and he was beginning to recover health and strength. That evening, one of the two men who had visited him the day before returned and asked him why he had not told people of his experience and of what God had done for him.

Armed with such testimonies, Derek and Lydia began believing that God would do even greater miracles at their hands if they would only trust Him. The opportunity to exercise this greater faith came not long after. One of the students at their school died unexpectedly. Derek and Lydia made their way to the girl's deathbed and found a scene that reminded them of an episode from the life of Jesus. The room where the girl lay was filled with mourners who tearfully poured out their grief in a frenzied African style. Derek took control and told all the mourners to leave. He and Lydia knelt on opposite sides of the girl's bed and began to pray. Within minutes, the girl shot up in bed and demanded, "Does anyone have a Bible?" Astonished, Derek handed the newly revived girl his Bible, and she immediately turned to Psalm 42 and began to read.

After a moment, the girl explained what had happened. When she died and her spirit passed from her body, two men appeared and took her on a winding road until she came to a place where there were bright lights and people singing. A man was preaching from Psalm 42. The two men then told her that she was to return, and she immediately found herself running back down the winding road until she awoke in her body with Derek and Lydia kneeling at her side. She had become so caught up in what the man was preaching from Psalm 42 that she immediately asked for a Bible so she could continue reading where he left off.

The story of these miracles filled both the school and the villages around Kisumu. The Kenyans came to regard Derek and Lydia with awe. Even the missionaries began to understand how their biases had hindered the work of God, and they began to treat the Kenyans differently. Before long Derek could not keep up with the invitations he received to preach the gospel and pray for the sick. Over the next few years, he would minister in hundreds of villages and hold extended services in dozens of rented facilities. He also grew bolder with his students and began telling them that they had to be filled with the Holy Spirit so that they too could perform miracles in the name of Jesus. Not long after, he was able to report in a newsletter that more than seventy-five of his one hundred students were baptized with the Holy Spirit.

Derek now found a kind of fulfillment in his work that he had never known pastoring in London. All of his gifts were employed, and all of his passions were engaged. He used his intellectual gifts in teaching classes and designing curriculum for the school. The same administrative skills that had made him a prized medical orderly helped him to lead the school to new heights. The enrollment doubled during his time, and his students went on to achieve magnificently, even leading schools of their own in time. Moreover, he preached the gospel throughout Kenya and met with astonishing fruit: thousands were saved, many were healed, and churches were planted that still existed decades later when he passed from this life. He was happy in a way that only graces a man when he is doing what he was made to do. He told Lydia that he expected he would spend the rest of his days in Kenya. He was forty-five at the time.

He felt that he was walking with destiny, and this made him dare to be creative. Like the educational strategist he was becoming, he began to think about the printed word and how it could impact a generation. Until now, his writing had been limited to newsletters. He began to sense that God wanted more, and he started writing articles and tracts to carry his ministry where he could not go. As he wrote in August 1960, "I have prepared a number of clear, short tracts, specially designed for young people. I find that these gain entry in many places where a Pentecostal missionary would not be invited. They have already found their way into quite a large number of schools in Kenya—and even one in Uganda—and from almost every school there comes a demand for more. As a result of these tracts, I have received letters from nurses, teachers, students, and others in many different places and institutions asking for definite information as to how to be saved or for other forms of spiritual help."

The success of the tracts fired his imagination, and he set himself to a larger work. In December 1960, he wrote to his supporters, "I have recently prepared a complete Bible correspondence course [now called the *Self-Study Bible Course*], based directly on personal study of the Bible by each student and designed to bring out in the most definite way possible all the main, basic truths of the full gospel message. Our mission press is at present installing a new off-set printing press, and as soon as this is complete we hope to produce the first edition of the course in English." Though he could not have known it, this course was not only an innovation that showed he was ahead of his time as an educator, but it was the foundation of one of the greatest works of his life.

Such successes did not come without difficulty, though. Derek's newsletters told the story. Each missionary had to do the work of many because there were far too few workers in the field. Lack of money was almost always a problem, and there was the unstable political situation to consider, which Derek described to his readers as a "volcano ready to erupt at any moment." Then there was the spiritual opposition. As Derek wrote, "There are undoubtedly powerful satanic agents and influences at work seeking to produce conditions of hatred, disorder, and bloodshed here in Kenya. In the face of such opposition, spiritual results can only be achieved by unrelenting labor in prayer, in ministry of the Word, and in fasting."

It may have been just such "agents" that nearly took the lives of Derek and his family. Derek and Lydia were driving on the road from Kisumu to Nakuru to visit George and Johanne Hedges one day when their car—a Morris Minor Traveler—swerved out of control. They later learned that a truck had leaked gasoline on the road, which made it so slippery that a car could barely stay on the road. The car with Derek and Lydia fishtailed violently from side to side and then plunged over a steep embankment. Lydia—who was nearly seventy at the time—was thrown from the car. Derek remained in the driver's seat, but the car came down with such force that he pushed the seat right through the bottom of the car. When Derek got out of the car to make sure Lydia was all right, he discovered a severe pain in his back. He told the rest in a newsletter.

> In Nakuru the doctor advised me to have an x-ray of my back, and this revealed that two vertebrae had been damaged in different sections of the spine. I spent five days in hospital where the doctor encased me in plaster from the loins to the neck. This plaster is due to remain in place for three months, during which period I am trusting the Lord to heal my spine completely and to give me an even stronger body than I had before.

Derek would heal completely in time, but the months in the body cast were frustrating indeed for a man of his energy. The truth is he had broken his back, and it is a miracle that he was not permanently crippled. Derek believed that the "agents" of evil were retaliating against him for the good that God was then doing through his life.

Such assaults were few, though, and Derek found he had much to be thankful for. God had given him many gifts during his time in Kenya. One of these announced itself as Derek and Lydia were sitting on their porch one evening. It was around five o'clock when Derek looked up to see a strange trio approaching the house: a black couple and a white woman carrying a bundle. After the customary exchange of greetings, the white woman said, "We hear you take children in. Can you do anything with this?" Derek and Lydia looked at the bundle in her arms and saw a tiny black baby girl who could not have been but a few weeks old. Derek explained that the family used to take children in, but that they were not doing so now.

The three said they were tired and asked if they could sit. As they did, they began to explain that the child's mother had died giving birth and that the baby was found all alone on the floor of a hut. It was a sad affair, for no one was willing to take the child in. Finally, as the three stood to leave, the baby put out her left arm toward Derek as if to say, "What are you going to do about me?" At that moment, Lydia gazed up at her husband's face and read his heart. Turning to the woman she said, "Give me a week to get a crib and some baby clothes, and you can bring her back." A week later, the woman returned with the child. So it was that Joska entered the lives of Derek and Lydia Prince.

Oddly, Joska would grow up in the Prince home much like an only child. The other girls had moved on with their lives. Anna had come to Kenya at the age of sixteen, finished her studies, and begun working as a volunteer nurse in Nakuru. It was then that she learned that the Pentecostal Assemblies were willing to pay for the children of missionaries who turned eighteen to leave the country. Kenya had not been a good experience for Anna. She not only missed the Western ways she had known in London, but she also found Kenya too primitive and dull for her tastes. She accepted the offer to leave and flew to Canada to enroll in a Bible school run by the Pentecostal Assemblies.

Elisabeth had come to Kenya as a fourteen-year-old and immediately enrolled in an all girls' school called Highlands School in Eldoret. In a paper she wrote not long after arriving, she described Kenya as "a land of sun and want." It was typical of her tender, poetic soul. When she finished her studies, she decided to return to England to study nursing as her sisters had before her, and she trained for three years at Hammersmith Hospital before becoming a psychiatric nurse.

When Derek and Lydia moved to Kenya, they expected that Kirsten, who had begun nursing school in England, would follow them when her studies were finished. She never rejoined her family, though. As she neared completion of her studies at Paddington General Hospital, she met a dashing young airman named Jim Fry. The two fell in love and married on Easter Sunday 1961. When Kirsten wrote her parents to ask their blessing, Derek and Lydia wrote back gladly giving approval, and they sent £25 as a wedding gift. Not long after, Jim and Kay moved to Singapore where Jim served in the Royal Air Force and Kay served as a nurse.

With the advent of 1961, Derek and Lydia began considering the matter of a furlough. It was the policy of the Pentecostal Assemblies to send their missionaries home for rest, training, and fund-raising after every five years of service in the field. In his newsletter of June 1961, Derek wrote, "Our plan now is to spend Christmas and New Year's in Scandinavia, then to move on to England early in 1962, spend some weeks there, and then on again to Canada, and perhaps also to the United States."

It happened much as Derek had outlined. He and Lydia gathered Joska in their arms and traveled through Denmark and England before arriving in Canada early in 1962. When they arrived, they had the joy of meeting Anna's new husband, David Selby, a man who would figure prominently in the Derek Prince story. Anna had been attending Eastern Pentecostal Bible College, the school she left Kenya to attend in 1958, when she met the tall, handsome David at Simcoe Street Pentecostal Church in Oshawa, Ontario. David had been working at a stamping plant, pressing out sheets of stainless steel into sinks, when he first saw Anna at a church function, and the two began dating in July 1959. Months later, David wrote to Derek and Lydia asking for Anna's hand in marriage. The gesture impressed Anna's parents, and they gave their blessing. David and Anna were married on July 8, 1961. Nine months later, Derek and Lydia arrived with Anna's Kenyan sister.

Not long after, Derek and Lydia attended a Pentecostal Assemblies conference in Toronto. With their sweet, black baby in their arms, the Prince family was the center of attention. Derek told the conference of their ministry in Kenya and of the tender way in which Joska had come to be theirs. He recounted the two occasions on which the dead had been raised and the hundreds of healings and miracles he had witnessed. The conference was electrified. The tales of their African ministry spread so rapidly that *The Toronto Globe and Mail* asked to interview Derek and Lydia about their lives and took a picture of Lydia and Joska, which came to symbolize beautifully the unusual pairing of the fair-skinned, aging Danish mother with the bright-eyed but midnight black Joska.

In his discussions with the leaders of the Pentecostal Assemblies about his calling and what it meant for his furlough, Derek had boldly insisted, "I am called to be a teacher of the Scriptures in the body of Christ." After so many years, he knew who he was. He was eager to use his gifts, and he sensed that God wanted him to impact the future leaders of the church. He seems also to have wanted time to write and to perfect the self-study Bible course that he had begun in Kenya. The Pentecostal Assemblies must have agreed, for by the fall term of 1962 Derek was teaching courses at the Western Pentecostal Bible College in North Vancouver, British Columbia.

Though the idea of teaching in an accredited Bible college must have stirred his teacher's heart, things did not work out as Derek had hoped. The problem was Lydia. She was in her early seventies and had wearied of living alone in a primitive country. If they were going to move to a western Canadian Bible college, Lydia had asked Derek to make sure that they could live close to the campus. She was too old to walk and too poor a driver to brave the Canadian roads. Moreover, she wanted friends and fellowship with other believers. She was tired of being isolated. Derek passed all these requests on to the Bible college president, and he agreed to do as Lydia asked.

None of the requests were honored, though. Derek and Lydia found themselves living miles from the campus in a rural house with no car. Moreover, Derek's teaching schedule was so tight that he had no time to do the very writing and studying that the furlough was designed for in the first place. He was frustrated and began to look for other options. By January 1963, after only one semester at the school, he had decided what to do. As he wrote the superintendent of the Pentecostal Assemblies in Canada:

> I have come to the conclusion that I need some further specialized training and also a base, where I can have time and quietness to concentrate on the work that seems to me important. After prayer and waiting to see God's way of providing these things, I have come to see that the best opportunities along this line are probably to be found in the United States, and it also seems that God has been opening doors for me in that direction. I have now accepted an invitation from a personal friend of mine, who is pastor of a Pentecostal church in Minneapolis, to join him there as a kind of resident Bible teacher. I feel that a position such as this will give me the facilities and the opportunities that I need.

The words are diplomatic, but they betray a deeper meaning and a bolder Derek than first appears. The fact is that Derek was leaving his denomination. He had become disillusioned with the Pentecostal Assemblies of Canada both because they had broken their promises and because they had treated the Danish Lydia and the British Derek with a stinging brand of national bias. Derek felt he had taken enough. He felt that the Pentecostal Assemblies of Canada had treated him poorly but that America offered him a stage suited for his gifts. He wanted to make a difference, to do the work he was called to do. So, in February 1963, Derek, Lydia, and Joska boarded a train in Winnipeg and left Canada for the United States.

When they arrived in Minneapolis, they were met with a surprise. The immigration official asked them why they wanted to enter the United States and how long they wanted to stay. Derek explained who he was and that they wanted to be in the United States for six months. The immigration official replied that it was impossible to get a visa for six months but that they could immigrate if they wished. Derek agreed, and with the completing of some papers, the Prince family became residents of the United States. It would prove to be one of the most strategic decisions of their lives.

9

America:

To Step Upon the Stage

" DEREK, WHEN DID you first hear the news?"
"I heard that President Kennedy had been shot while I was buying groceries in a Seattle store. They played the news broadcast over the store sound system, and I stood transfixed with all the other shoppers while we listened to reports of the assassination. Finally, the announcement came that the president was dead."

"How did you feel at that moment?"

"I felt almost immediately that the devil was trying to destroy America. Already, a renewal had begun in the United States, and it promised to become a very powerful move of God. I believed that the Kennedy assassination was part of an attempt of the devil to disillusion Americans and move the country toward a destructive, immoral counterculture."

"Did it occur to you that you had arrived in America at almost the same time that this horrible thing took place? In other words, did the assassination of Kennedy form any personal challenge for you?"

"Yes, it did. I began to think about all the lessons I had learned: lessons of intercession during El Alamein, lessons of fasting and renewal in London, lessons of racial healing in Kenya, and others. I felt as though my whole life had been preparation to step onto the stage of an America in crisis. It seemed that God was calling me to pray and to teach about prayer—particularly prayer for the government. Almost immediately, I began to have a vision for the nation, which was odd because I had only been in the country for a few months. I knew I wasn't the only one, but the themes the Holy Spirit had emphasized with me over the years seemed to prepare me perfectly for that very moment in American history."

The lives of great men normally reveal a pattern of strategic timing, as though providence has aligned the life of the man with the course of the age to achieve some higher purpose. Derek Prince's life is evidence of such grace. He was born in India just as the movement for independence in that land arose. He attended Cambridge in the wake of the First World War when great minds and tortured hearts were pondering some of the weightiest themes in human philosophy. He was there when Montgomery preserved the Middle East at El Alamein, there when Israel was born, and there when spiritual renewal swept a postwar England in decline. He was also there when America was remaking herself during the tumultuous decade of the 1960s.

It is this decade and the forces that converged within it that we must understand in order to grasp truly what Derek Prince meant to his age. He was forty-eight years old when he left Canada for America, and though he could not have known it then, his life had perfectly prepared him to answer the cry of a nation in spiritual upheaval. There were three streams then converging that would set the stage for Derek Prince in America: the baby-boomer counterculture, the Charismatic Renewal, and the technologies that spread both of these more rapidly than any previous movement in history.

To understand the spiritual climate of the 1960s, we should recall that the years prior to that decade were filled with a suffocating materialism. The Great Depression and World War II had meant sixteen years of hardship for Americans, who, with war's end, gave explosive vent to a craving for the trophies of technological advance and military victory. For several decades following the war, the American dream would be bound up with a frame house in the suburbs, cars with huge fins, the technology of comfort, and in short, "the good life." We perhaps remember the values of this age best from the film clips of the June Cleaver type of housewife proudly displaying her "modern, space-age" kitchen, the promise of a strong and noble society reflected in every shiny appliance.

The children of the World War II generation, those we now call "baby boomers," came of age in this era of triumphant materialism and found it without remedy for the aching emptiness in their souls. Sadly, the churches, filled as they were with the spirit of the age, offered no alternatives. The cultural Christianity so loosely woven through their parents' lives was too inconsistently external for this younger generation, who were desperate for a transforming spiritual reality.

This was, after all, the age of Eisenhower, a president who movingly proclaimed a national day of prayer and fasting, only to spend it playing golf. Ike had declared his belief that religion is essential to a republic, but then added, "And I don't care what that religion is!" Though it was during the Eisenhower administration that the phrase "In God We Trust" became the national motto, the place for God in the American psyche was tragically small. The postwar generation, entering adulthood as they were in the late fifties and early sixties, were hungering for an invisible reality they could not define and to which their parents seemed completely oblivious. Already their discontent was being heard in the writings of Allen Ginsberg and Jack Kourac, films like Marlon Brando's *The Wild One*, and an innocuous philosophy of nonconformity called "beat."

With the beginning of the 1960s, three events occurred that set the stage for the devastating blows the decade would bring. These were the birth of the Charismatic Movement, the rise of John F. Kennedy, and the removal of prayer from the public schools.

The first of these events resulted from the tender response of the heart of God to young America's quiet desperation. In the latter part of 1959, Rev. Dennis Bennett, a neo-orthodox Episcopalian priest in Van Nuys, California, received the baptism of the Holy Spirit, an experience long believed by most Christians of the day to be a uniquely first-century phenomenon. News of this joyfully transforming experience spread rapidly in the 1960s, particularly through the youth culture of the West Coast and then through it to the youth of the nation. What came to be known as the "Charismatic

Movement" had begun, and so had the battle to fill the immense spiritual vacuum of American society.

Then, in 1961, forty-four-year-old Harvard-educated John F. Kennedy became the thirty-fifth president of the United States. Kennedy captured the hearts of the baby boomers unlike any other president, largely because the presidents they had known—Roosevelt, Truman, and Eisenhower—had been distant grandfather figures to them. Kennedy seemed to be one of them, a handsome war hero and prizewinning author whose poetic, almost evangelistic, speeches called them to join in changing their world. Kennedy referred to Scripture more than any president in American history, but he changed the quotations to speak of democracy, freedom, and the American way of life. He spoke religiously of America's "calling" to venture into outer space, conquer poverty, win against communism, and take global responsibility through a program called the Peace Corps. Youth. Idealism. The New Frontier. Camelot revisited. Kennedy's vision, naïve and humanistic though it was, caused young America to believe they could change the world in their own strength, and they never saw the world or themselves in quite the same way again.

The third of these critical events is often overlooked. In the spirit of Kennedy's self-sufficient humanism, the United States Supreme Court, in the 1962 *Engel v. Vitale* case, told 39 million American school children that the twenty-two-word prayer with which they started their day was a violation of the U.S. Constitution. The offending prayer—"Almighty God, we acknowledge our dependence upon Thee, and we beg Thy blessings upon us, our parents, our teachers and our Country"—seemed innocuous enough. But the result of its removal, as David Barton has so clearly shown in his *America: To Pray or Not to Pray*, was that almost every area of American life mentioned in the prayer began to show unprecedented decline. Statistics on academic test scores, school violence, child abuse, teen pregnancies, alcoholism, violent crime, and sexually transmitted diseases—to name just a few—all revealed that the ruling principles of American life had changed dramatically. A wall of protection, constructed through prayer over several generations, was being dismantled.[16]

Thus, with the stage set by an intensified spiritual battle, the illusory hopes of secularism, and a weakened prayer defense, the first of the hammer blows occurred: November 22, 1963. The images are still clear in our minds decades later. Breathless announcers interrupting the broadcast day.

Jacqueline's pink dress and pill-box hat. The final announcement from Parkland Hospital. The shock of the nation. Little John-John tearfully saluting his father's casket as the caisson rolled by. The televised assassination of the president's assassin.

The much-debated question of who shot John Kennedy in Dallas' Dealy Plaza is not nearly as important as what it did to the nation. It was a collective trauma on an unprecedented scale, as though the whole nation had experienced a violent accident with all the fear, the uncontrollable emotion, and the desperate search for normalcy that follows such horrors. The gaping national wound that the death of Kennedy left on the American soul meant a loss of the troubled innocence that had characterized postwar society. Now, with the prince of Camelot slain, the young knights of Camelot were set adrift.

Then began the seduction of a generation. A mere ten weeks after the Kennedy assassination, an "assault" team landed at LaGuardia Airport in New York. Their reason for entering the country was to appear on *The Ed Sullivan Show*, riding a crest of popularity from hit songs like "Please, Please Me," "She Loves You," and "I Want to Hold Your Hand." From the very beginning they electrified young America, as films from their concert at Shea Stadium depict. Screaming, weeping, contorting youths were moved by forces beyond the music. Sixteen-year-old girls charged the stage, flattening policemen twice their size, while others simply passed out and had to be carried from the field. No one seemed more stunned by the commotion than the "fab four" themselves, but their music had touched the mourning hearts of Camelot's lonely young knights, and now the Beatles would become, however unwittingly, the generals—or perhaps just the sergeants—in a new kind of war.

Having hooked American youth as cute "mopped-topped" boys, the Beatles then underwent a transformation powered by drugs, sex, Eastern religions, pop-culture social consciousness, and superstar cynicism. This radical change can clearly be seen in the *Rubber Soul* album of 1965 and the *Sgt. Pepper's Lonely Hearts Club Band* album of 1967. The "four gay lads," as John Lennon once described them, had died; the picture of four graves on the cover of *Sgt. Pepper's* made this point emphatically clear for those who hadn't heard it in the music. What arose in the place of the early Beatles were psychedelic pied pipers who played their entire generation into a spiritual abyss.

The "new" Beatles led a bewildered army of millions into mind-altering chemicals, sexual experimentation, and Eastern mysticism—this last empha-sis a result of their relationship with the Maharishi Mahesh Yogi. By the time John Lennon quipped that the Beatles were more popular than Jesus Christ, he was, sadly, more right than he understood. The disciples of these new pied pipers had long ago discarded their parents' seemingly irrelevant Christian-ity and had begun, at the urging of Beatles' friend Timothy Leary, to "turn on, tune in, drop out."

The problem with Leary, the Beatles, and the other gurus of that era is that they seldom understood the forces they invoked. As they urged the recreational use of psychedelic drugs, they were unaware that ancient cul-tures had also used such drugs but for radically different purposes: to deaden the rational mind and thus open the soul to the influence of spirits. Hallu-cinogenic drugs for any other purpose was unknown before the 1960s. In fact, the biblical word *witchcraft* is often a translation of the Greek word *pharmakeia*, the term from which we get our words like *pharmacy* and *phar-maceuticals*. Without ever fully understanding it, the Beatles and their ilk had pried open a huge door to the demonic, merging culture and occult in a manner that would reshape their world.

It was no accident, then, that among Derek Prince's first spiritual experiences in America was a confrontation with demonic forces. Those who knew the course of his life and the nature of American culture in those days would have expected no less. Yet before we follow Derek's journey through those early years in America, we should also consider an innovation that would soon change his world: the invention of the cassette.

What was known as the "compact cassette" was first patented by the Philips Company in 1964, the year after Derek came to America. It was designed as an improvement over reel-to-reel tape recorders that were prov-ing too large and too slow to suit a high-speed society. Aware of what this new technology might mean, Sony and Norelco were early licensees of the patent for the cassette. In fact, the plastic case that virtually all cassettes were sold in was dubbed the "Norelco case" as a result.

Record companies were slow to accept the new audio format, though, and only released albums in cassette format after the record had been on the market for a while. This led one company to boast on its dust jackets, "Remember, it always happens on records first."

While the cassette was making only modest inroads into the marketplace, the 8-track cartridge was foisted on the American public. The appeal of the 8-track was its portability, and record companies, believing that this new technology was the wave of the future, spent enormous budgets to assure its success. There were problems, though. The 8-track was not only cheaply constructed and easily damaged, but it also could not be used to record. Americans soon soured on the once touted device, and the 8-track became a dinosaur faster than any other similar technology in history.

The age of the cassette then dawned. In the early 1970s, Maxell, a Japanese company, dramatically improved the quality of the cassette, and TDK followed their lead. Sensing a trend, companies like 3M, Ampex, and Sony, who had been making cassettes for years, shifted larger budgets behind the technology, and it was not long before the cassette became the medium of choice for the recording industry.

It was not the high-end cassette market that dramatically shaped Derek Prince's life, though. Once cassettes became the preferred medium for music, companies quickly realized that there was a growing market for home recording and duplication. Every cassette player was soon capable of recording, and it was not long before inexpensive tape duplication machines also spilled onto the market. The cassette tape revolution had begun.

This technological revolution quickly merged with the spiritual revolution already underway. When Derek Prince entered America, the Charismatic Movement was but a newborn babe. Within a few years, though, the movement would begin emphasizing Bible teaching, prophecy, and personal ministry to such a degree that Charismatic believers began to beg for recordings of almost every word spoken at a conference or a church service. In time it became a joke among Charismatics that a man's holiness was measured by how many white plastic cassette tapes with handwritten or dot matrix labels he had stored in his house. The joke betrayed the reality. The Charismatic Movement grew on the power of recorded speech, and the cassette was the accessible medium that gave that speech global appeal.

In fact, it is not going too far to suggest that the cassette tape defined Charismatic culture. The faithful took tapes the way their secular counterparts took medicine. Mothers played tapes on healing for their ill children, and families listened to their favorite teachers during mealtime. Purses and pockets spilled over with tapes in the wake of a conference, and entire ministries were devoted to aiming little white cassette tape missiles at the American soul.

It was a technological moment perfectly suited for the work of Derek Prince. By the time he set foot in America, it had been nearly twenty years since he had heard his God say, "You are called to be a teacher of the Scriptures, in truth and faith and love, which are in Christ Jesus—for many." Since that time he had honed his teaching skills in a Ramallah way station for orphans and soldiers, in a London house church, in a Kenyan teacher's training school, and in a Canadian Bible college. By 1963, Derek was eager to touch the world with the truths he had learned, and the cassette was just the tool to help him do it.

It is intriguing to note that Derek Prince entered America in the spring of 1963 a largely unknown Pentecostal preacher. He had spent the previous year in the backwaters of Canada and the half-decade before that in the backwaters of Kenya. He was unknown, undefined, and unemployed.

A mere seven years later, Derek had become one of the best-known preachers in the country. His gifts had chiseled a place for him in the emerging Charismatic Movement, and he had gained a national reputation as one of the most theologically sound yet spiritually electrifying teachers on the Christian stage. To understand these seven years is to understand what Derek would mean to his generation in the decades that came after.

He began his work in America as a teaching pastor at Peoples Church on Van Buren Street in Minneapolis. The senior pastor there was a man named Henderson whom Derek had met during the war. When Pastor Henderson learned of Derek's eagerness to serve as a teaching pastor in America, he realized what a man of Derek's education and experience might mean for his church and quickly extended an invitation.

For Derek, the opportunity seemed strategic. It not only gave him a chance to use his teaching gifts in a larger arena, but it also offered him time to work on the project that seemed dearest to his heart in those days: his correspondence course. His explanation of the project to a friend portrays both his passion for Christian education and his sense of the times.

> As things are now moving in the world both politically and spiritually, I do not feel free to commit myself to anyone or anything anywhere.…My main purpose in accepting a temporary appointment at the Western Pentecostal Bible College in Vancouver was to have time and opportunity to consider the question of my own future ministry and also to work on some kind of development or extension of the original "All Nations" Bible Correspondence Course which I produced during my term of service in Kenya. However things did not work out at the Bible college in Vancouver as I had been led to expect. Since then, during the period of my temporary association with the Peoples Church here, I have been able to work out, with the Lord's help, what I believe can be a practical and useful instrument of Bible teaching, both at home and overseas. It would take too long to explain my scheme in detail, but basically it would consist of the following:
>
> - A series of systematic, Bible teaching lectures recorded on tape, each lecture lasting not more than twenty-five minutes.
>
> - A set of outline notes with Scripture references to accompany each lecture.
>
> - A set of self-examination question papers, with answers included, on the pattern of "Programmed Instruction" at the end of each set of four lectures.
>
> In this way, the whole program would be self-contained and would provide within one system the three psychological requirements of good teaching: hearing, seeing, and doing.

Derek's educational wisdom shines in this letter. It is only 1963, and yet Derek not only feels an urgency to get what he has learned into the body of Christ, but he also realizes that this task cannot be fulfilled with conventional education. He understands that the average Christian believer does not have the time or the inclination to sit for hours in a classroom. Still there is the pressing need for deeper teaching than the average church provides. To meet this need, Derek designs something new: a self-study program that can be completed by any believer anywhere and at his own pace. It is just the kind of innovation that will, in time, place advanced teaching in the hands of thousands of believers and make the name of Derek Prince synonymous with the systematic teaching of God's Word.

It is also interesting in Derek's letter that he describes his role at Peoples Church as "temporary." He apparently sensed something others could not have foreseen. It would be natural for us to expect that Derek would remain in Minneapolis, thrive as a teaching pastor, and extend his teaching by tapes and the printed word to a nation in need. The fact is he was only at the Peoples Church a matter of months. His year of preaching in Canada and the stories of his work in Kenya that appeared in Pentecostal publications had given him some exposure among the Assemblies of God churches in America. One of these, a church in Seattle called Broadway Tabernacle, decided to extend an invitation to Derek to become their pastor. Derek and Lydia, feeling what they later described as a "spirit of adventure," decided to accept.

It was an odd decision. If anything springs from the pages of Derek's letters at the time it is a passion to be free of entanglement in order to teach as widely as possible the revelations that burned in his soul. In Minneapolis, he has the benefits of a large American city, and he has the freedom to teach a local congregation as well as to travel and speak widely in Pentecostal circles. He also has time to write the material that is stirring in his heart. Instead of building on his opportunities, he accepts a pastorate in Seattle, a move that seems to fly in the face of everything he was striving for at the time. It would prove, though, to be one of the great turning points of his life.

✖

Derek assumed the pastorate of Broadway Tabernacle in Seattle on September 15, 1963. He soon realized he had landed in a war zone.

The problem was not primarily with the congregation. They numbered several hundred people and were for the most part respectful, devoted, Pentecostal people who welcomed Derek and Lydia warmly. What disturbed Derek, though, was that, when it came to spiritual matters, the people seemed to be in a daze. As Derek later described the situation, "It didn't matter what I did, there was no real response. It was a baffling situation."

As Derek and Lydia prayed, they began to understand what they were dealing with. They sensed that God was leading them to Galatians 3:1, which includes the question, "Who has bewitched you?" Derek was surprised by the passage. The scripture seemed to indicate that the congregation was under some kind of evil manipulation. But where did it come from, and how had it spread?

In time, Derek and Lydia came to know the full story. It turned out that the wife of the previous pastor of the church had fallen in love with one of the church's board members. The two engineered a scheme by which they would each divorce their spouses so they could marry. The previous pastor was so wounded by his wife divorcing him and turning to another man that he simply abandoned the church and moved away, thus leaving his wife as the virtual head of the church.

The woman began to control the congregation, largely by means of manipulation and intimidation. When a dispute arose in the church, for example, she would say, "Now how many of you are for me? Put your hand up." Anyone who didn't raise their hand received a withering stare that seemed to have an almost supernatural effect. When Derek saw what she was doing, he could only describe her control of the congregation as "mesmerizing." He knew that the congregation would never be free to pursue God fully until this woman's spiritual grip on the souls of the people was broken. He and Lydia began to pray.

As they did, they were reminded of an experience that took place shortly after they arrived. A local Baptist pastor who barely knew Derek called him one day and said, "The Lord has shown me you are to minister deliverance to a woman in my congregation." Derek wasn't sure what the pastor wanted of him, but while he was still on the phone he quickly prayed, "Lord, is this from You?" and he sensed that the answer was yes. He told the Baptist pastor that he would meet with the woman, and the two made an appointment.

When the pastor arrived with the woman in need, Derek noted that she seemed like a perfectly normal American housewife. The other pastor immediately explained, "This woman has already been delivered of a spirit of nicotine, but there are more demons that need to come out." Derek was stunned that a Baptist would speak in such a manner, but he agreed to join the man in driving demons out of the woman. Settling into Derek's office, the three began to pray for deliverance.

The Baptist pastor took the lead, shouting at the top of his voice and commanding the spirits to leave. He seemed to believe that the louder he shouted, the more power he had. It didn't prove true. After only a short while, he was exhausted and the woman was unchanged.

Derek took over. He turned to the woman and began addressing the spirit in her. "In the name of the Lord Jesus Christ," he commanded, "what is your name?" Suddenly, a full, masculine voice issued from the woman's throat and said simply, "Hate." Just as Derek heard the word, he looked at the woman's face and saw the most perfect mask of hatred he had ever seen or envisioned. Then the spirit within the woman spoke once more: "Hate," it said again, "and I'm not coming out. I've lived here twenty-five years, and I'm not coming out."

Derek knew that spirits often fight back with fear and intimidation. He was too experienced in casting out demons to let such tactics succeed. Facing the woman, Derek felt his soul fill with a strength of faith he had seldom known. He commanded the spirit to leave. It refused, but Derek was undaunted. He and the other pastor prayed, read Scripture, and ordered the spirit to go. Suddenly, the woman's hands rose to her throat and began choking her. Derek and the other man knew that the spirit was using the woman's own body against her, and they began commanding the spirit to cease while physically pulling the woman's hands away from her throat.

Finally, the spirit fled and the woman relaxed. The struggle left her exhausted and with astonishing heat rising from her body. The two pastors sensed that there was more work to be done, though, and began immediately commanding the spirits within the woman to name themselves and leave. A spirit of infidelity named itself and then fled at Derek's command. Six or seven other spirits named themselves and left. One of them identified itself as a spirit of death.

When the work was done, Derek looked at the woman and saw that she was transformed. Her countenance had changed, and there seemed to be a gentle glow to her features that had not been there before. She was free, and everyone knew it.

This experience was both glorious and troubling to Derek. He was thrilled at the victory over demons and thrilled to see the woman set free. Still, he knew that the experience challenged something he had come to believe. Pentecostals had long taught that while the unsaved could have demons living in them, Christians could not. Standard Pentecostal theology maintained that any demonic powers that might once have dwelt in a Christian were driven off at the moment of their salvation, when the Spirit of God took up residence in the believer's soul. Since the Spirit of God and the spirits of evil cannot reside in the same vessel, Pentecostals believed that no evil spirit could indwell a true Christian.

Derek was beginning to realize that while the Spirit of God might live in the spirit of a born-again man, the man's body and soul could still be a haunt of demons. Christians who gave themselves to sin or who had come to Jesus with particularly grievous strongholds of evil needed help driving the demonic from their lives. Derek knew that most of the church world wouldn't agree. Most non-Pentecostals didn't even believe that demons still operated in the modern world, and most Pentecostals believed they operated only in the lives of the unsaved. He could already see that taking the position that demons can indwell Christians wasn't going to be popular. Still, he now knew it was true, and he knew that in an increasingly demonized age this knowledge was too precious to keep from God's people.

It was this experience with the demonized woman that moved Derek and Lydia to start wondering if their congregation didn't have demonic troubles as well. As these thoughts were first crossing their minds, though, it happened. One Sunday morning Derek was preaching boldly about Elijah. He began saying that it doesn't matter what the devil does, God has the answer. Satan has his pharaoh, but God has His Moses. Satan has his prophets of Baal, but God has His Elijah. Just as Derek said these words, a woman let out a horrible, piercing scream and began writhing on the floor. The congregation let out a corporate gasp and then sat stunned as the woman contorted violently. Derek paused in his sermon but seemed calm. He waited, scanned his spirit for a nudge from God, and then simply called some of the congregation's leaders to the front and announced, "Now we will minister to our sister."

The contest began. One of the ladies Derek had called up to help began demanding that the demon in the woman give its name. The spirit refused and continued its torment. The lady then screamed at the demon with greater volume. Still, the spirit would not obey. Finally, with the lady exhausted and the congregation deeper in shock, Derek asked some of the deacons to take the writhing woman to his office.

While Lydia and some of the church leadership ministered to the troubled woman in the office, Derek tried to calm his overwhelmed congregation. After a few moments, though, Lydia looked around the door of the office and said aloud to Derek, "You'd better come in here quickly." Realizing he could do nothing more for the stunned congregation, he simply said a prayer and dismissed them. As he walked toward the office to help in delivering the woman, a couple approached him. "Mr. Prince," they said, "that is our daughter in there. May we come with you?" Derek thought for a moment, couldn't think of any reason to say no, and replied, "By all means."

Now, the demonized woman, Derek, Lydia, some deacons, and the demonized woman's parents were all jammed in Derek's tiny office. Immediately, the parents began relaying their daughter's story. She had recently been embroiled in a sinful relationship, her mother explained. Derek listened and quickly realized that the tormented woman was being seduced by spirits intent upon ruining her life and the lives of her family. He quickly began commanding spirits to name themselves. The first one identified itself as a spirit of flirtation. Derek commanded it to go, and it did. Then another named itself as a spirit of petting. It too went out of the woman, and then the floodgates seemed to fly open. As Derek later described it, "Spirits began identifying themselves and flying out of that woman like passengers handing their tickets to a stewardess before boarding a plane." Derek would demand the spirit's name, command it to go, and the spirit would flee. Before long, the exhausted woman was freed of demonic control. Derek charged her to go home and repair the damage her immorality had done.

Derek and Lydia now realized that their new church was filled with sweet, Christian people who were frequently under the influence of demons. As troubling a thought as it was, it was impossible to deny given what had happened on that Sunday morning. Even some of the most skeptical leaders in the church were now convinced that demons were real, that Christians could be controlled by them, but that Jesus had given His church the power to drive them off. Seizing the moment, Derek began teaching his flock about the power believers have over demons. He recounted the victories he had seen in Kenya, challenged his congregation to new levels of holiness, and began praying for those who were willing to be free.

Word of changed lives spread. At first people came from Seattle and the surrounding regions. Then, as victory followed victory in the lives of troubled people, seekers came from other American states and even parts of Canada. Sensing that he was pioneering something critical in the body of Christ, Derek and Lydia, dutifully, prayed with everyone they could. There were astonishing victories. The drug-addicted, the bitter, the angry, and the tormented all made their way to Derek, and most were permanently delivered.

It was exhausting work, though. Derek and Lydia seldom got to bed before two in the morning and rarely had time for anything but preaching and casting out demons. Their home life was constantly disrupted, and this was largely because they chose to hold deliverance sessions in their living room to preserve the privacy of those who sought help. Little Joska quickly learned the routine. In the wee hours of one morning, the deliverance session ended with Joska crumpled in a corner and her head in her hands. When Derek called to her, she shot straight up and asked, "Did you get them all out?"

It was during this season of dramatic ministry that Derek first came into contact with an organization called Full Gospel Business Men's Fellowship International (FGBMFI). Begun in 1952 by Christian businessman Demos Shakarian, FGBMFI was designed as a movement of businessmen who met to share their changed lives with other businessmen. The strategy was simple: each member would invite someone from the business community to a meal during which other businessmen would explain what Jesus had done for them. Though the movement grew slowly at first, it eventually ballooned when well-known preachers—men like Oral Roberts and Gordon Lindsay—held special meetings to promote the cause. By the mid-1960s, the organization had exploded into more than three hundred chapters with a total membership of more than one hundred thousand men.

When the movement's leaders heard Derek's teaching tapes, they knew he was just the kind of man they needed. Though Derek still had a thick British accent—which reminded his American listeners of the

BBC announcers they had heard during the war—his teaching was precise, unemotional, systematic, and practical. It was just what a movement such as FGBMFI needed. Businessmen often didn't relate to the loud, sentimental preaching of the average Charismatic minister. Derek was a refreshing change, offering a clear, organized message that businessmen could understand.

Derek also got results, and businessmen, who were trained to think in terms of the bottom line, liked seeing "real world" benefits. This was because Derek not only taught but he also prayed for people and received spiritual insights about their lives that left them changed. After teaching on curses, for example, Derek might look at a woman and say, "Madam, I sense that your father often told you that you would not amount to anything. I'm here to tell you that it isn't true." Then, placing his hands on the woman's head, Derek would pray against the curse and command spirits that had enforced the curse in the woman's life to come out. There might be a shriek or a violent shaking for a moment, and then the woman would be calm. All who knew her would acknowledge in the days after that she had been deeply changed. When Christian businessmen and their wives heard of such transformations, they wanted Derek to join their work.

It was usual for a FGBMFI conference to schedule Bible teachers during the day and businessmen's testimonies at night. Derek first found a home in the movement as a teacher in the daytime sessions. To the delight of crowds throughout the country, Derek gave balanced, systematic instruction on themes like the power of God's Word, the need for the baptism of the Holy Spirit, prayer, holiness, and the power to cast out demons. His ministry was wildly popular, for people had seldom heard such solid exposition of the Scriptures or experienced such unemotional yet amazingly fruitful ministry following the teaching. Throughout the network of FGBMFI, Derek Prince came into huge demand, and, given that by 1972 the membership of the organization had grown to more than three hundred thousand, this was no small achievement.

Derek now found himself straddling his growing reputation in FGBMFI and his duties as the pastor of a local church. He was feeling an old frustration: the tension between the "teacher-at-large" he felt called to be and the responsibilities of a good shepherd. Increasingly, he had come to see his Seattle church as a "middle class social club that meets on Sunday morning."

People came to church, paid their tithes, heard the weekly sermon, and went back into their lives until the next Sunday. There was little change and even less impact on the broader world.

This frustration moved Derek to consider other directions for his ministry. Early in 1964, he was approached by the fledgling Oral Roberts University about taking a faculty position. The offer must have thrilled him. What better situation could he have than to be on the faculty of a Charismatic university where he could teach all that he had learned without restraint and yet still have the freedom to travel and speak around the country? Clearly, Derek wanted the position. He would not get it, though, and the reason why is telling.

On his application for the ORU position, Derek had listed as a reference the director of the Pentecostal Assemblies of Canada, a man named G. R. Upton. When the provost of Oral Roberts University, J. D. Messick, contacted Mr. Upton for information about Derek and Lydia, he received a kind letter in return but one that included a condemning paragraph that probably brought ORU's consideration of Derek to an end. Though he spoke glowingly of Derek's teaching and administrative skills, he then wrote:

> All of his past history would indicate that he does not remain long in any one position or location. And so far as we can ascertain from our experience with his family, we found that certain problems have always developed with regard to Mrs. Prince's association with those about them. I am writing to you confidentially. Mr. Prince has unusual ability; and if he is engaged there are the prospects of certain personality problems developing, if one is prepared to take those risks in securing the advantages of his services.

It is hard to know what Mr. Upton intended. He had to know that this paragraph would end Derek's chances of being on the ORU faculty. Perhaps he was given to sour grapes over Derek's departure from the Pentecostal Assemblies of Canada. It is also unclear what problems had developed around Lydia. She was certainly as bold and plainspoken as a human being could be, but she does not seem to have left a trail of offense wherever she went. Still, this episode in Derek's life is important for two reasons. It demonstrates that the Charismatic Movement was growing up and valuing good teaching like never before, and it shows that Derek Prince was quickly gaining a national reputation as a solid, Spirit-empowered teacher of God's Word.

The rejection by ORU was far from a stinging rebuke, but it did make Derek wonder where best to live out the powerful brand of ministry God seemed to be giving him. He began to contemplate a move out of the pastorate, and he put the matter before God in prayer. He decided that if God wanted him to leave the pastorate, He would have FGBMFI invite Derek to be a banquet speaker at their special Fourth of July conference in Philadelphia. Derek prayed and waited, and the invitation came. As usual, his time of ministry in Philadelphia thrilled the attendees and took his already rising reputation to new heights. The crowd was also touched by seeing a British scholar sitting on the platform with his Kenyan daughter on his lap while attending a meeting designed to remember the founding of America. Derek never forgot the moment, both for what it symbolized historically and because it was the confirmation he needed from his God that his pastoral work was done.

Immediately after the meeting in Philadelphia, Derek returned to Seattle, resigned his pastorate, and prepared to move to Chicago. One of the senior leaders of FGBMFI was associated with a church called Faith Tabernacle, which stood in the Park Ridge section of Chicago, and he had invited Derek to teach there while continuing to travel as a popular speaker. Derek accepted, and in late summer of 1964 he moved his family to the Midwest.

The Princes would spend four years in Chicago, a trying season that proved to be far from the easiest of their lives. The astonishing demand for Derek's teaching ministry kept him away from home for weeks and sometimes months at a time. Often, he took Lydia with him. This left Joska, who remained behind so often that first Johanne and her family and then Elisabeth moved into the home to care for their little sister. Clearly, there was little family routine. To make matters worse, when the Princes first moved to Chicago, they lived in an apartment in a troubled part of the city. It was largely a Puerto Rican neighborhood that was beset by a great deal of crime and violence. This was not unusual, for in the late 1960s the cities of America were becoming cauldrons of unrest.

Chicago was the beginning of Joska's troubled relationship with American culture. She was only eight when the family moved from Seattle, and she must have felt the change deeply. A new lifestyle in a new city is a challenge to any child, but Joska had more obstacles than most. She would have been far darker than most of the blacks her Puerto Rican neighbors had ever seen, and yet her father was a tall Englishman and her mother was a short, plump Dane. It was confusing to her new friends. What was more, her parents were far older than the parents of her friends. Derek was almost fifty, and Lydia was in her mid-seventies at the time. Joska remembers to this day the questions, the embarrassment, and the snickers of her Chicago playmates.

After a year in the apartment, the Princes moved to a better section of the city, and life improved for Joska. Still, she wrestled with who she was. Though she delighted in the love of her parents, she also began to realize how being black set her apart—from her parents, from her friends, and even from the culture at large. She saw other black children on television, and it made her want a sister the same color she was. Her parents told her, though, that it wasn't possible. It may be that Derek missed the larger issue in Joska's soul. She was beginning to realize that as a Kenyan girl living in America with white parents, life would never be as it was for other girls her age.

At the same time that Joska was finding her world a bit more troubling, Derek and Lydia were beginning to hit their stride. Freed from the pastorate and widely in demand, Derek felt that he was just beginning to live out the true calling on his life. Wherever he spoke, he not only taught the Bible, but also he told his audiences of his life's journey, of the truths he had learned, and of the challenges and the victories he had passed. His message was as much who he was as it was what he said. This intensely personal brand of ministry began to make him a father to the spiritual renewal then underway in America, just the kind of elder statesman the ungainly Charismatic Movement needed.

To understand how this was so, it is important to understand the brand of ministry that was common among Charismatics in those days. By the late 1960s, the renewal was still in its infancy, but it had lived long enough to grow a certain style of ministry. Like the Pentecostals before them, Charismatics had disdain for overly doctrinal teaching. Most Charismatics had been in mainline churches when they stepped into the renewal and tended to associate highly structured preaching with the deadness of their former churches.

Ministers in the early Charismatic Renewal soon learned that their audiences gravitated to a casual, exhortational style of preaching. The goal was changed behavior and spiritual power, not understanding. A sermon would usually begin with the reading of Scripture, but the speaker might never explain the text or refer to it a second time during his talk. Instead, he would most likely illustrate an opening point with personal anecdotes and the testimonies of people in the congregation. Humor, personality, and spiritual force were the keys to pulpit success.

Though this style of ministry was effective in launching the movement, in time it left hungry Charismatics yearning for greater depth. The very idea of the Charismatic Movement—with its focus on the work of the Holy Spirit, tongues, miracles, demons, and spiritual power—demanded a fresh understanding of Scripture. Exhortation moved men to act, but spiritual power came through believing truth, and this required teaching. Many began to understand that the old Pentecostal idea that "if you get your learning, you lose your burning" was silly. Charismatics began to value knowledge that led to faith and thus to power. This created a demand for "anointed" teaching followed by effective personal ministry—prayer for the sick, casting out demons, giving revelations about people's problems. It was just as Charismatics realized what they truly needed that Derek Prince stepped into view.

What Derek offered his growing audiences in America was exactly the kind of biblical truth that had sustained him through the years: in the sandy furnace of northern Africa, in the backwater of Palestine, on the teeming streets of London, and in the spiritual wilderness of Kenya. Having no church culture to shape him, Derek had quite naturally approached Scripture with the same logic and systematic investigation that made him a respected scholar. He understood that the Bible was God's Word, filled with spiritual power for those who believed it, but he also knew that God had used men to write the Bible. This meant that the elements of history—religion, language, culture, politics, and race—all have effect on the interpretation of Scripture. Decoding these came naturally to Derek as a scholar of classical literature.

When he stepped on the American stage, then, Derek combined three elements that were rarely merged in a Charismatic leader: mastery of the biblical text, a sensitivity to the voice of God acquired through years of experience, and a clear, systematic style of teaching. Audiences who heard him for the first time learned more of the Bible in one session than they might have from a dozen other sermons. Yet, they witnessed no fewer miracles or dramatic moments of ministry than occurred with other, more exhortational ministers. What was more, many Charismatics who had secretly wondered if what they had come to believe was truly biblical found under Derek's teaching that Charismatic doctrine grew organically from the pages of Scripture. This only deepened their faith, made them bolder in spreading their message, and matured the movement as a whole in a way that was desperately needed as the tumultuous decade of the 1960s neared its end.

Derek's effectiveness in ministry led to financial success for the first time in his adult life. With the increased income he was earning from his speaking, he bought the first house he had ever owned. It was a simple, suburban home near the church in the Park Ridge section of Chicago, but it was dear to Derek and Lydia.

In fact, it was this house that led, in part, to Derek Prince moving to the city that would become the launching pad for his international destiny. Early in 1968, Derek had been asked to speak in Florida, and when he did he was amazed by the beautiful scenery and inviting climate. His years in Chicago had been among the coldest and snowiest on record. Derek hated the cold and often jokingly commented that he ought to repent because he was "a sun worshiper." Africa had worked its way into his soul and given him a love of warm, sunny climates.

As he reflected on the beauty of Florida, it occurred to him that his ministry was such that he could live anywhere in the country. He seldom spoke in Chicago by this time because he was always on the move throughout the United States. He could live most anywhere so long as there was a large enough airport to get him to his meetings. It was just as he was beginning to suggest the idea of a move to Lydia—and was secretly house-hunting on his trips to Florida—that his son-in-law called him while he was on the road. George Hedges, Johanne's husband, asked Derek if he was sitting down because he said he had bad news. The house next to Derek's had caught fire and was completely destroyed, but the blaze had also badly burned Derek's house. No one was hurt, he said, but the damage was extensive.

Derek realized that rebuilding his house would not only be expensive, though there was insurance to cover the bill, but it would make the house unlivable for quite some time. He saw the crisis as an opportunity, though, and suggested to Lydia that the time had come for a move. When he described the glories of Florida and the lives they might have there, Lydia couldn't resist. In 1968, Derek sold his house in Park Ridge, put $5,000 down on a $25,000 home, and moved his family to the city that would become more associated with the Prince story than any other in America: Ft. Lauderdale, Florida.

10

A Teacher for Our Time:
To Heal the Broken Stream

"DEREK, IT STRIKES me that you first entered America the year that Kennedy was shot and the country began unraveling. You then rose to prominence just before the country celebrated her bicentennial. That set you up for huge impact on the United States, and yet you still feel your primary calling is Israel. Can you help me understand?"

"I did not see it clearly at the time. I was simply doing the next thing the Lord told me to do. Yet I believed then as I believe now that Britain lost her empire because she turned her back on the Jews. As you know, I was there as a witness to that betrayal in the events leading up to 1948. I realize now that the Lord may well have placed me in America when He did to reconnect the American church to her spiritual roots and to awaken her to the priority of Israel. Had America turned her back on Israel along with everything else she was enduring in the 1960s and 1970s, she might have perished as a nation."

"Can you explain what you mean by America's spiritual roots?"

"As a Britisher, I had known only a little of the history of America's beginning. I knew there were Christians who helped settle the nation, but to say the truth, that did not seem unique to me. There had also been Christians instrumental in settling South Africa and Australia, too. Yet in 1970, the city of Plymouth, Massachusetts, celebrated the 350th anniversary of the landing of the Pilgrims. I have described this in *Shaping History Through Prayer and Fasting*. But the sponsors of that event invited me to give a series of addresses at the Church of the Pilgrimage there in Plymouth, and they also introduced me to the writings of the Pilgrims.

"I started reading *Of Plymouth Plantation*, by William Bradford, one of the leaders of the Pilgrims. He described the Christian motives of the Pilgrims and how they prayed and fasted constantly. I began to understand that the early settlers of America entered into a covenant with God for the land. I realized that it is a covenant that must still exist in the heart of God, and I knew then I was to awaken the American church so that they would renew that very covenant. It was clearly a divine moment. You must remember that in the early 1970s the country was still reeling from the '60s and still suffering the disillusionment of Watergate. God seemed to be saying, 'You have leaned to your own ways in running this country. See what it has produced? Now, return to My ways.'"

"Did it seem odd to you, as an Englishman, to be calling America to her founding vision?"

"You must remember that America's early settlers were English. An 'American' would not exist for almost two hundred years."

"OK, you got me there. But how did it feel to you at the time?"

"I felt it was perfectly as the Lord would have it for an Englishman with an African daughter to speak to the nation about her history."

"Did the American church hear you?"

"Some did. Sadly, the renewal of those years seemed to go in two directions. Some wanted to welcome the power of the Holy Spirit, renew the ancient covenant, and thus change the course of history with what God was doing. Others seemed to want a blessing only for themselves. This gave rise to the extremes of prosperity and prophecy, so called. I think I see signs that those who wanted to change the world under God's hand are now making great strides, but there will always be, I suppose, the Charismatic sub-culture that only tends to itself."

"Can you remember how you felt about the Charismatic Movement when you first came to America?"

"It was like watching a child play with adult toys. Rather than seeing the outpouring of the Spirit as a call to maturity, to the person of Jesus, people leaned toward the thrills and the experiences of revival. People gathered around dynamic personalities whether they had any depth or not. The movement was fragmented, and no one could speak for the whole. It was tragic because God was doing powerful things in the lives of many, and there would have been much more had there been unity."

"Is that what you were trying to heal when you helped to launch the Discipleship Movement?"

"Yes. We wanted to bring unity and order, hopefully of a kind that would lead to maturity. I must say that I believe that God ordained the Discipleship Movement, but that the response of some people to it was very carnal. It was right in its original motivation, though. Ultimately, selfish ambition destroyed it."

"Even your own selfish ambition?"

"Yes, I am sad to say."

"And what did Lydia think?"

"She loved the men we ministered with in Ft. Lauderdale, but she sensed there was something wrong with the direction we were going. She kept telling me it had a wrong spirit attached to it."

"Can you remember her specific words?"

"To say the truth, no. But I've been told that not long before she died she turned to a friend with whom she had been discussing discipleship and said, almost in tears, 'They've got my Derek.'"

When Episcopalian priest Dennis Bennett received the baptism of the Holy Spirit in 1959, a new spiritual movement was born. True, there had been Pentecostals since the beginning of the century, and there had even been a neo-Pentecostal movement called "the Latter Rain" that arose immediately following World War II. This movement was led by what might be called "progressive Pentecostals," men like Oral Roberts, Gordon Lindsay, and T. L. Osborn, who wanted to make the power of Pentecostalism relevant to a modern world through publishing, film, television, and a more contemporary ministry style.

Still, when Dennis Bennett experienced what had once been the exclusive province of Pentecostals, a new day dawned. The Spirit began to move in denominations any Pentecostal would have deemed apostate—Episcopal, Catholic, Presbyterian, and Baptist, to name a few. Before long, seekers in every major denomination were receiving this transforming gift of the Holy Spirit, praying in tongues, and believing that miracles ought to grace the daily lives of the faithful. In time, the Full Gospel Business Men's Fellowship International began printing booklets with titles like, *The Acts of the Holy Spirit Among the Lutherans* or *The Acts of the Holy Spirit Among the Churches of Christ*. It seemed to many that God intended to reforge the church in America through the heat of spiritual renewal.

Sadly, these hopes would not live long. As the renewal moved into the mainline churches, the denominational authorities began pondering how to respond to this new phenomenon. Charismatics, many of whom remained in their traditional churches after receiving the baptism of the Holy Spirit, hoped that their churches would welcome them and the new expressions of faith they practiced. It was not to be. Almost immediately, denomination after denomination began speaking out against the renewal, and many Charismatics found themselves made increasingly uncomfortable in their former spiritual homes. Many were asked to leave if they would not renounce their Charismatic ways, and some were forced out of churches their grandparents had helped to build.

Rejected by the mainline denominations, then, the Charismatic Movement quickly reformed itself into a flotilla of home groups, Bible studies, prayer meetings, and conferences. Doctrinal distinctives faded to the background in meetings where refugees from most every Christian denomination worshiped in a passionately Charismatic style, listened to the teaching of the Scriptures, spoke in tongues, received revelations, and prayed for healing or deliverance from demons. The flagship of this flotilla was clearly the FGBMFI, but it provided little direct oversight to the thousands of smaller meetings that were fed by its conferences, publications, and cassettes.

There were benefits to this informality in the Charismatic Movement. Small meetings assured that individual needs were met and that the hurting were well-loved. Evangelism became a matter of simply inviting the lost into a home where a more mature leader would teach the Bible and perhaps present the truths of salvation. There were no time limits, no constraints. A meeting that convened in the early evening might stretch late into the night or shift emphasis as the needs of people and the sense of the Spirit's will dictated. In truth, the early Charismatic Movement anticipated much that later came to be associated with "seeker-sensitive" baby-boomer spirituality.

There were also dangers to this informality. In a movement in which any member might have a revelation, disorder often reigned. Eschewing structure, authority, and often leadership, Charismatic groups frequently suffered from competing revelations or doctrinal excesses, and no one was empowered to correct or discipline. As these groups grew in size, teachers or prophets with notable gifts were often invited to minister. Usually, these guest speakers brought the power of the movement to groups that would otherwise only know it in diminished fashion. Lives were changed, and the gatherings were refueled for service to others. Sometimes, though, these leaders had impure motives or planted the extremes of the movement in the local group. When this happened, deep wounds, broken relationships, and general confusion reigned.

When a teacher like Derek surveyed the Charismatic scene in the later 1960s and early 1970s, there was much to celebrate but also a good deal to prompt concern. Many Charismatics had overreacted to their former mainline churches and had discarded from their belief system anything that smacked of tradition, organization, or the very idea of doctrine. What little systematic truth survived often did so in horribly misshapen form. A truth that a biblically sound teacher might proclaim in a Full Gospel Business Men's meeting would often undergo disastrous reworking by the time it made its way to a local prayer meeting or Bible study. Doctrinal extremes, spiritual excesses, and social chaos often prevailed. For a man of order, system, and spiritual purity like Derek, things could not remain as they were. Something had to change, Derek believed. It might require extreme measures to make it happen.

�֎

When Derek and Lydia moved with Joska to Ft. Lauderdale in 1968, their increasing fame brought them into contact with an organization called the Holy Spirit Teaching Mission. Begun as a prayer meeting in the home of

Christian businessman Eldon Purvis in 1966, the mission evolved into an annual teaching conference that drew leading Charismatics from all over the United States. By 1969, the mission was sponsoring seminars in California, Georgia, and Ohio in addition to its meetings in several Florida cities. It also sponsored a four-week leadership course four times a year in Montego Bay, Jamaica, as well as several teaching tours and cruises. In June of that year, the mission started a monthly magazine called *New Wine*, which soon became one of the most influential publications of the Charismatic Movement.

The men who led the mission by the time Derek arrived in Ft. Lauderdale were a diverse lot. There was Don Basham, a former Disciples of Christ pastor who was transformed by the Charismatic Renewal and who became a popular speaker in Full Gospel Business Men's conferences. In 1967, he had decided to leave the pastorate and give himself to a ministry of writing and teaching. This landed him in Ft. Lauderdale in January 1968, a move largely prompted by the search for a more accommodating climate. Basham was a sensitive, creative soul whose messages were clear biblical truth laced with humor and moving stories. He was the guiding spirit behind *New Wine* magazine, and his literary gifts reached many souls his preaching never could.

Another leader of the mission was Bob Mumford. A Pentecostal by background, Mumford had an extensive academic background that he merged with a dynamic, entertaining speaking style to become one of the most sought-after speakers in the Charismatic Movement. His sense of humor, his desire to empower Christians to impact the broader culture, and his eagerness to heal the Charismatic Movement placed him before huge crowds and also brought him to the attention of Eldon Purvis in Ft. Lauderdale. In 1970, Purvis invited Mumford to move to Florida to be part of the Charismatic work there, and Mumford accepted.

The other leader of note in the mission at the time Derek arrived or shortly thereafter was Charles Simpson. A man of impressive administrative gifts, Simpson had been a Baptist pastor when he encountered the ministry of Ken Sumrall, a fellow Southern Baptist pastor who had embraced the Charismatic Movement. After receiving the baptism of the Holy Spirit himself, Simpson began traveling and ministering throughout the nation, having gained wide attention for his recorded testimony, an insightful yet humorous talk entitled *A Southern Baptist Looks at Pentecost*.

When Derek encountered these men, he felt that he had found brothers in arms. He and Lydia had ministered as a team for more than two decades by the time they arrived in Ft. Lauderdale, but they had seldom felt connected to other ministers. The Holy Spirit Teaching Mission welcomed them and brought them into contact with like-minded leaders who were also Charismatic, also gaining popularity throughout the country for their speaking ministry, and also concerned about the state of the renewal.

In the last two years of the 1960s, while Derek continued to answer his full speaking schedule, he also began to merge into the mission's events. He wrote for *New Wine* magazine, spoke at their conferences, and taught at the extended training sessions the organization sponsored. Increasingly, Derek felt he had found a spiritual family. He was no longer alone, in life or in leadership, and this endeared him to the growing team of Charismatic leaders then forming in Ft. Lauderdale.

In 1970, a crisis in the mission embedded him even more deeply in relationship with the other men. Under Purvis' leadership, the mission had accrued more than $36,000 in debt. The board of the mission and its leading personalities, like Derek, were stunned. In time, they would also discover that Purvis was a practicing homosexual. Not only did these revelations mean likely damage to the Holy Spirit Teaching Mission but also to the ministries of those who were identified with it. Derek was among them. As he later said, "We wanted out of it. Our names were associated with it."

Horrified by what they had discovered, Derek, Mumford, Basham, and Simpson gathered in a hotel suite at the Galt Ocean Mile Hotel on October 8, 1970. After discussing the crisis for a short while, the four knelt to pray. As Derek later recounted, "God did something very sovereign and supernatural. When we rose, everyone knew without speaking a word or asking a question that God had in some way united us together spiritually. . . . It was not something we asked God to do; it was not something we anticipated."

Mumford agreed: "On a hotel room floor, Don, Charles, Derek, and I encountered God and encountered one another. It wasn't a choice—it was an assignment."

That assignment, though, was unclear. Still, the four men soon found themselves assuming control of the Holy Spirit Teaching Mission. In 1972, the organization changed its name to Christian Growth Ministries (CGM) to reflect its deepening emphasis on teaching and training. Each of the men wrote for *New Wine* and spoke at CGM's conferences, yet maintained their individual ministry organizations.

With time, a doctrinal emphasis began to emerge that distinguished CGM from other Charismatic organizations. In 1972, Mumford wrote a series of articles entitled "Lawlessness," which focused on the need for practical obedience to God and submission to His delegated authority in all spheres of life. That same year, Simpson wrote an article entitled "Covering of the Lord," which argued that a believer is "covered" or "protected" by submitting to a God-ordained authority. And in a 1973 sermon by Mumford, everyone present at the Governor's Club of Ft. Lauderdale was given the unqualified charge, "You need to find a shepherd." The emphasis of CGM was clearly becoming the centrality of the shepherd/sheep relationship.

For Derek, the idea of every believer living under the guidance of a God-ordained authority had strong appeal. He not only saw this as the answer to the Charismatic Movement's excesses and immaturity, but he also believed that doctrinal sophistication and biblical depth could come from such mentoring relationships as well.

The fact is, also, that Derek was not as in touch with the emerging emphasis as men like Mumford and Simpson were. Throughout his life, Derek had maintained a capacity for detachment, an ability to be present in body but absent in mind. Though he agreed with the basic values of CGM and with what he knew of the other men's ministries, he was too absent and too preoccupied to focus on the possible extremes of the emerging CGM doctrine. It would prove to be one of the few black marks on the record of his ministry.

Derek's growing association with CGM increasingly made Lydia uncomfortable. By the early 1970s, she was in her eighties and had seen it all. An already blunt woman, she had become even more outspoken with age and with her deepening sense that Derek was becoming part of something that had the potential to compromise all that God had been preparing him for through the years.

When Eldon Purvis proved to be a homosexual, Lydia burst into a meeting that Derek, Basham, Simpson, and Mumford were having and demanded, "Is *this* your discernment?" She was disturbed that such spiritual men should be deceived, and she worried that there were bigger deceptions to come.

During the years of the early 1970s, when Derek was tightening his relationship with the other men of CGM, Lydia was working on her book, *Appointment in Jerusalem*. Because she spoke English better than she wrote it, she dictated the book to Derek, who in turn put her thoughts into the refined English he knew well. The work should have been a joy, the rewarding reflections of a fruitful life shared with a loving husband. Instead, the air was thick with tension as Derek and Lydia worked on the book. Their disagreements over the doctrines of CGM had begun to tear at the fabric of their relationship.

By this time, the Princes had been in America nearly a decade, and it had not been the easiest of seasons for Lydia. True, she had enjoyed an ever-increasing level of prosperity as Derek's ministry grew, and she had become something of a mother to the Charismatic Renewal. Still, she seemed alternatively disturbed and thrilled by the lives they were living.

Part of her discomfort was surely due to the constant emphasis on the twenty-six years that lay between she and Derek. The fact is that he had grown into a handsome older man. He was trim both from fasting and athletics. He loved basketball, tennis, and jogging on the beach. The Florida sun tanned his already lean, muscular body, and this combined with his still dark hair and his 1970s full sideburns made him a dashing figure. Lydia, on the other hand, began to look evermore like exactly what she was: a Danish woman of eighty years who had lived a hard life. Pictures of the two at the time immediately suggest a mother with her son, something their early photos do not. It was not uncommon for someone to turn to Lydia after Derek had preached and gush, "Your son did a marvelous job."

Perhaps it was comments like this that often made Lydia seem irritable. A minister once walked by Lydia sitting alone in a hotel lobby and kindly asked, "How are you doing, Mrs. Prince?" Lydia glared at him like he had denied Christ and snapped, "How am I supposed to be doing?" It was the first time the two had ever met. If someone hugged her—for hugging was common in Charismatic circles—and happened to pat Lydia in mid-embrace, she would immediately pull away and protest, "Don't pat me. I'm not a dog." Comments like these were largely reserved for American women, whom Lydia found to be an odd breed. "American women are always talking. Always cackety, cackety, cack," she complained.

It may also have been that Lydia was breaking out of the narrow, Pentecostal conformity she had known all her life. She had been a missionary, a pastor's wife, and a hard-working Christian mother most of her eighty years, and she may have found welcome relief in the freedom that was becoming a beloved hallmark of the Charismatic Movement. She seemed to be returning to who she really was and with a vengeance. Once when Derek was teaching at a conference in Philadelphia and some friends took the Princes out to lunch, Lydia casually ordered a beer. This was not unusual for Charismatics from, say, a Catholic or a Presbyterian background. But for Lydia, Derek Prince's wife and well-known Pentecostal, to order a beer during a Christian conference was sure to set tongues wagging. Clearly, she did not care, nor was it the last time she had a lager with her goulash in public.

Yet, to the confusion of those who were tempted to dislike her, Lydia could also be astonishingly gentle and deeply spiritual. She gravitated to the young, particularly the hippies and the troubled youths who made their way to Derek's meetings. The same Lydia who avoided hugs from overdressed pastors' wives held hurting hippie girls in jeans and fringed leather jackets as long as they would stay.

She was also known for her love of animals. She never stopped talking about her two dogs, Sammy and Susie, as though they were human. Derek had bought them for Joska, but Lydia took them as her own. She often prayed for animals, too. A stray cat wandered into a friend's yard, and Lydia, seeing a protrusion from the feline's belly, held it tenderly, prayed for it, and made everyone thank God the next day when the animal seemed to be healed. She did not have equal success with horses. A friend's horse died after Lydia prayed for it, and Lydia was so depressed that Derek chided her with, "You won't let a horse get your victory, will you, my dear?"

What almost everyone would remember of their time with Lydia was that she was amazingly perceptive spiritually. It was not uncommon for her to turn to someone she had never met before and say, "You know, if you will forgive your mother for what she did to you when you were five, you will be set free." She once walked by as a man who would become one of the Princes' longtime friends, Jim Croft, was praying for a woman to be delivered of demonic control. Lydia took one look, pointed to an amulet the woman was wearing around her neck, and said, "If she will get rid of this, she will be free." The woman removed the amulet, Croft prayed again, and deliverance came instantly. And as much trouble as Lydia seemed to have with adults, she had nearly none with children. She routinely held them against her matronly body as she prayed for them to be healed of asthma or gently led them into the baptism of the Holy Spirit.

Derek, knowing her depth of perception and having the ability to read her face with amazing precision, insisted that Lydia sit on the front row directly in front of him whenever he spoke so that she was always in his line of sight. If he made a point that was unclear or if he was feeling like he was slogging through mud as he spoke, he could take one look at Lydia to see the situation registered on her face and to know that she was praying. It comforted him, made him a better teacher, and inspired him to give his all when she was there.

In the first half of the 1970s, Derek needed Lydia more than ever. His ministry exploded. His speaking schedule was astonishing. One week he might be appearing at the Tennessee/Georgia Christian Camps in Eatonton, Georgia, and the next he would be at a Charismatic Catholic meeting in Green Bay. He spoke in Brethren churches, Assemblies of God sanctuaries, and Episcopal cathedrals. He laid hands on the sick and the oppressed in hotel ballrooms, in house church meetings, after highly liturgical services, and at training centers from Bangor to San Diego.

His fame spread in large part because of his books. He had published his *Self-Study Bible Course*, which met with wide acclaim, and before that his Foundation Series, a kind of Charismatic systematic theology, had become the rage among the more intellectual followers of the Holy Spirit. In 1973, he published *Shaping History Through Prayer and Fasting*, which framed many of the intercessory movements that grew up in anticipation of the nation's bicentennial and in answer to the crises of the early 1970s. In time, Derek's books would gain a reputation as the intellectual fuel of a spiritual movement and would be reprinted around the world.

One of the reasons that Derek's ministry expanded so dramatically in the early 1970s was the presence of his son-in-law, David Selby. At Derek and Lydia's invitation, David and Anna moved to Ft. Lauderdale with their children and took over the administrative work that Derek had been doing largely on his own. There were books to print and sell at Derek's conferences, tapes to duplicate, and newsletters to print and mail. The ministry grew from a backroom project to a guesthouse and then finally to a headquarters with a warehouse for storing materials. David's technical skills and gentle manner with Derek helped the growing organization to run smoothly and freed Derek to do the things he was made to do.

The "teaching letter" of those years reveals much about the ministry. Each letter was actually a stapled newsletter of several pages with a picture of Derek and Lydia on the front sheet and the words "A Personal Message" overhead. Inside, Derek offered light commentary on contemporary events, gave news of prayer events and trends, and offered his materials along with his schedule. There were also tidbits of personal news, of how a grandchild was doing, or of the joy the family felt when they gathered for a holiday. This drew the letter's readers into the Princes' personal world and accounts for the intense familiarity many of Derek's followers felt for him and his family.

It was just this sense of intimacy that fueled what came to be known as the Shepherding Movement. When the doctrines of submission to ordained authority and "covering" merged with the desperate need for order and leadership in the Charismatic Movement—and all of this joined with the exceptional gifts of men like Prince, Mumford, Basham, and Simpson—a new movement was born. The Shepherding Movement, also called the Discipleship Movement, would accomplish good in the lives of many, but it would also bring devastation to thousands and become one of the most damaging controversies in American Christianity.

The movement had no official beginning, but it may well be traced to the summer of 1974 and a series of meetings held by the men of CGM and a group of Charismatic Catholic leaders led by Steve Clark and Ralph Martin in Montreat, North Carolina. As *New Wine* magazine reported, "Over 2,100 pastors, leaders, elders, and shepherds gathered...for one of the most significant and powerful weeks the body of Christ has ever experienced. Leaders from around the nation and around the world gathered." The presence of Billy Graham at one of the meetings heightened this sense of history, and by the time the sessions concluded, *New Wine* was able to report:

> It was clear that the Spirit was speaking one message to his people: become rightly related to each other! The conference included teachings on authority and submission but also emphasized unity in

the church and the need for leaders to work together to build the house of the Lord....Those attending the conference came away with a sense of awe at the power that had broken men into tears, convicted them of their need for one another, and formed new and tight joints throughout the body of Christ.

Before the Ft. Lauderdale men could leave the conference, dozens of other men approached each of them to ask if they might become their disciples.

Among the leaders at the conference in Montreat was a man who would soon join the Ft. Lauderdale team. Older and more experienced than the other four, Ern Baxter was known for his sound teaching and engaging personality. He was born in Canada, later served famed evangelist William Branham, pastored a number of churches, and by the early 1970s was a noted speaker in the American Charismatic Movement. Baxter connected to the men of CGM at the Montreat meetings in 1974 and moved at their invitation to Ft. Lauderdale early in 1975. He was perhaps the best orator of the five and brought a depth of historical knowledge and theological sophistication that rivaled even Derek's.

Increasingly, men around the country began submitting themselves to Derek, Basham, Mumford, Baxter, and Simpson. Many moved with their families to Ft. Lauderdale and began living out the kind of relationships they had heard described on the tapes sent by CGM. Those who couldn't move to "the Charismatic Vatican" began to organize their prayer meetings and their Bible studies to assure proper covering and lines of authority. Even mainline churches were challenged to "get in right order" and submit to one of the famous teachers from Florida.

In March 1975, a historic conference was held in Atlanta's Red Carpet Inn. All five teachers brought together the men they pastored directly, and the doctrines of shepherding were imparted to their souls. It was a decisive moment in Charismatic history. Men signed written covenants of commitment to their pastors and took Communion not only as a remembrance of Jesus but also as a sacrament of devotion to their human shepherds.

Perhaps because he had secret reservations, Derek was "there in body, but absent in spirit" at the Atlanta meeting. These words, which are his, well describe his unfocused approach to the entire movement. Though observers would soon note a Prince/Basham wing of shepherding—focused more on deliverance, prophecy, Israel, and other Charismatic themes—as opposed to a Mumford/Simpson wing—focused on "Kingdom" matters like proper government—Derek seems to have begun distancing himself at heart from the movement almost from the start. The fact is that he nevertheless remained publicly in support of the movement, and this dichotomy is hard to understand. Derek's defenders have suggested that he was simply too busy to know about the excesses that were occurring with mounting frequency. They have also insisted that Derek was more concerned with teaching than he was with structure and government. In his later years, Derek himself would offer similar explanations. While he would never contend that he had no part in the movement's beginning, he did often suggest that of all the Ft. Lauderdale teachers, he was more distant, more disconnected, and therefore less responsible.

Clearly, such contentions angered his fellow teachers and for good reason. To them, Derek seemed as much an instigator as they were. Derek's own news-letter confirms that this was true. In his teaching letter of winter 1975, Derek not only anticipated the National Shepherding Conference in Kansas City, Missouri, scheduled for September of that year, as an "epoch-making" event, but he also described the start of a church in Ft. Lauderdale, Good News Church, as a place where "rightly structured personal relationships" would be taught. Clearly, he believed in the shepherding ideal, taught it internation-ally, and encouraged those who held its firmer line.

If Derek's heart did indeed fade early on from the Shepherding Movement, it was likely for the same reason that Derek faded from life for a time: on October 5, 1975, Lydia Prince died. She had not been feeling well for some months, and Derek had not known if it was physical or emotional. In fact, Johanne and Magdalene had moved to Florida in part to care for their mother.

The work on *Appointment in Jerusalem*, now finished, had been gruel-ing, and Derek wondered if that might have tired her. Perhaps more of a concern, she was worn with worry over what the Shepherding Movement might mean for Derek's ministry. When the other teachers had come to the house one evening, she rose from her bed in her nightgown, embraced them each warmly, and told them that she loved them. Clearly, she was trying to overcome her resentments, particularly for Mumford whom she saw as the instigator of a "cult."

At three in the morning on October 5, Lydia awoke and told Derek she felt ill. Derek called Johanne and said, "We have to take your momma to the hospital." On the drive, Lydia's condition did not seem to be severe. She giggled once, and when someone asked her why, she said that Jesus had just told her He was pleased with her. She then began giving Derek instructions about endorsements for her book, a project she was very proud of. At the hospital, nurses put her in bed, administered a battery of tests, and gave her breakfast. Privately, the doctor in charge took Derek aside and said there wasn't much he could do. She was an eighty-five-year-old woman whose heart was giving out. Derek kept the news to himself.

Derek drove home to tell Joska what was happening, have breakfast, and phone the rest of the girls. Later that afternoon, the hospital called to say they should all return. Standing in a row by her bed, the girls—Joska, Johanne, Magdalene, and Anna—all spoke to Lydia and told her of their love. Then they prayed. Lydia prayed as well, first in English, then in Danish, and then in tongues. Over and again she gave thanks to her God, specifically expressing her gratitude for the blood of Jesus. She also blessed her daughters, each by name: "Bless Joska, sweet Joska. Lord, bless Joska." Then, when Derek sensed she was fading, he told her they all loved her. Over and again Lydia thanked her God for the blood of His Son. Her last words were in tongues. Soon after, Derek heard the heart monitors go flat, and he knew Lydia was dead. The sound of the monitors would haunt him the rest of his life.

Lydia's funeral would draw most of the major ministers in the American church. For the Pentecostal Dane who had ministered alone in the backwaters of Palestine, police would stop traffic throughout Ft. Lauderdale and air traffic controllers would scurry to land the chartered flights needed to get the grieving to her side. With all of her daughters in attendance, Lydia was buried with the first copy of her life's story in her hands.

At the funeral, the congregants laughed and wept at the tales of her boldness and her strength. One story suffices. When Lydia was being interviewed for consideration as an American citizen, the officer in charge asked her if she would bear arms for her new country. Though the question was silly for a woman her age, Lydia thought for a moment and said, "If it was for my girls, I'd fight like a lion."

Moved by her spirit, the officer said, "Madam, you are a remarkable lady." And so she was.

Lydia's death devastated Derek. Joska still remembers the animal-like cries of grief that sounded from her father one night as he wept for his dead wife. He was with friends, and they were trying to comfort him but to no avail. The gut-wrenching torment in his soul formed itself into uncontrollable sobbing and screeches so heartrending that his comforters found themselves undone and unable to offer Derek any solace. And they wept together.

After Lydia's death, the Princes' dear friends, Jim and Prudence Croft, came to live with Derek and Joska. This was a standard shepherding practice, one in which a disciple would live with his shepherd and serve him. In this case, it was also a dire necessity. Partly out of the desire of the grieving to stay busy and partly because of his growing fame, Derek began to travel more than ever. This left Joska at home, and someone had to see to her needs.

Joska had not known an easy time in Ft. Lauderdale. Part of this was her age. Like any teenager, she had the usual conflicts with her parents. She skipped school, argued with her Pentecostal mother about the Beatles albums she cherished, and fought over clothes, pierced ears, and curfews like most any other American girl of the age.

But Joska suffered far more than her parents knew because of her color. She had come to Ft. Lauderdale at the age of nine and found herself the only black child at her elementary school. This was hard, and she yearned for a school with children of her own kind. Then she went to a mixed-race middle school and found this harder still. She clearly wasn't white, but she was also too different from the other blacks to fit in. Her features were more purely African, and her skin was a beautiful, deep ebony that set her apart from American blacks. Tragically, this only made her an object of ridicule among her own race. Then four years of high school came, and her horrors multiplied.

In what should have been among the best years of her life, the American high school experience, Joska found herself a victim of astonishing cruelty and hate. When she walked down the halls of her school, boys who thought her African features unattractive would begin barking and shouting insults. They stole her books, mimicked her walk, and jeered at her. Joska worked to avoid her nephews and nieces during the school day so that the other students never learned she was related to whites. To keep from riding the bus with the white children from her upscale neighborhood, she rode her bike halfway and then walked to make it look like she lived in a black neighborhood near her school. Her great fear was that one of her parents would show up. What would her tormenters do with her white father or her eighty-year-old white mother? When Derek came to pick her up from school, Joska hid. He never knew why.

With her high school experience proving so traumatic, Joska moved to Kansas City not long after Lydia's death to live with Derek's friends David Rose and his family and to finish high school. Life improved for her. She received her diploma, began living independently, and in time joined her father for a trip to Europe and Israel, on which she saw the pope. She spent her eighteenth birthday in Jaffa, Israel, and, having learned to love the land as her father did, returned the next year to live on a farm called a *kibbutz*. It is hard to find a more unusual life than Joska's, but she emerged from her winding path a woman of great grace and beauty.

Lydia's death signaled the start of a painful season in Derek's life. As he later understood it, his grief over Lydia opened the door of his soul to the loneliness that had stalked him all his life. It is not hard to understand how this was so. With his wife of nearly thirty years no longer near, his daughters grown and out of the home, and the press of ministry keeping him constantly on the road, Derek began to feel like the hunted prey of a tormenting spirit. He found himself battling the depressive blackness at every turn: in a lonely hotel room, in tortured late night hours, in the temptations that reached to the unanswered longings of his soul, and in the echoing quiet of his now empty house.

To make matters worse, the controversy over discipleship began to cost Derek friendships at the very time he needed them most. People who had been his most ardent supporters now sensed a spirit of control about his ministry and began to pull away. Some would never return. Others, like his daughter Johanne, would always love him but felt that discipleship drove a wedge between them that was never removed. It was painful, both for Derek and for those who had devoted their lives to him and now felt betrayed. It left him feeling fragile, needy, and even more alone.

It did not help that these years of private struggle were filled with his most public battles. In 1975, the same year that Derek entered an almost debilitating season of grief over Lydia, many of the major leaders in the Charismatic Movement took public stands against discipleship. Pat Robertson, head of the highly influential Christian Broadcasting Network, not only spoke out against shepherding but also banned the CGM teachers from his network and erased all recordings of their previous appearances on CBN shows. Robertson then proceeded to call shepherding "witchcraft" and stated on the air that the only difference between what the "Ft. Lauderdale Five" were doing and the death cult of Jonestown was the Kool Aid.

It got worse. That same year, the flamboyant but hugely popular Kathryn Kuhlman refused to take the stage at a Jerusalem Conference on the Holy Spirit when she learned that Bob Mumford was also scheduled to appear. It was a humiliating blow, both to Mumford personally and to the whole Shepherding Movement. This was nothing compared to what came next. Demos Shakarian, the founder of Full Gospel Business Men's Fellowship International—the organization that had launched virtually all of the CGM teachers to national acclaim—now decided that they were all heretics to be shunned. This was as close to a denominational split as the Charismatic Movement was capable of.

Chaos reigned and bitterness prevailed. Attempts to heal the rift died in despair. Late in 1975 at Ann Arbor, Michigan, and again at Oklahoma City in 1976, leaders gathered to convince, rebuke, and declare. The meetings evidenced more heat than light, and the Charismatic Renewal continued to tear itself apart.

Overblown myths fueled both camps. Those opposed to shepherding told of men who could not write a check or bed their wives without permission from their pastors. The emphasis on tithing to shepherds personally rather than to churches or ministries fueled the myth that greed powered the whole movement. Then there were the tales of men who served their shepherds but let their wives and children go hungry, or of attractive women who were kept near their shepherds while their husbands were assigned elsewhere. As with most controversies throughout history, myths took on the air of fact in the retelling and, in this case, fed a Charismatic need to see the other side as demonically influenced rather than simply in error.

Those who spoke for shepherding understandably felt falsely accused. When Pat Robertson's daughter suffered cruel headaches, he concluded that she had come under a curse sent by Ft. Lauderdale prayer meetings. Others concluded that Kathryn Kuhlman's untimely death occurred for much the same reason: the followers of Basham, Prince, Simpson, Mumford, and Baxter had "released a spirit of death over her life." Such views escalated the controversy over shepherding from a disagreement about theology and church leadership into a battle between good and evil. The Ft. Lauderdale men consequently saw the opposition to their movement as an assault of Satan on a pure work of God.

The real damage, though, was being done to the average believer, to the hungry souls who filled living rooms, store fronts, and hotel ballrooms in pursuit of Jesus. They wanted simply to be righteous and to sense the nearness of their God. If this meant submitting to the wisdom of an older believer, they would do it. If it meant battling spirits that drove them to lust or addiction, they would fight until they were free. Whatever was required—listening to tapes, confessing verses of Scripture, submitting to authority, buying the right books, praying the right formulas, or giving everything they had—they would do it if they could only live a better life and feel the love of God.

Sadly, both camps in the shepherding controversy failed them. Leaders who opposed the movement were often as motivated by territorial concerns as they were theology and largely because their own ministries were threatened. A gathering of discipleship devotees in Kansas City drew more than fifty thousand souls, a massive number by any ministry's standards at that time. Moreover, name-calling frequently passed for biblical examination, and personal animosities masqueraded as spiritual discernment. There were few critics of shepherding who conducted themselves so as to rescue hurting Christians from the grip of error.

In the same way, the Ft. Lauderdale Five were moved by a kind of ambition that blinded them to the destructiveness of their movement and by a brand of spirituality that kept them from seeing their critics as the unpaid guardians of their souls. The more they were opposed, the more they banded together and concluded their opponents were "of a wrong spirit" or "blinded by the spirit of the age." As Derek later said, "We each were filled with self-ish ambition and did not realize until too late the damage we had done."

✕

It is possible that what ultimately became Derek's break from the Shepherd-ing Movement actually began in the tension over his choice of a second wife. Derek had never intended to offend. In fact, he later admitted his greatest sin in the discipleship mess was a fear of being thought disloyal. Yet, when his fellow shepherds did not approve of his decision to marry, the strain cre-ated fracture lines that would, in time, lead him to sever ties with the other men in the Ft. Lauderdale Five.

Derek had never done well alone, and the agony of living as a single man was ever on his mind. By the late 1970s, he was more than sixty years old. He found little that attracted him in women of his age, and, even if he had, the pace of his life prevented any meaningful relationship with a woman from developing. The young men who tended him often heard him declare that he would never marry again. Secretly, though, they knew that he was only trying to convince himself. No one they knew needed to be married like Derek Prince.

It was just about this time that Derek joined a number of other leaders on a trip to Israel. A dear Catholic friend, Cardinal Suenens of Belgium, was celebrating his fiftieth year in the priesthood with a trip to the Holy Land, and Derek felt honored to go along. After the rest of the group left Israel, Derek stayed behind to pray about the course of his life and ministry.

He decided also to visit an organization that had been distributing his books in Jerusalem. Not long before, he had received a letter from the orga-nization, and he wished to thank them personally for their work. He remem-bered, too, that there had been a handwritten note on the side of the letter. It read: "I want to thank you for your ministry. It has meant much to me over the years." It was signed "Ruth Baker."

When he inquired about this woman at the organization's offices, he was told that she was at home at her apartment because she had seriously injured her back. Derek had experienced a great deal of success in praying for people's backs to be healed, and he decided to go and minister to this woman named Ruth. He and his driver wandered the streets of Jerusalem for some time looking for her address and were just about to conclude that God was not in their plan when Derek looked up and saw the house they were looking for.

When they entered the apartment, Ruth was lying on the sofa in her living room in obvious pain. After a moment's conversation, Derek laid his hands on her and felt that God gave him an encouraging word about Ruth's future, which he shared with her. Her countenance lightened immediately, and Derek then began praying for her back. When he was done, the three exchanged further pleasantries before Derek and his driver left.

On his last night in Israel, Derek tried to go to bed at his usual time, but as soon as he lay down he felt the nearness of his God. He also heard the Voice again, the same one he had first learned to respect in the deserts of Africa those many years ago. The Voice reminded him of scriptures and of the promises he had been given over the years. Then Derek slept. In the early hours of the morning, a vivid picture appeared. He was awake now, but an image formed before him as though it were a dream. He saw a hill sloping steeply upward before him, and it reminded him of one that sloped up to Mount Zion at the southwest corner of the Old City of Jerusalem. He sensed immediately that this image represented his path back to Jerusalem.

Even more intriguing, though, was the vision of the woman. She was seated on the ground just at the point where the path he had seen started up the hill. With her blonde hair and Western features, she was clearly a European. Yet, she was wearing a green Oriental-style dress, and she was bent forward in a strained, unnatural position that suggested pain. Suddenly, Derek realized the woman was Ruth Baker.

He was confused for a moment and turned the matter over in his mind. Yet as soon as he did, certainty came. As he later wrote, "Before I had even formulated the questions, I knew the answer. It did not come to me through any process of reasoning. It was not even something God spoke to me. It was just there, settled in an area of my mind to which doubt had no access. God intended the woman to become my wife."

Returning to the States, Derek was excited but concerned. He knew many people who had wrongly thought God told them who to marry and who had made horrible messes of their lives. He must be cautious. After much prayer, he decided to write Ruth and see where it might lead. In his letter, he told her that if she was ever in the States, she might want to visit a church in Kansas City known for its love of Israel. Not long after he mailed the letter, he received one in return from Ruth saying that she and her daughter were soon leaving Jerusalem for the States and assuring that she would visit the church in Kansas City. She also gave a phone number where she could be reached.

Derek strained to hide his excitement. He quickly rearranged his schedule so he could meet Ruth in Kansas City. Not long afterward, he found himself in the home of a pastor friend talking again with this intriguing Ruth Baker. On the first day, the two talked as people do who are just getting acquainted. On the second day, though, Ruth made an appointment to discuss a problem with Derek and appeared wearing an unusual Arab dress of just the kind and color he had seen in his vision. Ruth then apologized but explained that the pain in her back was lessened if she sat on the floor against the wall. When Ruth positioned herself as she had described, Derek looked at her and saw to his amazement that she looked in every detail as the woman had appeared in his vision.

As he later wrote, "I was unable to speak. I could only stare at her in awe. Then a warm current of supernatural power surged through my body, and I was filled with an inexpressible love for this woman, who was still outwardly a stranger. For a few brief moments we sat there in silence. Then, with an effort of my will, I mastered my emotions and began to inquire about the problems that had caused her to seek my counsel."

Derek was smitten but was now more cautious than ever. Thankfully, he had to leave immediately for a ministry tour in South Africa, yet all the time he was there he could not get Ruth off of his mind. He knew two things: he loved this woman, and he intended to marry her. He decided to send Ruth a telegram asking that she meet him at the King David Hotel in Jerusalem at a certain day and time.

When the appointed day arrived, Derek met Ruth in the lobby of the King David, and the two had breakfast together. All the while, Derek plied her with questions about her life. He was fascinated with her, but he was also probing for the signs of God's confirmation in her story. The details tumbled out. She was a descendant of the early Pilgrims, grew up in the Midwest, had served in the Marines, and was a Messianic Jew. Each of these truths only endeared Derek to her more. She had been married, she explained, and was now divorced. Derek leaned in. He had clear views about divorce and remarriage. There were only two biblical reasons for a proper divorce—adultery and abandonment—and without these Derek knew he could never marry Ruth. As she explained the tortured path of her marriage, Derek came to understand that Ruth was free to marry again. Relieved, he pressed on with his myriad of questions.

Into the late afternoon, Derek and Ruth sat on the veranda of the King David and explored each other's lives. Finally, Ruth explained that Derek's questions had worn her out, and she could answer no more. She needed a rest. Derek knew his moment had come. He drew a breath, looked into Ruth's questioning face, and told her of the vision of the woman and the hill that led to Jerusalem. "That is why I invited you to meet me in Kansas City," he explained, "and why I've invited you here today. I believe it's God's purpose for us to be married and to serve Him together. But you can't decide on the basis of a revelation God gave me. You have to hear from Him for yourself."

Ruth did not seem shaken by what she heard. With a gentle tone in her voice, she replied, "After we had been together in Kansas City, I told the Lord that if you were to ask me to marry you, I would say yes." Both of them felt immediately that a lifetime commitment to one another had been made.

Later that evening, Derek explained that he now had to check his feelings for Ruth with his brothers in Ft. Lauderdale. "We've agreed not to make major personal decisions without consulting one another," he explained. "For that reason I'm not free to go any further with my commitment to you until I've spoken to my brothers. However, I believe God has made His will plain, and He will work it out." The next day, Derek returned to the United States to tell the other Ft. Lauderdale men about Ruth.

It did not go well. When Derek explained to Basham, Simpson, Baxter, and Mumford what seemed so obviously God's will to him, they saw only the problems. Ruth was divorced, they reminded him, and for a visible Bible teacher to marry a divorced woman would only diminish his ministry and lead others astray. Moreover, Ruth had serious physical problems and would be more of a burden than a help, not to mention that she was nearly twenty years younger than he was. Nothing about the relationship seemed right. The men would not approve the marriage.

Derek was undone. This rejection by his friends was a bitter pill. He thought seriously of casting aside the counsel of his fellow leaders and pressing ahead with what he believed was God's will. Yet to do so violated all that he had taught and all that their movement was built on. He relented. He called Ruth and told her what had happened. Later, in Jerusalem again, he sat with her and explained all the objections the other men had. "I feel we need to break off all contact with one another," he explained, "except the contact we can have by prayer." Ruth agreed, and when Derek saw her drive off in a taxi, he felt a bit of winter return to his soul.

To this point, everyone who lived this tale agrees that these are the facts. It is what happened from this point on that rankled Derek's peers and left them feeling, even years later, that they had been played. Unable to let the matter rest, Derek continued to press the men to reconsider. Some of Derek's friends took this as a godly appeal. Others thought it was arm-twisting, an unrighteous attempt to wrest consent where it had not been given.

It is hard to know what happened behind closed doors. What is certain is that on October 17, 1978, Derek Prince and Ruth Baker were married with more than six hundred people in attendance. Every one of the Ft. Lauderdale leaders took part and gave no sign of their dissent. Clearly, this seeming unity betrayed a private reality. As the Discipleship Movement came unraveled, the anger over Derek's marriage to Ruth surfaced. As one of the group later revealed privately, "That marriage was far from God's will. Derek wanted it and Derek got it, but it was never God's will. I think, for the discerning, time told the tale."

11

Remembrance:
An Evening With Derek Prince

"DEREK, I HAVE to ask you some difficult questions. Are you ready?"

"As much as I can be, I suppose."

"When you tell the story of falling in love with Ruth, you say that you submitted your desire to marry her to the other Ft. Lauderdale men and that when they objected you acquiesced. Then you say they changed their minds, recognized the marriage as God's will, and gave permission. Surely you know by now that these men felt their arms were twisted and that they never did think Ruth was right for you. They say you badgered them into giving permission. I'm sorry to state it so bluntly, but how do you answer this?"

"I can only say that as far as I know my heart I intended to entrust the matter to God and hear His will through my brothers. I did believe marrying Ruth was the will of God. I thought that the other men looked only at the outside of the situation—that Ruth was divorced, that she was not the most healthy of women, that I had previously said I would never remarry. It seemed to me that God worked in their hearts to change their view. If that was not the case, I never knew it. I think the fact that all of them attended our wedding and gave their blessing formally should speak for itself."

"Are you aware that some of the men see your marriage to Ruth as the first in a series of betrayals? They think that you entered into covenant with them, then kept yourself at a distance, forced them to approve your remarriage, and then abandoned them while criticizing the Discipleship Movement. I know I am treading on painful memories, but can you answer this view?"

"I am surprised that anyone would hold this view. I had often been a negative voice in our discussions. For quite some time I had been concerned about personal ambition—which I think ultimately killed the work—and about inexperienced men being put in positions of authority. The men knew my concerns. And I've already addressed the marriage issue. I thought they approved. Their actions seem to verify this."

"But can you understand why they would feel as they do?"

"I think time has worked a distorting effect on memory. I did not leave the movement over Ruth. I left because I could no longer support it. I thought we were becoming a denomination. The truth is, I had been more distant from it than the other men. My first wife had died. My ministry was rapidly growing and in an overseas direction. I had also remarried. All of this pulled me away. I simply was not as involved as the other men. I don't say this to shed blame. What kept me connected to the movement was my fear of being disloyal. I think I may have taken this too far. I probably should have left much earlier."

"How did the end come?"

"It was rather undramatic. I simply drifted away. My departure received almost no mention in the press or in *New Wine*. I didn't feel any need to write about it in my newsletter, either. So, it looks more significant all these years later, but at the time it was rather unremarkable."

"What were your failings in the movement, Derek?"

"I believe that the movement was God-ordained and right in the original motivation, but I think selfish ambition took control. In my case, I wanted to be a popular and recognized Bible teacher. I saw the Discipleship Movement as a means to that end, just as the other men saw it as a means to achieve their dreams as well. It was sin for all of us. We messed it up, but the beginning was right and of the Lord."

"How do you think now about the pain the movement caused?"

"It is one of the saddest notes of my life. Ern died hurting and in virtual isolation. Don, the most tender of us all, certainly died of a broken heart. Bob suffered health problems for years. All of this was due to the strain, I'm sure. But I care most about those who were wounded in those days and so turned away from the Lord. It is a hard thing to bear. I've asked the Lord to bring them all home again."

"So you left in 1983. What happened next?"

"Well, to say the truth, the best years of my ministry began. The anointing of God was stronger than ever, Ruth was a marvelous aid, and the world opened up to me. We were on the radio. The books were becoming even more popular. Ruth and I were splitting our year between our home in Jerusalem and world travel. I think the years and lessons of my life converged in that next decade and a half. I believe I fulfilled the commission of the Lord like I never had before."

"What do you remember most from those years, Derek?"

"Probably the Spirit's work through me. The hand of the Lord was strong upon me during that time. There were many miracles, and the teaching I did had exceptional grace attending it. When I think back on those years, what I remember most, though, are the hungry faces, the millions of faces of people who were desperate for the Word of God. What a privilege I had been given. All my years were preparation to answer that moment in that hungry generation. I will see those faces in my mind until the end of my life."

It is a Friday night somewhere in America, and Derek Prince is about to speak. The year is 1988.

On this last night of a conference, the crowd is eager. Momentum has been building, and everyone is certain that Derek Prince will have the "word of the hour," that he will capture in one teaching what God is doing on the earth and how true believers should respond to it. He has done it before.

It does not really matter what this particular conference is about. The topic might be any of a dozen favorite Charismatic themes: "How to Walk in the Anointing," "True Prosperity," "Deliverance From Demons," "Your Prophetic Destiny," "The Tongue and Its Power," "Knowing the Will of God," "Healing for the Soul," "Walking Under Authority," or "How to Maximize Your Marriage," to name a few. Given the year, the conference may well be on God's will for Israel or the timing of the Second Coming. It has been forty years since the birth of Israel, after all—a biblical generation. Surely God is going to do something special this year, and Derek Prince will know what it is.

It also does not matter exactly where this conference is taking place. The scene could be most anywhere Christians gather, from the Hilton in Denver to a community center in West Texas, from a Methodist church in Boston to a Catholic cathedral in St. Paul, Minnesota. Or Murfreesboro, Tennessee. Or Ann Arbor, Michigan. Or Dallas, Texas. For that matter, it could be anywhere in the world: a school in Christchurch, a hotel in London, a city park in Nairobi, or a chapel in Berlin.

It doesn't really matter where we are on this Friday night in 1988 or why we are here. What really matters is this: Derek Prince is about to speak.

The crowd has been gathering for some time. They are an amazingly diverse lot, a cross-section of the Charismatic Movement. There are housewives and businessmen, construction workers and airline pilots, pastors and newly released prisoners. There are husbands and wives, families with children, and singles enjoying a date. There are rows of teenagers sitting with their college-aged youth pastor and whole sections of blacks who have come on their church's bus and now sit together like extended family.

There are men with crew cuts sitting beside women with large hair and men with shoulder-length hair and beards sitting beside women with crew cuts. A young man in the middle section has dyed his hair blue and formed it into spikes using Elmer's glue. Two rows behind him are five girls the same age sporting high school letter jackets and long, wet hair. They have just come from volleyball practice and are glad to have made it in time to find seats together. Sitting around them is an Episcopal priest, a policeman still on duty, two homeless men brought by the local street mission, and the pastor of the largest Pentecostal church in town accompanied by his well-adorned wife.

There are people from every possible religious and theological background here tonight. Some have spent years in the cults that arose in the 1960s and then turned to Jesus when the more avant-garde gave no answers. Others have come into the Charismatic Movement straight from their secular lives: perhaps through the spreading power of Christian television or the ministry of a dynamic local church. Most, though, have spent years in mainline denominations before "coming into the fullness of the Spirit," as they would say. Sitting here tonight are Baptists who once thought that Pentecostals were mentally unhinged and Episcopalians who once thought them heretics. There are Presbyterians who used to think all Charismatics were on par with snake handlers and Methodists who were open to anything but the miraculous. Now they are here to listen to a former Anglican Pentecostal/Charismatic pray in tongues while he heals the sick. They laugh together at their former foolishness and tearfully hug those they once condemned.

In the third row, sitting expectantly, is a man in a clerical collar. He is a Catholic priest, still an unusual site at a Charismatic meeting. He is watching the crowd with a peaceful smile and is occasionally interrupted by the unannounced hug of a fellow conferencee. Since the Charismatic Movement is as much about love as it is about truth, the non-Catholics in the room are happy to see this priest. Some have left denominations that insist the pope is the Antichrist and the Catholic church is the whore of Babylon. Now, filled with the Holy Spirit and ready to love anyone who calls Jesus Lord, they are thrilled this priest is here. To drive the point home, a former Presbyterian greets the man with a crushing hug and is followed by a newly Charismatic member of the Church of Christ and a woman who attends the First Assembly of God in Des Moines, Iowa. Later, they will tell friends about the time they hugged a Catholic priest. It is a sign of what God has done in their lives.

The priest himself has quite a tale to tell. A ruffian in his youth, he was drawn to the church by the love and manly ways of a Jesuit who went to seminary in Washington DC. The Jesuit loved basketball, told good jokes, and fought tears when talking about the mission of the cross. This impressed the future priest and began to stir something in his heart. He felt it during the Mass and when the father talked to him while wearing his robes. There was a pull, an otherworldliness that somehow was familiar. It made him press into God, and when he did, he began to feel a drawing. Some said it was a call. He knew what he wanted to be: a priest at the altar of Jesus.

He went to seminary at Notre Dame and served in a number of small parishes until he landed at a prominent one in Cincinnati. It was there that his crisis began. He was popular, and his parish was well tended. But he knew there was something missing inside. Duty had killed devotion. Over lunch with a fellow priest, he heard that other priests often felt the same way but that a renewal was quietly sweeping through the church. It was changing hearts and filling clergymen with new passion. Some even said miracles had occurred. A Roman Catholic layman named Ralph Martin was holding conferences to introduce Catholics to a relationship with the Holy Spirit. There were other leaders in this renewal, as well, but they had all been influenced by the same man: Derek Prince. The priest was intrigued and immediately decided to hear this man as soon as he could find him.

Now, the priest is sitting quietly, remembering his journey, and barely able to contain his excitement. He senses he is going to receive something tonight. An answer of some sort, a reply to his ache.

Come, Holy Spirit. Tonight. Touch me through Your servant Derek Prince.

In the back on the right is the woman from Des Moines, Iowa. Having hugged the priest she is now sitting quietly, dabbing tears from her eyes. She is here. She never thought she would be.

It had taken some time to convince her husband to let her go. He never had understood, really, why she wanted to hear this man Derek Prince. But the teacher's words had set her free, and she had to come. Tapes and radio broadcasts weren't enough. She needed to be there in person and, if God was willing, to ask this Mr. Prince or his wife to pray for her themselves.

She had grown up in an army home with army chapels as her only tie to faith. Then, she had married a dashing young lieutenant. Twenty years and three children later, she found herself straining for life. She was in trouble. She loved her family, but she just could not give them her every waking moment anymore. She began to drink, and her heart began to roam. Just when she might have made a horrible mistake, a friend told her to talk to a chaplain. She had refused. Most chaplains were dull, cloying men. Her friend understood, but this one was different. So she made an appointment and went to the chapel. Two hours later, she emerged born again.

Jesus became the love of her life. Every moment she could she spent praying, reading, and trying to learn more. In a newsletter she found on a friend's coffee table she learned about this Derek Prince and his radio ministry. She tuned in and heard the kind of teaching her soul longed for. It was clear and wise, balanced yet deeply spiritual. She listened every day, ordered books and tapes, and devoured what this man had to teach.

Then she learned of this conference. It was an answer to prayer. She had long believed she needed help, that there was some kind of weight, maybe a spirit, that lived in her soul. A curse, perhaps, from her harsh father, or an assignment of evil against her passion for God. She would go, if her husband would let her, and get the help that she needed. Then she would be free. Her husband would see the change and maybe join her. Maybe then they could be one in the things of God. Maybe they could even serve Him together, like Derek Prince and his lovely wife Ruth.

So she is waiting, moved that God has made a way and praying that tonight will be the turning point. Perhaps one of those dramatic moments of change she has long heard are possible will happen to her in this place.

O God, meet me, Your handmaiden. Make me fully Yours on this night.

On the other side of the room, making his way to his seat, is a middle-aged man with a beard. His hair is brown and beyond his shoulders. His eyes are blue, laughing, and seem to be always near tears. He is not tall, but he is wiry and strong. His muscular arms extend from the faded blue laborer's clothes he has not had time to change. While he talks to an elderly lady in the aisle by his seat, he does not notice that the high school girls in the letter jackets are pointing him out. They are chattering, giggling, signaling his way. They have just realized who he looks like: he reminds them of Jesus in jeans.

Though they could not have known it, this is just what he hopes he will be. His dreams have not always been so noble. He entered his late teens just as the 1960s were heating up and remembers sitting with friends late into the night listening to the Beatles and smoking weed. Then he graduated to heroin, something he turned on to at Woodstock. He can't explain it, really, but he felt more love among the dropouts and druggies than he ever did at home. So he followed the river of lost souls to California, and his life became a series of flop houses, coffee shops, drug dens, and dives.

In the early seventies, he needed a change, and he hitchhiked back to the East Coast. He was lonely and walking the backstreets of Philly one day when a sweet-looking girl walked up to him, handed him a flower, and said, "Jesus loves you, and so do we." Gazing behind her he saw a band of youth who looked just like him. They gestured him along, and he followed them back to their place, a kind of half-church, half-bunkhouse called "The Joint."

It turned out they were Christians but not like any he'd seen. They had all been dealers or hookers or thieves. But they had all been changed and talked about new lives. He didn't understand, but they loved him anyway and told him that a few days later a man was going to be speaking in their place who would probably set him straight.

So, he waited and basked in their welcome and grace. Two days later hundreds of people crammed into their center to hear an older man with a British accent. His name was Derek Prince. He must have been sixty, but he talked about his own youth and about doing goofy things like painting his toenails pink. He said that the youth were close to the kingdom of God, that they had thrown off the stifling materialism of their culture and were just where God wanted them to be: ready for truth at any price. So he taught about Jesus and how He heals broken lives out of love.

Our young man couldn't take it. When the older man came to an end and asked people who wanted to know Jesus to meet him at the front, this young man flew to his side. He prayed to receive Jesus and welcomed the Spirit into his life. Soon after, he found himself praying new words he had never heard before, and just when he was feeling so light he thought he might fly away, he realized Derek Prince was staring him down.

"You have a spirit, young man," Mr. Prince announced abruptly. "It is a spirit of loneliness, and I know it well. If you are willing, it will come out. Is this what you want?"

The young man barely understood, but if there was something more that needed to happen, he wanted it. He nodded yes, the kindly man placed his hands on his shoulders, and commanded a "foul, lying spirit" to come out. The younger man crumpled. It felt like someone had reached into his stomach and pulled out a long sheet of gritty material. It almost hurt, but just as it grew intense, it stopped. He sat on the floor, feeling a strangeness and aware of someone praying for him from behind. It was the kindly man's wife, and she was quietly praying, "Love, Lord. More love for this child." And the young man wept—for hours—but he never felt lonely again.

Now, he is here on this night because he wants all that God wills to do. He has made it to as many Derek Prince meetings as he could over the years, and each time he has been changed. This time he yearns for the next step with God, for whatever the Spirit will do. And Derek Prince is the vessel, a man who will listen to God and let the Spirit do His thing.

Lord, meet me here as You have in the past. Make me the clean vessel You've called me to be.

There are a thousand stories in the room just like these. Some are new and have never heard Derek Prince. Most, though, have been changed in a crucible of their lives by the words this man spoke or the prayers this man prayed. And though they know that Jesus is their source, that it is His truth and His power that has changed them, they do not hear this truth in as undiluted form when others speak as they do in the ministry of Derek Prince. So they come, by the thousands, and they hope. And now they are here.

It is time to worship. A bearded man playing guitar leads singing with the help of two women and a second man on piano. They lead choruses that are so commonly sung in Charismatic churches that there is no need for a hymnal or lyric sheets. Everyone knows them, and even if they don't, the words are so simple they can easily be learned by the second time around. And there will be a second time. And a third. And probably a fourth. Charismatic choruses aren't sung like hymns. The point is not to finish the song; the point is to enter the presence of God. Songs are sung until the goal is achieved.

Without pause, the bearded man leads the singing from one chorus directly into another. He has chosen songs from the Charismatic liturgy, tunes that come from the movement's informal canon of worship. There is a rowdy, Hebraic-sounding tune called "Jehovah Jireh," which is about how "my God shall supply all my needs." Then there is a sweet, tender round about how "as the deer panteth for the water, so my soul longeth after thee." The lyrics are taken directly from Psalm 42. In fact, many of the older choruses are word for word from the King James Bible, which was very much the style in the early days of the Charismatic Movement when people seemed to want to sing nothing but the Bible.

The final song is a folk version of "Amazing Grace." The last verse is sung simply as "Praise God" over and again to the tune of the classic hymn. Everyone can sing this: the priest at his first Charismatic meeting, the man who is just out of jail, the woman who has never been in a church but was brought by a friend, the youth who lean more toward U2 but are now feeling in the flow.

Most of the people have their hands raised and their eyes closed, singing their hearts into the face of God. If they open them even for a second, they will notice that Derek Prince and his wife Ruth have slipped into the front row. They are worshiping, kneeling, crying out to God—lost in their own stream of devotion.

The singing comes to an end, and everyone stands quietly still. They are waiting for God to speak, for a prophecy or a spiritual language to sound over the crowd. There are a few coughs and the sound of shuffling feet. Then a voice from somewhere behind: "'My children, know that I love you most dearly. Know that I have brought you to this place and this time, for this is a time of deliverance and this is a time of My choosing. Rest in Me in this place, and I will perform that which I have promised. And you will leave here changed to the praise of My glory,' saith the Lord." There are shouted "amens" and "hallelujahs," and when another quiet moment or two has passed, the bearded worship leader bids everyone sit down.

A man steps to the podium and adjusts the microphone. He is a local pastor or a prominent Christian leader of some sort, perhaps a radio personality or the Christian weatherman on the local station whom everyone will know. He welcomes the crowd and reminds them of how exciting it is to have so many different Christian denominations and movements represented tonight. There is applause and shouts of amen. He tells them to stand and greet those around them. This takes ten minutes or so and creates so much noise and commotion that the man has difficulty regaining control. He doesn't mind. There is love in this room and the kind of spiritual excitement that makes the commotion worth it. He waits, jokes about how heaven will be just like this, and urges them to be seated.

When he has told them how they can get tapes after the service and how they can put their names on a mailing list, he turns to his final task: introducing Derek Prince. In what has become a standard Charismatic style, he tells the crowd of a troubled time in his life and how a friend gave him a tape by Derek Prince. Tears fill his eyes. He relates how he was set free by what he heard on that tape and how his family was changed. He hopes the same for everyone present. Now he regains control and says that it is his honor to introduce God's man of the hour, Derek Prince.

Derek steps to the podium, and people immediately notice that he is a trim, stylishly dressed man, particularly for his age. He is seventy-three, after all, and not only does he look good for his years, but he is also unusually trim for a preacher. People are used to a bit of corpulence from the clergy, but Derek breaks the mold.

Some Charismatic preachers are known for a joking and talking stream of consciousness for nearly half an hour before they say anything of weight. Here again, Derek breaks from the pack. He is focused. He has been in prayer all day and has been meditating upon his talk. Like a loaded gun that aches to fire, he is ready to set his aim. Still, he is warm. He talks about the spiritual power of the meetings in the conference and of his regard for the men who are in charge. He has been eager to spend this time with them, he says, and before he begins his teaching, he would like to call up Ruth.

Derek leaves the podium and steps to the side of the seat where Ruth Prince is sitting. He offers his arms and she, unsteadily, rises and takes small steps at her husband's side until she reaches the podium at the front of the stage. She is not elderly, but she does have severe circulation problems in her legs and often feels them weak and wobbly. Derek stands beside her as she greets the waiting crowd.

She is an attractive woman with a full figure and bright white teeth that flash readily when she smiles. Her voice is high but pleasant, and she speaks with the firmness of a matriarch to her tribe.

What immediately strikes many in the crowd is that her head is covered by a scarf that matches her dress. Those who may have seen her before the meeting probably did not notice the scarf. It was wrapped about her shoulders and would have looked like a stylish adornment to her dress. This is what she intends. When she steps into a service, though, she raises the scarf over her head and binds it loosely about her neck. For her, this is more than a matter of style. It is her spiritual duty.

Despite the Charismatic emphasis on freedom from human convention and traditional ways, Derek Prince and his wife believe that women should cover their heads in spiritual services. This is confusing to some, a false doctrine to others. Derek believes that St. Paul's injunction in the Book of Corinthians that women should cover their heads in church was not merely addressing a first-century problem of prostitutes and misbehaving women; it is the rule of God for all time. Ruth seldom appears without head covering, then, even if it is a bandana wrapped around her head while she prays for the sick in Uganda. In fact, she has virtually invented a style of dress that allows her to look stylish on the street but still be ready to cover her head in an instant of need. Other women follow suit, and it is not uncommon to find ultra-modern Charismatic churches all over America in which women cover their heads while in worship.

Sometimes these women copy the style but fall short of the meaning. In one Nashville church, barefoot young women in halter tops and shorts cover their heads with a shawl while dancing before their God. This is the legacy of Derek Prince, though he would wince at the inconsistent application of his views.

Ruth merges gentleness with authority as she tells of her prayer life with Derek and something God has shown them this day. She has a mystical air. To some, it is endearing and makes them wish they knew God as she does. To others, it is a style, a chosen affectation, and one they hope the women in the Charismatic Movement won't take as their own.

She is deferential, though, and speaks submissively of her husband and his gifts. Her final words are of her excitement at what he is about to share and how she, now, must get out of the way. As the crowd thunders their approval, she makes her way slowly to her seat on her husband's arm and sits down, returning her thanks to the audience with a smile.

Derek returns to his podium and announces his subject. Perhaps this time it is "Our Debt to Israel" or "Life's Bitter Pool" or "The Marriage Covenant." He may tell his personal story in the oft-repeated "From Philosophy to Christ" or he may do a primer on driving off demons called "The Basics of Deliverance." If this last topic is his choice, he will certainly joke that the subtitle is "Everything you ever wanted to know about demons but were afraid to ask."

Whatever his subject, Derek will announce it with a seriousness that rivals a declaration of war. He does not regard what is about to happen as entertainment or merely the fodder for another series of tapes. He has prayed, labored, and struggled for this truth he is about to teach. It has been hard won, perhaps in the agony of military defeat in the Second World War or the poverty of a Kenyan village or the personal fight with a demon of despair. He has mined these truths, paying dearly for their presence among the people of God. In his mind, he is here to set a people free. There is no more important matter at hand.

Because he feels the gravity of this moment, he is sure to say something about how vital his message is for this particular audience. It is not uncommon for him to announce, "I cannot think of any audience in the world for whom this message is more important than you," or "It is certainly the will of our Lord that we are about to consider this text at this time." They are the words of a man who feels himself destined, of a preacher who speaks as one rescuing dying men.

He reads his text, then. As the man of system that he is, he gives a one-sentence outline of his plan: "I wish first to consider the origin of demons, and then the means of their defeat before I discuss the myths about evil spirits that keep the people of God bound." This thesis statement is in nearly all of his talks. It is the valuable holdover from his life as a scholar, the imprint of Cambridge philosophical dialogue upon this now American Charismatic preacher.

If the members of this audience are typical, they will focus their ear for a moment on his pleasant British accent. It is familiar to most of them from the tapes and radio broadcasts they listen to by the hour. In fact, many in this crowd have spent more time listening to the voice of Derek Prince than they have any other human being. His accent seems to be one with his character and the truth that he teaches. It was not always so. When he first came to America, his accent was strong and often kept Americans from understanding him. Now, it has mellowed, as he has, and become a smooth, almost otherworldly conduit to truth. It is not unlike the Bible recordings by a British narrator that have become so popular. Something about spiritual things spoken in a British accent sounds holy to Americans, perhaps a holdover from the days of Hollywood Bible films, and this makes Derek's manner of speech seem like an extension of his message.

He has planted himself behind his podium. If custom proves true, he will not leave that spot until it is time for ministry. Instead, he turns from side to side, sometimes moving his feet as he turns and sometimes simply twisting from the waist. He moves so he can see his audience, not so that they can see him. He is visual, piercing. Often he complains about the lighting. He wants to see what the Spirit is doing as he speaks.

If he doesn't move, he does gesture. His favorite is the pointed finger, which more often than not is pointed upward, like a mother telling a child, "I will tell you *one* thing!" His other favorite hand motion is a sweeping gesture. It comes when he is speaking of the flow of history or the entire tale of the Bible. "In the whole of human history," he might say, sweeping his right hand from one side to the other just over his podium, "there is nothing to equal Paul's letter to the Romans."

There is nothing overt that happens as he speaks, but it is not long before some in the audience have an experience that is new. There are connections happening in their minds. It is as though some force is taking Derek's words and drawing lines from his themes to scriptures they already know, teachings they have already heard, and ideas that have occurred to them in prayer. A matrix of truth becomes embedded in their mind. They understand more than they ever have, easily seeing the world in terms of the truth Derek describes. Later, when they are home, it will not be as clear, and they will realize that Derek's teaching ministry is as much about the environment that is around him as it is the specific truth he teaches. Some call it being "under the anointing," and others speak of a "spirit of revelation." No matter its name, it is the most defining aspect of Derek Prince's speaking ministry: people envision while he speaks what they have not before and cannot as well afterward. So they stay close—through tapes, books, radio, and conferences—until what once was new becomes a permanent part of their mental system. It is why millions of them worldwide unashamedly claim Derek Prince as their spiritual father, the man who planted those transforming truths in their lives.

He is winding to a close now. Some wonder what he will do next. There are times when he invites people to receive Jesus for the first time. When this is the path he chooses, he often asks everyone to close their eyes, and when they do, he tells briefly of his own salvation. As he does, tears come when he recalls a lonely British soldier finding Jesus in a Scarborough barracks all those years ago. So now he offers the same salvation to others.

It is more likely, though, that he will assume his listeners are saved and that he will minister to the crowd as a whole. If he has spoken on deliverance, he will have the people who want to be set free stand and repeat words after him. Then he will command the demons to go. He will do the same with healing or the cleansing of past wounds or the imprint of a curse. This is a method he has learned from the press of ministry. He had to do something. He used to remain for hours after he taught, ministering to each individual in need. It exhausted him and left him feeling there was a better way. So he started leading his huge crowds in mass ministry sessions, and he found the results were just as good without the strain.

Still, it is likely he will sense the Spirit's leading to pray for a few one-on-one. There will certainly be a prophetic word or two for people he calls out of the crowd. Then he will pray for healing. With the crowd looking on, he will call a woman forward from the crowd, and she will confirm what he sensed to be true: she has a severe back problem. Derek will ask her to sit, and then he will explain that while he has special grace to pray for backs, the Lord has shown him that most back problems are a result of people's legs being uneven. He will ask her to push the small of her back to the rear of her chair, and then he will ask her to take off her shoes. She will be embarrassed. Derek Prince is now kneeling before her with her feet in his hands, and she cannot suppress a giggle. Derek knows the drill. He jokes that she should not be nervous, that he has smelled feet around the world. The humor works. The woman settles, and the prayer begins.

Derek will ask people to gather around who want to see. There is an inch difference between the length of the legs, and now he is going to pray. He commands the short leg to lengthen. It does. The nearby crowd applauds with glee, and the woman rises from her chair and gratefully hugs Derek and Ruth with tears streaming down her cheeks. As she returns to her chair, people reach out from the crowd to touch her and congratulate her on the blessing she has received.

Time is passing, though, and after others receive prayer, it is time for the service to end. The crowd is in disarray. There are people weeping in the arms of those who came with them for the joy of the healing they have received or the deliverance they have just found. Others are quietly worshiping to the tune the piano player has been quietly offering while ministry has been underway. Many in the room, though, are kneeling and praying for this powerful moment to continue in the lives of those not here.

The man who introduced Derek now steps to the podium and calls everyone to sing a closing song. Derek and Ruth, with the help of ushers, gather their Bibles and make for the door. The crowd interrupts the speaker to applaud. They have not had a moment to thank Derek Prince, and they risk being rude to offer their love. He waves an arm in reply before slipping out the door with Ruth on his arm.

The crowd will end with singing, and then they will rush to the tables. Their first concern is the tapes. Each person present can think of a dozen others they wish had heard this teaching. Tapes are the key. Thousands of tapes will be made, with the duplicating machine whirring at full speed to answer the crowd's demands. If there are two thousand people in this meeting, there may well be ten thousand tapes sold.

Then there are the books. Derek has dozens in print, and each of them has a title that promises changed lives. Truckloads will sell with orders for more arriving at Derek Prince Ministries by mail in the weeks to come. Indeed, so many Derek Prince books have sold that after his death people who know nothing of the course of his life or even that he has passed away will remember a moment in their journey when a Derek Prince book intervened.

Now there is a new way to replay the evening: the videocassette. Many will order this medium and gather loved ones in living rooms to relive the moment and the power. Though these will never surpass the reach of the audiocassette, they will let Derek live long after he is gone.

The tapes, the books, and the videos will go from this conference to the nations of the world. Mothers will mail them to children at college, and pastors will send them to friends overseas. Cell groups will gather in suburban living rooms to play the tape of this evening's events. Preachers will teach as their own what Derek has imparted in churches around the world, and thousands of phone calls will begin with "You *have* to hear what Derek Prince said!"

And on the videotape, the voice of an announcer tells the story. He says that Derek Prince Ministries takes "the inspired Word of God to the ends of the earth," that they are devoted to "reaching the unreached and teaching the untaught." Derek—"one of the leading Bible expositors of our time" with "more than thirty books in forty languages and radio broadcasts that reach half the world—travels the globe with his wife Ruth, teaching God's Word, praying for the sick, and providing insight into world events."

And so it was in 1988.

12

If I Forget You, O Jerusalem:
Home

"**D**EREK, HOW WOULD you like to be remembered?"

"As a teacher in the body of Christ and father to a movement that survives me. I want Derek Prince Ministries to last until Jesus returns, always seeking out new ways to penetrate the nations with God's Word."

"What is the most important truth you have learned about life?"

"God is faithful. He keeps His word. He is a rewarder of those who diligently seek Him. I cannot emphasize this enough. It is the greatest truth of my life: God is faithful."

"What is your greatest regret?"

"That I did not forgive more quickly. I have had long seasons of wrestling with unforgiveness in my life."

"Can you name one of them?"

"When Full Gospel Business Men's Fellowship came out against deliverance and then rejected me for discipleship, that hurt. I felt it was personal and more about control and competition than it was about truth. I seethed over that for a long time, and it damaged me. I wish I had been a better man."

"What is your biggest concern for the church today?"

"The church should not be part of the world. When the church is not part of the world, what the Holy Spirit does is good, but when we ask the Holy Spirit to bless what is carnal or a mixture, it is not good. I'm concerned the carnality in the church and the worldliness are going to grieve the Spirit and hinder what God wants to do in the last days."

"Do you have specific concerns for America?"

"In America, the most necessary message is separation from the world, of which there is very little. Americans are a nation of businessmen. I don't see this in any other nation. This is not a criticism. Sometimes it is a necessity. But if business doesn't follow biblical principle, then it is unfortunate, and the American church is veering that way."

"What about England?"

"I believe that England may be the first Western nation to fall to Islam. It is already happening. This is due to the loss of true Christianity and a lifting of God's grace because of how Britain treated the Jews. I'm afraid I do not have much hope for England unless she undergoes total, national repentance. One of the things that has led to this state is the British passion for niceness. If you want to be 'good' in the United Kingdom, you never say anything bad about other people. But often that means you're not acknowledging the truth. Britain desperately needs the truth, but some who love her will have to be very un-British to give her the truth she needs."

"Do you have anything to say to the next generation?"

"I hope I have said it with my life. I will tell you this, though: each new generation must be very careful about what it accepts from their parents' time. It is true that we want to receive good from those who have come before us, but we must also understand the difference between living truth and ensnaring tradition. I have a great deal of hope for the youth I see today. They truly are young lions who roar after their prey. They are hungry for truth and willing to pay the price: in fasting, in prayer, in labor, and in devotion to the Word of God. It gives me great joy to pass what God has done through me to such willing vessels."

One of the pleasant yet unusual truths of Derek Prince's life is that he reached the zenith of his influence and fame in the latter decades of his life. Not all men are so blessed. Some peak early in their lives and then drift or decline until the end. Some never peak at all. Others rise and fall repeatedly, their life's path resembling the outline of a small range of mountains. Derek Prince's life rose gently, and though he rejected any discussion of fame in reference to his work, he did welcome the mounting influence of his life as evidence of God's grace.

The natural reasons for this continuing rise in his last two decades are easy to understand. He had come to America armed with lessons of prayer for nations and deliverance from strongholds of evil just when the church and the country desperately needed them. He was the right man with the right message at the right moment in time. Later, he emerged from the discipleship debacle largely unscathed. This was both because of his distance from the movement during its worst days and because he was perceived as the hero of truth who left once the whole thing went wrong. He therefore became an elder statesman figure at a time when the Charismatic Movement was led largely by younger, more untested men. Perhaps more, the level of spiritual power in his life only heightened as he aged. This was evidence of his devotion to prayer, to fasting, and to obeying the Voice that had long been his guide.

In addition to these critical factors, he also made some brilliant decisions that took him where he had not been before. In February 1979, Derek announced to readers of his newsletter that he was starting a daily radio show called *Today With Derek Prince*.

> For several months, I have been impressed that the Lord wanted me to undertake a new outreach through radio. After much prayer, God made it clear to both of us that I should plan a daily broadcast, from Monday to Friday each week, dealing briefly with specific themes, of which some are covered more fully by my books and tapes, while others are completely new. I began my ministry in the U.S.A. in 1963 on radio, with a systematic Bible teaching program which eventually took the form of my seven "Foundation" books, and has

thus gone on blessing thousands of people ever since. I feel confi-
dent that there are many people today who could be reached and
blessed no less effectively by my ministry through radio.

This decision to start a radio broadcast would prove to be one of the
most important of his ministry. It was a perfect fit both for him and the
times. Derek's teaching style was perfectly suited to filling twelve and
one-half minutes of airtime with concise, transforming truth. Moreover,
the age of Christian radio was just then emerging in America. It was not
long before his supporters caught the vision and empowered *Today With
Derek Prince* to become one of the most influential teaching broadcasts on
Christian radio.

Derek recorded his show in a studio with Ruth and an engineer as his
audience. He rarely made a mistake or had to start over, and he had an
uncanny ability to end right on time. Only once in his radio career did
he make a false start. He was teaching in the sound booth with Ruth
watching him from the other side of the soundproof glass. As he had with
Lydia, Derek drew from the attention of his wife while he spoke. On this
occasion, Ruth, who was usually adoring and attentive, decided to file
her nails while Derek spoke. Flustered, Derek stopped in mid-teaching
and yelled through the glass, "What are you doing?" The engineer and
Ruth both looked up at Derek in shock. He had never interrupted himself
before. All three erupted in laughter, and then, when they had composed
themselves, Derek started his teaching over again—Ruth's nail file safely
tucked away in her purse.

Today With Derek Prince would become the flagship venture of Derek
Prince Ministries. In most every city of any size in America and in many
cities around the world, the distilled teaching of Derek's life was broadcast
at a time and in a format calculated for greatest impact. Believers were
not only treated to a brief but nurturing tour of God's Word, but they also
came to know Derek's life in a way that endeared him to them and fostered
respect. Wisely, Derek offered his books on the air and announced parts of
his speaking schedule. His ministry grew dramatically. More importantly,
millions were fed a rich spiritual diet in a format that penetrated their
busy lives.

A second decision that strategically extended Derek's work was the start of the Global Outreach program (GO). At the end of 1983, Derek and Ruth sensed that God was telling them to make Derek's books and tapes available to leaders in foreign countries who might not otherwise have access to them. The program began with Derek writing twenty-three leaders he already knew around the world and offering them books and tapes without charge. The overseas leaders were ecstatic, and the idea captured the hearts of contributors in America. Two years later, the GO program had sent material to more than five hundred leaders in fifty nations on six continents. At its most successful stage in the early 1990s, the program gave over two hundred thousand books and tapes to more than sixteen hundred international leaders in one hundred ten nations.

The impact of this is hard to exaggerate. The GO program gave Charismatic leaders in emerging nations training and refreshing they urgently needed. Churches were strengthened, ministries were fashioned, and the Charismatic Movement in dozens of nations was matured on the strength of Derek's solidly biblical teaching. In Charismatic churches Derek would never know about—perhaps in Zimbabwe or Indonesia, for example—his tapes were used for the Sunday sermon, his books were used to prepare leaders, and his name was given to newborn babes. It is not uncommon to this day to find a Derek Sun Yee or Abdullah Derek Khan preaching the gospel somewhere in the world.

A third influence on the growth of Derek Prince Ministries in the last years of Derek's life was more a trend than a decision. Decades before, when Derek was newly born again, he had heard God say, "It shall be like a little stream. The stream shall become a river, the river shall become a great river, the great river shall become a sea, the sea shall become a mighty ocean, and it shall be through thee." Yet there was something more: "But how thou must not know, thou canst not know, thou shalt not know."

Throughout his life, Derek took this latter phrase as a guarantee of humility. His ministry would be effective, but it wouldn't be all his doing. Derek could almost hear God saying, "If I allow you to know how I am going to affect the world through your ministry, you will simply get in the way. I will use methods you would never dream. Stay in your place and do what I tell you to do. I will do the rest." Thus, he came to accept that God's plan would prevail if he would only obey.

It paid off. Aside from the astonishing success of his radio program and the vast reach of the Global Outreach program, Derek's impact on the world was dramatically extended by ideas that originated with other people. It was humbling, perhaps, but the results were sometimes so historic that Derek could not deny this was God's way. Typical of these, and certainly among the most successful, was Ross Paterson's plan for China.

In the early 1960s, Paterson was a student at Cambridge University when he first heard Derek speak. He then became a missionary to Taiwan with his wife, Christine. The two were often sustained on their lonely mission field by Derek's books and tapes. They returned to England in 1979 and became pastors in the northern city of York. During a season of fasting and prayer, Ross was walking around an abandoned horse track one day when he heard his God say these words: "Take Derek Prince to China."

He immediately made his way to northern Ireland where he had heard Derek was speaking and asked some friends there to introduce him. When he explained to Derek what he intended to do, Derek eagerly agreed and promised to help as much as he could. Ross then used his connections with Overseas Missionary Fellowship, the former China Inland Mission, to gain access to the Far East Broadcasting Company (FEBC). He asked if they would be willing to air Derek's radio teaching, and, in time, they agreed. Ross soon found himself typing out Chinese translations of Derek's messages.

The early days did not always go smoothly. The FEBC translators often reworked Ross's translations into paraphrases that missed the original meaning. In time, though—as their trust grew—they began allowing unaltered translation. The broadcast became one of the most popular radio shows in China. Three years after the start of the broadcasts, the FEBC was so pleased with the success that they asked if Ross could provide more material. Since that time, the theme of every Derek Prince radio tape and sermon has been played on Chinese radio in both Mandarin and Cantonese, as well as other dialects.

On the strength of his success with radio, Ross then worked to get Derek's books into China, as well. In conjunction with ministries in Hong Kong and Taiwan, he engineered the translation of the Foundation Series into Chinese. This moved Derek, a few years later, to announce that he wished to give the nation of China a present: a million copies of the Foundation Series. With time, that goal was achieved, and now more than five million copies of Derek's books have been distributed in that land.

Not a man easily satisfied, Ross has since turned his attention to distributing video compact disks of Derek speaking in hopes of feeding the ballooning small group movement in China. These VCDs will be quite a shock for many of Derek's followers, though. Surprisingly, most of them believe he is Chinese. In order to air Derek's teaching on Chinese radio, Ross gave him the name "Ye Guang-Ming," which means "Clear Light," and asked a Chinese believer to read the scripts of Derek's teaching. Chinese Christians who have been listening to Derek's teaching for years know nothing of the name Derek Prince and will certainly be amazed to see a tall Englishman on VCDs that are supposed to depict their favorite teacher, Ye Guang-Ming!

Ross Paterson's efforts in China met with such success that Derek once said, "If the Lord took everything away from me, the last thing I would let go of would be China." Yet there were similar victories in dozens of other countries—France, South Africa, Russia, Latin America, New Zealand, and India, for example—and largely because valiant believers offered themselves as champions of Derek's teaching in their lands.

Among all the forces that lifted Derek to greater heights in his latter years, Ruth must surely be given her due. Few in Derek's life devoted themselves to him as she did. Few sought as fiercely to drive him to his best. And few were as resented and misunderstood as she was.

Ruth endured opposition from the moment she entered Derek's life. There was, first, the rejection by the Ft. Lauderdale men. Though kind, they saw her as a burden and a divorcee who would taint Derek's name. Then there were family members and friends, who suspected that Ruth, who had never been well-off, eyed Derek's prosperity and fame.

Some thought they saw signs that God was confirming their fears. When Ruth first came on the scene, Johanne had a dream in which Ruth was pushing Derek in a wheelchair. They were in a building something like Grand Central Station in New York. Suddenly, Ruth pushed Derek violently down a great flight of stairs. All the while, Derek was screaming Johanne's name. When Johanne awoke, she was understandably horrified by the nightmarish scene. Her dread only deepened sometime later, though, when Don Basham's daughter told her that she had dreamt the same thing. Such images did not inspire a warm welcome for Derek's second wife.

Sadly, Ruth did little to endear herself. Though, to her credit, Ruth saw it as her calling to protect Derek and drive him to the greatness she dreamed for him, many people remember her as controlling and small. She regimented Derek's schedule and eating to the last detail, imposing huge burdens both on him and those about them. When she and Derek visited the homes of family or friends, Ruth announced upon arriving the precise time meals would be served, what the menu would be, and when Derek would take a nap or a walk. Sometimes her demands were mailed to family members in advance. When family members called the house and asked for Derek, they were told he was sleeping or in prayer. Later Derek would ask why people never called.

Once when the two of them went shopping with friends, Derek—who had a wicked sweet tooth—put sugary delights in the shopping basket that were not on his diet. His friends giggled: Derek was being typically male. Ruth was not amused, though. At first, she simply took the offending foods from the basket and put them back on the shelf. Finally, she grew so enraged that she exploded at Derek in terms everyone in the store could hear.

Because of this overprotectiveness that bordered on isolation, many people describe Ruth as a frustrating combination of control and insecurity. She was at times petty, raging, and harsh. She dominated Derek's life in a way that many around him came to believe hindered his work for God.

Perhaps, though, there is another way of understanding this woman. No life is revealed in one dimension. Human beings are complex and difficult to define. To see them as anything near what they are requires a warm blend of humility and mercy, a compassion that checks the rush to judgment and grants truth a moment to be heard. Surely, any sense of honor for the life of Derek Prince requires a gentle second look at the woman that he loved.

It may be that Ruth's hurtful ways were the outworking of an inner pain of her own. There is a revealing story that comes from a meeting of the international council of Derek Prince Ministries at Nuremburg. There had been some tension between Ruth and a man at the meeting. Things grew heated. During a break, Ruth approached the man and continued pressing her views. Derek walked up to the two just as the man was telling Ruth that she was a bit overbearing. Ruth looked to Derek to disagree, but instead he nodded assent: "Yes, Ruth, you are sometimes hard to bear." Ruth burst into tears and then, in a painfully transparent moment, looked pleadingly at Derek and said, "You never tell me you love me, and you always criticize everything I do."

If these words genuinely represent a hidden pain of Ruth's heart, it may well explain some of her crashing ways. Derek Prince shone brightly for her before the two ever met. He was one of the luminaries of her Charismatic world. When he first made his way to her Jerusalem apartment to pray for her, she was humbled by the mere honor of his presence. Later, when they fell in love and married, an insecure, overwhelmed Ruth took it as her duty to care for Derek and make him even more than he was. She only knew one way to do this: the Marine way—discipline and control. But she wanted love in exchange, and when it did not come to her satisfaction, she drove herself—and Derek—even harder. This meant more ironclad routine, more offense, and more distancing of friends. Derek surely felt the squeeze and may have expressed his discomfort in the criticism of which Ruth complained. The two may have entered a vicious cycle: Ruth trying to protect and regulate Derek's life to earn his love, and Derek resenting the domination and withholding the affection Ruth craved.

Whatever the case, it falls short of the truth to paint Ruth as the Jezebel of the Derek Prince story. Like Lydia, she could be harsh and abusive but also a lady of great tenderness and depth. We should remember that she ministered at Derek's side for more than two decades, praying for the sick, teaching the Scriptures, and enduring the hardship just as he did. She held the sick and the dying to her chest, hiked through jungles to preach God's truth, and endured the criticism that all leaders receive. Yet she never lost the tender touch. When Kirsten's beloved cat died one year, Ruth sent her a card describing the agony of loss and how she shared the pain. Kirsten, who was more used to the demanding houseguest, could barely reconcile the two Ruths in her mind.

There are other stories that are as equally in conflict with the darker image of Ruth some prefer. Only one is needed. Derek and Ruth were in a van on their way to a meeting in Pakistan. Suddenly, the van began to careen wildly and seemed as though it was about to crash into an oncoming truck. Seeing the danger, Ruth unfastened her seat belt and threw her body over Derek to keep him from harm. When the van righted itself and moved back in its lane, Ruth moved back into her seat and fastened her seat belt again, all without comment. The message was clear: Ruth saw her life in terms of Derek. She would give her all to him. His work, his ministry, was more important than anything else, even her own life. A woman who thinks like this is bound to give offense to others, but surely she can be honored for serving a higher cause.

At the end of his life, Derek was asked about Ruth and her domineering ways. With the tears forming in his eyes that were always present when he spoke of his wives, he said, "I know she was not perfect, but my ministry in those years was due in large part to her labors. She got me where I needed to be and cared for all the details that would have escaped me. I was a healthier, happier man because of her, and if she hurt those whom I love, I can only hope they understand."

Regardless of how Ruth is remembered, it is certain that only an exceptional woman could have kept up with Derek Prince toward the end of his life. By the early 1980s, Derek and Ruth had decided to spend up to half of their year in Israel to identify with the Jews and encourage their return to the land. This meant that the remaining half of the year was spent ministering abroad. It sounds like a leisurely arrangement, and Derek and Ruth may have decided upon it in part to find some well-earned rest.

It was not to be. Rarely did they spend a full six months in Israel, and even when they did, there were meetings, tours, bombings, and regional wars to endure. When they were abroad, their schedule was astonishing given that Derek was nearing his eightieth year. One six-month period, pieced together from his newsletters, tells the tale. From July to late November, Derek and Ruth ministered in Amsterdam, Ornskoldsvik in Sweden, Singapore, Karachi in Pakistan, Scotland, Ireland, Austria, Germany, and five conferences in the United States.

That Derek's schedule was almost ridiculously full in those years is testament to the demand for his teaching. By the late 1990s, Derek was viewed as a pioneer of many of the truths that were then proving of impact, a father to just the kind of movement he had hoped to launch. Indeed, there were so many biblical themes that he embedded anew in the Christian world that it is sometimes difficult to recall a time when those themes weren't well known.

His chief theme in his latter years was love for Israel. He believed that the church had failed to understand the meaning of the return of the Jews to the land and that this was largely due to the replacement theology in the body of Christ. For centuries, most Christians believed that while the Israel of the Old Testament was the chosen people of God, the ministry of Jesus signaled a change: the church is Israel now. In Derek's view, this false doctrine gave rise to much of the anti-Semitism in world history. Instead, he taught that Christians ought to recognize their debt to Israel, understand that the birth of the nation of Israel in 1948 was of huge biblical significance, and do all in their power to bless the Jews and aid them in returning to their land.

The truth is that Derek understood the whole of his life in terms of Israel. He had been baptized in the land, had been witness to the creation of modern Israel, had adopted Jewish daughters, and felt a call to turn the Christian church to her Jewish roots. He saw it as deeply prophetic that life in Jerusalem should mark both the beginning and the end of his ministry. This was more than just an accident of geography: it was the fulfillment of the purpose for his life. Asked on his deathbed what his last commission from God had been, he said hoarsely, "To pray for the peace of Jerusalem."

Derek's second major theme was the truth and power of God's Word, the Bible. At a time when Charismatics often left being biblical in order to be spiritual, when experience ruled over thought, Derek helped draw the movement back into biblical boundaries. He was as devoted to spiritual experience as any Charismatic could be, but he understood that Christian spirituality should grow organically from Scripture. Rather than simply viewing the Bible as a collection of inspiring statements, as many Charismatics did, Derek understood it as a tapestry of truth woven over centuries, a revelation of God through the record of human experience. He called the movement, then, to a passion for the Bible, right methods of interpreting Scripture, and sound doctrine as the path to spiritual power.

Yet, as certainly as he demanded a scholarly approach to Scripture, he also understood that the words of the Bible are filled with spirit and life. He believed that Scripture ought to be stored up in the heart, proclaimed in power over the circumstances of life, and held before God as the spiritual language of prayer. He and Ruth often made "proclamations," both in private and with their audiences, in which they spoke aloud scriptures that pertained to a certain need or a battle for victory. There were proclamations that pertained to health, mental acuity, salvation for the lost, God's will for nations, the restoration of Israel, defeat of the devil, and strengthening of marriages, to name a few. This practice was the outworking of Derek's belief that the Bible, once properly understood, could be applied in faith to the real world to produce change.

Indeed, this was the foundational belief of much else that he taught. He urged what he did about demons because he found it first in the Bible and then his experience confirmed it. But he would go no further in driving off the demonic than the Bible allowed, and he urged others to do the same. He taught about the power of curses or the grace of God to heal or the spiritual power of human words or the value of intercessory prayer or the spiritual life of nations—all because he saw it first in Scripture and then applied it in faith to change human lives. This was the keystone of his ministry: he was biblical in order to be spiritual and spiritual because he was biblical.

It is not going too far to contend that his theology may well have been, in part, a positive stamp of his Platonist beginnings. He loved the ideas of Plato, he said, because they taught of a perfect world beyond the natural. Yet to understand these ideas, Derek had to do the hard work of classical scholarship. Once he became a Christian, he brought both the scholar's skill and the Platonist's mysticism, perhaps even dualism, to his understanding of Scripture. Thus, he loved language but kept his eye on its spiritual power. He understood sickness as something real but always believed there was a spirituality to illness that held the key to its cure. He believed in good government, but he understood that the course of nations is shaped in a spiritual realm. The same could be said of his view of authority, marriage, the future, the church, and a score of other topics on which he taught.

By the time Derek came into his latter years, these perspectives had become mainline in the Charismatic Movement. Indeed, some spoke of a neo-Charismatic Movement: the portion that embraced spiritual experience but was as much given to sound teaching and doctrine as any Presbyterian or Baptist could be. Derek had given birth to this movement, and many hundreds of thousands knew it by the late 1990s. It is a pleasant thought that Derek was honored as the father he wanted to be well before his death. One pastor who introduced him said, "Surely Derek's presence with us tonight is a victory lap. May he have many more before he goes to be with the Lord."

It would be going too far, perhaps, to say that Derek Prince's personal ministry ended with the death of Ruth, but there is no question that her passing signaled a dramatic decrease in his life. Their last Update tape together—the cassette tape of news and teaching they now sent to their supporters in place of a newsletter—was filled with plans and dreams they hoped to achieve.

Ruth, however, succumbed relatively quickly to a thoracic problem that was never clearly diagnosed and died on December 29, 1998, in Jerusalem.

Derek was understandably devastated but at the funeral made one of the most critical declarations of his life. He had sensed an unclean force arising in his soul from the moment Ruth died, a bitter blaming that he knew would eventually distance him from his God. At the funeral, just after Ruth's casket was lowered in the ground, Derek felt moved to step forward and kneel by her side. Speaking so all in attendance could hear, he thanked God for all that He had done for Ruth and told his heavenly Father that he trusted Him and that he was content with all that had happened. As Derek later said, "It was a significant moment in my life. I knew I could never go forward with the lament I felt over Ruth. I would always blame God, and the door of my life would have been shut. This was the only way I could continue." Ruth's gravestone, at the Emek Rephaim cemetery in Jerusalem, displays the words that capture Derek's faith at the time. They say simply:

RUTH PRINCE
1930–1998
A LIFE LAID DOWN

The remaining years of Derek's life were far from aimless. He worked closely with David Selby to chart a course for Derek Prince Ministries. He occasionally taught when he felt able and each time gave evidence that the fire and the gift still lived. When he was in Jerusalem, he attended an Anglican gathering called Christ Church. It was his favorite place of worship and the only Christian church within the walls of the Old City. He also encouraged believers in the land of his heart and met with Christian leaders from around the world who sought him out whenever they could.

The beginning of the end, though, came on March 28, 2001, when doctors discovered a tumor growing on Derek's head. Unless its course was reversed, he was told, he did not have long to live. Derek entrusted himself to God but submitted to the treatments the doctors recommended. There would be radiation treatments and huge doses of steroids that would cause Derek to balloon to nearly twice his normal size. At times, it seemed as though he was winning, and in these short seasons he planned for future ministry and began sketching out books he hoped to write. Then the hard days would return and leave him frustrated that he could not do the things he dreamed.

In his final months, he lived in a home he had purchased in Jerusalem and which he shared with the family of Eliyahu Ben Haim, a long-time friend. Though his body faded, his spirit never dimmed. He still had his fire. When the mullah from the mosque near his house sounded the *salat*, the Muslim call to prayer, Derek routinely looked toward the window and spouted Scripture in return. He never seemed too ill to joke with a friend, humorously argue with his devoted help, or engage in spirited conversation about trends and ideas. He was aware to the last, a great mind and a fiery spirit indwelling a body that had come to its end.

He died on September 24, 2003, while he slept in the land he had loved all his days. It should not go without mention that he left this life in a year some have marked as "The Passing of the Fathers." In the same year Derek went to be with his God, Bill Bright and Kenneth Hagin, both leaders of major Christian movements, died as well. It is fitting that this should be so, for it signifies not only that the pioneering fathers are passing away, but that the passionate sons should take up their torch.

Epilogue

THERE IS A passage in the historical books of the Old Testament that tells us that upon occasion the eyes of God "run to and fro" throughout the earth to strengthen the hearts of those who are fully committed to Him. (See 2 Chronicles 16:9.) If this is true—and for the earth's billion and a half Christians and Jews it must be—then it may also be true that the eyes of the Lord roam the earth for other reasons as well. Perhaps God scans the earth to remember the suffering or take righteous pride in those who serve Him or enjoy His creation as the Scriptures indicate He may sometimes do.

If there are indeed other occasions on which the eyes of the Lord go to and fro throughout the earth, then it may well be that He sometimes looks around the world to take pleasure in His work through one of His servants. There would be much to please Him in His work through Derek Prince as it survives today.

As God scanned the nations of the earth, there would be the churches, of course. Thousands of them have been founded, guided, matured, or empowered through the work of God in Derek Prince. There would also be the ministries of every kind, from those that feed the hungry of the nations to those that train the leaders of the world. Perhaps as pleasing would be the truths—of the power of God's Word, of the victory over evil, of the future glory of Israel, of God's will for families, and a thousand other themes—that Derek fathered in his time.

These truths have been sent into the earth in a dozen different forms, and God's eye might move over them as well. In a U.S. Army tent in Iraq, soldiers gather around a CD player to hear a lesson on prayer for the nations. The voice on the CD belongs to another soldier, and he is teaching lessons he learned in a different war, in a different army, many years ago. In a community center in central Africa, the image of Derek Prince is projected on a whitewashed wall. The lesson today is holiness, and the words carried by the British voice are changing the culture of a newly Christian African tribe. And in a magnificent office in Dallas, an international Christian figure is reading a small booklet written by Derek Prince. This leader will absorb the lessons in the booklet, make them his own, and preach them in one television broadcast to nearly as many people as Derek Prince addressed in his entire life. Surely God is pleased as His eyes behold His work.

Yet all this may only be the beginning. Derek Prince is dead, but his God and the truths he pioneered in his generation are not. They live, perhaps as passionately as ever given the work of those whom Derek inspired. There are the thousands of pastors, statesmen, businessmen, authors, entrepreneurs, missionaries, artists, professors, and servants of every kind who see themselves as an extension of God's work in Derek Prince. There is also, of course, the valiant devotion of Derek Prince Ministries, which lives in books, tapes, Web sites like www.derekprince.org, CDs, and videos as an offering to the world.

And as Derek's story becomes better known, there may be even more to delight the God who gave us Derek Prince. There will be men and women who know only a "winter in their soul" but who find the loving thaw that God can give. There will be servants of God with difficult marriages who endure the valleys to realize the heights because they have seen what such character can do in the life of Derek Prince. There may, too, be leaders who have risen and failed but who know that the best is yet to come because a man named Derek had his failures but found his best life on the other side of each of them.

Perhaps most of all, decades from now there may be a people who take "God is faithful" as their battle cry, who defy destructive extremes, laud the words of the Bible, embrace the power of the Holy Spirit, disdain the oft-traveled path, use their minds to the glory of God, and call the nations of the earth to their best. If there is such an army one day, they will surely remember that much of what they know was taught by a man named Derek Prince. Perhaps they will also remember what the truths they love cost this man and so will live lives of equal weight in their day. Then the eyes of the Lord may rest upon them, and the heart of the Lord may take pleasure in them, just as He surely takes pleasure in His work through Derek Prince.

✖ Appendix
The Life and Ministry of Derek Prince

August 14, 1915	Born in Bangalore, India
October 12, 1915	Baptized at St. John's Church, Bangalore
1920	Returned to England with his mother
July 1929	Entered Eton
Summer 1934	Left Eton and toured the Continent
October 13, 1934	Admitted to Cambridge
June 1937	Awarded a BA in philosophy from Cambridge
1940	Elected to a fellowship at King's College, Cambridge
September 12, 1940	Joined the army at Boyce Barracks, Crookham
1941	Awarded an MA in philosophy from Cambridge by proxy
July 1941	Began noncommissioned officer course at Scarborough, Yorkshire
	Born again while living in Scarborough
December 1941	Transferred to Egypt
August 23, 1942	Baptized in Jordan River
October 1942	Participated in the Battle of El Alamein
November 1941	Went to a military hospital on the Suez for a year
November 1943	Transferred to Sudan
November 1944	Reassigned to Palestine, at Kiriat Motzkin

May 1945	Assigned to No. 16 British General Hospital, Jerusalem
April 17, 1946	Married Lydia Christensen and became father to Lydia's eight daughters
June 6, 1946	Discharged from the British army
August 1948	Escaped to England during the Israeli War of Independence
August 1949	Pastored a small Pentecostal church at his home near Hyde Park
Late 1949	Resigned his fellowship at King's College, Cambridge
1957–1961	Served as principal of Nyang'ori Teacher Training Center, Kisumu, Kenya
1958	Adopted Joska
December 1961	Left Kenya with Lydia and Joska
1962	Taught in a Canadian Bible school
1963	Immigrated to United States and became the teaching pastor at Peoples Church, Minneapolis, Minnesota
September 15, 1963	Became the pastor at Broadway Tabernacle, Seattle, Washington
Late summer 1964	Moved to Chicago, Illinois
1965	*Self-Study Bible Course* published
1966	Foundation Series published
1967	Entered full-time traveling ministry
1968	Moved to Ft. Lauderdale, Florida
June 1969	*New Wine* founded

	Entered into relationship with Charles, Don, Ern, and Bob
May 1971	Derek Prince Publications opened offices in Ft. Lauderdale, Florida
October 5, 1975	Lydia Prince died
	Appointment in Jerusalem published
October 17, 1978	Married Ruth Baker
February 1979	Radio ministry *Today With Derek Prince* began
1981	Moved to Jerusalem with Ruth
1982	Ross Paterson received word to "take Derek Prince to China."
1983	Renounced the Discipleship Movement
1984	*Living Sacrifice* (in Chinese) began airing under Derek's Chinese name Ye Guang-Ming (later in five Chinese dialects)
	DPM–South Pacific office opened in New Zealand
	DPM–South Africa office opened
	Global Outreach Leaders Program began with twenty-three leaders in third world countries
1985	For Derek's seventieth birthday, contributions were received to begin Spanish and Russian broadcasts
	DPM–Australia office opened
	DPM–Canada office opened
1986	DPM–UK office opened in Northern Ireland, later moving to Britain

	The Workman God Approves started airing in Chinese
	Derek Prince Interpretiruet Biblia started airing in Russia
1987	German missionary to Mongolia heard English broadcast (from Seychelles) and began to translate program into Mongolian
1989	DPM–Netherlands office opened, overseeing Eastern Europe and CIS countries
1990	*Blessing or Curse: You Can Choose* published
1991	DPM–Germany office opened
May 1993	Moscow conference (thirty-four Bible schools opened in following years)
November 1993	Ministered at ICCC in Mannheim, Germany
May 1994	Conference in Almaty, Kazakhstan
June 1994	Ministered in Budapest, Hungary
November 1994	Traveled to South Africa, Indonesia, Malaysia, and Singapore
1995	Global Outreach Leaders Program free distribution reached 200,000 books to 124 pastors and leaders
	Began legally printing Spanish books in Cuba
September 1995	Conference in Ismir, Turkey
November 1995	Jubilee Celebration in Ft. Mill, South Carolina
March 1996	Ministered in Singapore and Indonesia

August 1996	Ministered in Lublin, Poland
October 1996	Conference in Bahrain; ministered in Germany
December 1996	Ministered in Cuba
January 1997	Ministered in Bogota, Colombia DPM–Switzerland office opened
May 1997	Ministered in Lucerne, Switzerland
October 1997	Ministered in Toulouse, France and Portugal
1998	DPM–France office opened Ministered in India for the first time
July 1998	Ministered in Cornwall, England at Barnabas Camp
December 29, 1998	Ruth Prince died *They Shall Expel Demons* published
March 1999	Ministered at Lydia Fellowship in Lake Junaluska, North Carolina, and in Palm Harbor, Florida
April 1999	Ministered at Wellington Boone conference in Richmond, Virginia
June 1999	Ministered at World Outreach Church in Murfreesboro, Tennessee
July 1999	Returned to the United Kingdom
August 1999	Ministered in Malvern
November 1999	Ministered in Kensington Temple, London
January 2000	Returned to Jerusalem Ministered in Vancouver, British Columbia

April 2000	Ministered at Cornerstone Church, San Antonio, Texas
May 2000	Ministered at Lakewood Church, Houston, Texas
June 2000	Ministered at New Covenant Church, Ft. Lauderdale, Florida
2003	DPM–Israel office opened
September 24, 2003	Died in his sleep in Jerusalem
2004	First Derek Prince Ministries National Conference, Charlotte, North Carolina (speakers included John Hagee and Kirbyjon Caldwell)
	Derek Prince Ministries Training Week held for pastors around America, Charlotte, North Carolina
	DPM–Norway office opened
2005	*Self-Study Bible Course* revised and expanded with studies by Derek previously not included
	Video masters of Derek teaching from the early 1970s, once thought lost forever, discovered in a DPM warehouse and converted to DVD teaching materials
	DPM expands ministry on the Internet with www.derekprince.org streaming audio and video teaching from Derek
July 4, 2005	*Derek Prince Legacy Radio* began airing

Acknowledgments

M Y DEEPEST GRATITUDE is to the daughters of Lydia and Derek Prince. In the years required to write this book, they have been gracious hosts, surrogate mothers, and kind friends. Each of these dear ladies has opened their lives to me in a most unexpected way. They did not know me, and they could have kept me at arm's length, this big American to whom they were being asked to share their most tender memories. They might have resented the intrusion and kept their treasures locked away. They did not. Instead, they gave themselves to remembrance. By the hour, they have wept, laughed, and—always shoving food my way—given themselves to this powerful story. I am changed by their grace.

My own team of editors and researchers has made invaluable contributions to this project as they have to my life. Great minds and generous hearts like those of George Grant, Beverly Darnall, Jonathan Mansfield, Lores Rizkalla, Mark Buchanan, and Eric Holmberg have given this book life it did not have under my own hand alone. Dr. Brad Blankenship helped me understand Derek's medical history and provided astonishing insights into what that history may have meant for Derek's life. Sam Chappell and Rick

Myers have managed my world, and Susan Levine has scheduled my travel with such marvelous wisdom and skill that this and many other projects were made possible. Thank you, my merry band.

One of the great delights of my life has been working with the devoted people of Derek Prince Ministries. This book was their idea, and through the long years needed to give their dream birth, they have been welcoming family, caring friends, and professional comrades. David Selby, Derek Wesley and Marykay Selby, Christopher and Christi Selby, Jack and Jeanette Alongi, Peter Wyns, Pat Vitolo, and the rest of the DPM staff have given themselves to this book as they have to the work of Derek Prince, and I am touched by their sacrifices. My love, particularly, to Anna, who shares my addiction to calamari and a good laugh.

There have been hundreds of people who have been graciously willing to sit and talk with me about the life and ministry of Derek Prince, far too many to list here. Of particular note are Pat Robertson, Bob Mumford, Alice Basham, Jim Croft, Barry Segal, Bob and Nadine Feller, John Beckett, Ray and Jill Lockart, and Scott Ross. Where this book captures a story not previously told, it is credit to direct conversations with them.

Some of my sweetest and most rewarding hours during this project were spent in the archives of Eton College. Archivist Penny Hatfield gave of her expertise and her time in a manner that has deeply impacted this work and is a credit to her institution. The staff of the King's College Archives at Cambridge University were equally helpful, as were the staff at the India and Orient Room of the British Library in London. Thank you all for putting up with my clumsy questions and disturbingly American ways.

✖ Notes

1. Lawrence James, *The Rise and Fall of the British Empire* (New York: St. Martin's Press, 1994), 220.

2. Rudyard Kipling, "If—," *Rewards and Fairies* (England: Doubleday, Page and Co., 1911). Public domain in United States.

3. Tim Card, *Eton Renewed: A History from 1860 to the Present Day*, (London: John Murray, 1994), 224.

4. Anton Chekhov (1860–1904), Selected Quotations, Dr. Fidel Fajardo-Acosta's World Literature Web site, http://fajardo-acosta.com/worldlit/checkhov (accessed July 29, 2005).

5. Henry Wadsworth Longfellow, "A Psalm of Life," 1893.

6. T. E. B. Howarth, *Cambridge Between Two Wars* (London: Collins, 1978), 17.

7. Rudyard Kipling, "A Dead Statesman." Used by permission of A. P. Watt Ltd. on behalf of the Natural Trust for Places of Historic Interest or Natural Beauty.

8. F. Scott Fitzgerald, *This Side of Paradise* (New York: Scribner, 1988), 288.

9. Ibid, 73.

10. Howarth, *Cambridge Between Two Wars*, 175.

11. Walter Savage Landor, "Finis," copyright © 1901, from *The Oxford Book of English Verse*, edited by Arthur Thomas Quiller-Couch, (Clarendon: Oxford, 1919), 576.

12. Richard Deacon [Donald McCormick], *The Cambridge Apostles: A History of Cambridge University's Elite Intellectual Secret Society* (New York: Farrar, Straus, 1986), 60.

13. Murray N. Rothbard, *Keynes, the Man*, originally published in *Dissent on Keynes: A Critical Appraisal of Keynesian Economics*, edited by Mark Skousen (New York: Praeger, 1992), 171–198.

14. Deacon, *The Cambridge Apostles*, 85.

15. Larry Collins and Dominique Lapierre, *O Jerusalem!*, first Touchstone edition (New York: Simon and Schuster, 1988), 17.

16. David Barton, *To Pray or Not to Pray*, fifth edition (Texas: WallBuilder Press, 2002).

Books Available From
Derek Prince Ministries

Appointment in Jerusalem

Atonement: Your Appointment with God

Baptism in the Holy Spirit

Blessing or Curse: You Can Choose

Choice of a Partner, The

Derek Prince: On Experiencing God's Power

Divine Exchange, The

Does Your Tongue Need Healing?

End of Life's Journey, The

Expelling Demons

Extravagant Love

Faith to Live By

Fasting

Fatherhood

First Mile, The

God Is a Matchmaker

God's Medicine Bottle

God's Plan for Your Money

God's Remedy for Rejection

God's Will for Your Life

Grace of Yielding, The

Holy Spirit in You, The

How to Fast Successfully

Husbands and Fathers

I Forgive You

Judging: When? Why? How?

Life's Bitter Pool

Marriage Covenant, The

Orphans, Widows, the Poor and Oppressed

Our Debt to Israel

Pages from My Life's Book

Partners for Life

Philosophy, the Bible and the Supernatural

Power of the Sacrifice, The

Prayers and Proclamations

Praying for the Government

Promised Land

Prophetic Destinies: Who Is Israel? Who Is the Church?

Protection from Deception

Receiving God's Best

Self-Study Bible Course (revised, expanded)

Shaping History Through Prayer and Fasting

Spirit-filled Believer's Handbook, The

Spiritual Warfare

Surviving the Last Days

They Shall Expel Demons

Through the Psalms with Derek Prince

Transformed for Life

War in Heaven

Who Is the Holy Spirit?

A complete list of Derek Prince's books, audio teachings, and video teachings is available at www.derekprince.org.